STORMING
THE
HEAVENS

HISTORY AND WARFARE
Arther Ferrill, Series Editor

STORMING THE HEAVENS

*Soldiers, Emperors,
and Civilians in
the Roman Empire*

ANTONIO SANTOSUOSSO

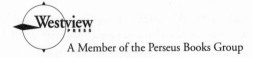

Westview
PRESS

A Member of the Perseus Books Group

Copyright © 2001 by Westview Press, A Member of the Perseus Books Group

Published in 2001 in the United States of America by Westview Press, 5500 Central Avenue, Boulder, Colorado 80301–2877, and in the United Kingdom by Westview Press, 12 Hid's Copse Road, Cumnor Hill, Oxford OX2 9JJ

Find us on the World Wide Web at www.westviewpress.com

Library of Congress Cataloging-in-Publication Data

Santosuosso, Antonio
    Storming the heavens : soldiers, emperors, and civilians in the Roman Empire / by Antonio Santosuosso.
        p. cm. — (History and warfare)
    Includes bibliographical references and index.
    ISBN 0-8133-3523-X (hc)
        1. Rome—Army—Political activity. 2. Rome—Politics and government—30 B.C.–476 A.D. 3. Social conflict—Rome—History. 4. Rome—Army—Recruiting, enlistment, etc. 5. Rome—History—Military—30 B.C.–476 A.D. I. Title. II. Series.

DG276.5 .S26 2001
937'.06—dc21
                                                                                00-068537

The paper used in this publication meets the requirements of the American National Standard for Permanence of Paper for Printed Library Materials Z39.48–1984.

10   9   8   7   6   5   4   3   2   1

For Alma with love

Contents

List of Figures

Acknowledgments

W hen Rob Williams, then an editor at Westview Press, suggested in 1997 that I continue my analysis of the history of warfare as a follow-up to *Soldiers, Citizens, and the Symbols of War*, on ancient Greece and middle-republican Rome, it was almost inevitable that I would return to a civilization that I had endlessly studied as a student, teacher, and scholar. *Storming the Heavens*, even more than my previous book, has been a journey home, to the land I left decades ago as a young man and to the roots of Mediterranean and European civilizations. At times this voyage back, like all such returns, has been tinged by a bittersweet longing for times past—for instance, my first visit to the Roman Forum. The Forum's cracked, chipped stones, the wildflowers appearing here and there, the broken columns, and the ruined temple walls made me a prisoner of things past, sweet and sad, while my throat seemed to tighten and tears appeared in my eyes. But the journey back to one of the foundations of our civilization has not always been nostalgically sweet, for Rome also embodied the cunning, cruelty, and exploitation of which humankind can be capable. There is probably no better subject area than warfare to transmit the greatness and cruelty of the ancient world. I have written this story keeping in mind the largest audience possible—scholars, students, the general public—anybody who treasures the past even if they tend to disagree with its value system.

The memory of my father as a soldier, as well as the remembrance of my mother, continue to inspire me, for both taught me to love books and to be mindful of my heritage. Also, my two loving sons, Derek and his family and Kevin, have continued being a source of silent encouragement. When I felt low, my weekly and sometimes daily talks with my beautiful granddaughter Dakota, who is four, or just the sound of the voice of her younger sister, Georgia, were sources of peace and stimulation to work even harder on projects that they may enjoy one day. But I owe the greatest debt to my wife, Professor Alma Colk Santosuosso, who has been my constant and loving companion in our European research trips, visiting battlefields, libraries, and musty archives, sometimes in combination with her own research on medieval music and sometimes momentarily neglecting her own work to provide me with support. Moreover, her careful reading of my manuscript resulted in constant suggestions and constructive criticism. Finally, a distinct word of thanks to Arther Ferrill and the other scholars and colleagues who have read various versions of my work, and to Carol Jones, who has guided its publication at Westview Press. In addition I wish to thank Michelle Trader, the production editor at Westview, as well as Paula Waldrop and copy editor Jon Taylor Howard. My students in my course on warfare at the University of Western Ontario gave me the opportunity to test, revise, and test again some of the ideas contained in the book.

I acknowledge modest financial support from the Agnes Cole Dark Fund, Faculty of Social Science at the University of Western Ontario, for one of my research trips to Rome. Unless otherwise specified, I have drawn the art myself using photo-illustration software.

Unless otherwise specified, all translations are from the Loeb Classical Library.

Introduction

S*torming the Heavens* begins in the second century B.C., when the Romans established clear supremacy over most of the Mediterranean world, and ends with the melancholic collapse of the empire in the fifth century A.D. I have tried to view this fascinating, dramatic tale from different angles, treasuring especially the voices of those who lived when the empire existed. My goal has been to integrate the emperor—the manager of war—and the military forces within the social, economic, religious, and symbolical context. Several powerful themes have emerged: the monopoly of military power in the hands of a few, whether an oligarchy or the emperor as the embodiment of the oligarchy; the connection between the armed forces and the most cherished values of the state; the manipulation of the lower classes so that they would accept the oligarchy's view of life, control, and power; the absence of real class conflicts; and imperialism's subjugation and dehumanization of people and the arrangements that made possible their subjugation, whether they were Gauls, Britons, Germans, Mideasterners, or Africans.

As enemies were cowed into submission, Rome, after a century, faced an internal situation that endangered its supremacy throughout the empire: social turmoil in the very heart of the Roman territories among an increasing number of dispossessed farmers; a scarcity of manpower for the army; and inevitable conflict with allies who had fought side by side with Romans to establish Rome's dominion in the Italian peninsula and elsewhere.

In the later half of the second century B.C., once the land redistribution reforms of the Gracchi (Tiberius and Gaius Gracchus) had failed, the ruling order had no alternative but to open the army's ranks to all citizens regardless of background. Although necessary, this measure soon became a harbinger of destruction and chaos. The rank and file, now mostly from the lower classes, switched allegiance from the abstract entity of the state to the commanders who provided a living and the loot. The army was democratized—but not the leadership. The highest order—the senatorial aristocracy—still retained its function as the manager of Roman war, for the soldiers never translated their struggle into class terms. Yet the upheaval was

1

immense. Ambitious aristocrats fed on one another; in the process their troops became armies of pillagers, their targets citizens like them. All this played out on a stage where other violent events had long been taking place. First, non-Roman allies from central Italy and the peninsular south took the field against Rome upon being refused citizenship yet again; then an army of slaves, led by the Thracian gladiator Spartacus, became so dangerous that the primacy of the state and its security verged on collapse.

By the middle third of the first century B.C., the allies had finally been accepted as citizens and the slaves were crushed, but the Civil Wars ended only when Augustus (63 B.C.–A.D. 14) finally defeated, in 31 B.C., the last contenders to the supreme power: Marcus Antonius (a fellow Roman popularized as Marc Anthony) and Cleopatra, the queen of Egypt. Earlier, under Julius Caesar (100–44 B.C.), Augustus's granduncle, the rank and file were acclimating themselves to a new ideal as defenders of Rome's best values. It was an ideal that Augustus cherished and then enforced by bringing fundamental changes to the army and the empire. Augustus became the sole manager of war: He cut the legions from about sixty total to twenty-eight and then twenty-five; established a fund providing troops with a secure source of income; and centralized, in his own hands, the administration of the provinces where most of the armed forces were posted. The soldiers, except for the imperial guard and the units in charge of public duties (policing and fire fighting, for instance), went to man the frontiers or the most dangerous internal spots of the empire.

Augustus's dominion seemed to restate the values of old, for he tried to preserve the arrangement of the past, wherein the commoners were in a subordinate position while the highest orders—senatorial aristocrats and equestrians—maintained their prestige and at least the semblance of political power in their hands. In reality, however, the changes were profound. The center of power was still apparently in the Senate, but in truth it had passed to the emperor or his delegates. He also retained the might of the sword, for he was the armed forces' paymaster; he, not the Senate, controlled most of the resources and legions stationed at the frontiers. The process was sanctioned ideologically and religiously. Literary works, visual creations, and religious rituals became an integral part of the imperial image.

During the same period, Roman supremacy extended to the whole Mediterranean, and to all lands west of the Rhine and south of the Danube, while Emperor Claudius (10 B.C.–A.D. 54) completed the conquest of Britain. Before he died in A.D. 14, Augustus instructed the Roman people to be satisfied with and defend what they had already acquired. It was an ideal he had come to accept only after the destruction of three legions in the Teutoburg Forest in A.D. 9, but this did not guarantee that his successors would adopt a defensive stance. Aggression remained the fundamental principle of Roman policy until well into the third century A.D.; it was assumed that legionaries should not only confront any invader that approached imperial lands but also enter enemy territories, retaliate against those left behind, and punish those who had escaped destruction during the invasion.

Rome's supremacy was never in danger during most of the first two centuries A.D. The situation started to change in the latter part of the second century, but thanks to Marcus Aurelius (161–180) and Septimius Severus (193–211) Rome still managed to push back the barbarian threat at the frontier. Still, the more serious danger emerged from within. In the last years of the second century and for a good part of the next, most emperors became the puppets of soldiers, especially of the pretorians, the emperor's personal guard. The pretorians kept their role as bloodied emperor-makers even after Septimius Severus disbanded them in A.D. 193, for the newly formed pretorian guard reacquired the power of its predecessor.

The army that emerged from Septimius onward was forged from a new mold: Its pay was raised; the permanent legions were increased; more troops were stationed in Italy (there was even a legion located a few kilometers from Rome—a radical departure from tradition); and aristocrats began to be elbowed out of command positions. But probably the most influential novelty was the erosion of the central position of Rome and of the Italian-born in the army. For instance, the new pretorian guard was formed with legionaries coming from the frontier, whereas before it had been almost a complete monopoly of native Italians. During the subsequent decade more changes were implemented. The influx of Italian-born soldiers had steadily declined since Augustus's time; now they almost disappeared except (for the most part) in command posts. Moreover, a troubling situation developed at the frontier under pressure mainly from the Germanic tribes in Europe. Emperor Diocletian (c. 245–313?) tried to stop the threat with stronger fixed defenses, but when that did not work Constantine (c. 272 or 273–337) adopted a defense in depth, that is, fortifications in stages that slowed the enemy so that a mobile army could face it in a decisive encounter. Probably beginning with Severus or more likely with Gallienus (d. 268; emperor 253–268), the Roman troops were being divided between those who served at the frontier—usually less paid and less qualified—and those in the mobile field armies—better paid and better qualified; the task of the latter was to face the invaders after they had pierced the frontier. In the process, the role of the infantry—the backbone of earlier Roman armies—eroded and was taken up by the cavalry.

The empire survived, though sometimes in tatters, frequently pierced but more often repositioned in a menacing stance. The end came in the fifth century A.D. not because of Adrianople 378—when Emperor Valens fell before the Visigoths who crossed the Danube—and the barbarian populations who were permitted to settle within the imperial territory, but because by the second half of the fourth century there were not enough resources for a relentless war effort, especially in the western region (the territories had been divided into the Western Empire and the Eastern Empire since Diocletian's time). This was so because the Germanic tribes relentlessly poured across the borders, undaunted by defeats and always hoping to lay hands on the rich spoils of the empire. In the meantime, an oppressive taxation system, and a society with privileges for the few and burdens for the rest, were among the ails that would eventually bring death to the empire. The eastern region of the empire, richer and less menaced, lasted another thousand years (its capital, Constantinople, finally fell to the Turks in 1453). In A.D. 476 the last emperor of the West, Romulus Augustulus—the "little Augustus" in more ways than one—was deposed. Roman supremacy had ended.

I

All–Rich and Poor,
Well-Born, and Commoners—
Must Defend the State

*[Marius] enrolled soldiers, not according to the classes in the man-
ner of our forefathers, but allowing anyone to volunteer, for the
most part of the proletariat. Some say that he did this through lack
of good men, others because of a desire to curry favor, since that
class had given him honor and rank. As a matter of fact, to one who
aspires to power the poorest man is the most helpful, since he has no
regard for his property, having none, and considers anything honor-
able for which he receives pay.*

Sallust, *The War with Jugurtha* lxxxvi.2–3

Once he learned that the barbarians—Germans mainly but also some
Celts—were approaching the mountains, the consul Gaius Marius (ca.
157–86 B.C.) crossed the Alps quickly. Thousands of legionnaires had already fallen in battle to these tall, ferocious, blue-eyed warriors.[1] Now divided into two main groups, the barbarians had decided to invade the Italian northern plains. One group, the Cimbri, were coming from the north
through Noricum (the region northeast of the Alps). The other group, the
Teutones, facing Marius, were coming from the west, the land of the
transalpine Gauls. The year was 102 B.C.

Marius had gained his military reputation in North Africa against the Numidian king Jugurtha, who, chained and dejected, had been exhibited in Marius's triumph in Rome and would soon lose his mind in a Roman dungeon. In Africa the consul had also won his soldiers' hearts and loyalty. His sense of justice, firmness of character, and willingness to share deprivations with his soldiers and reward them for their bravery had endeared him to the troops. Moreover, he was a leader who brought great financial gains. His triumphal procession had displayed 3,007 Roman pounds (eleven ounces each) of gold, 5,775 pounds of uncoined silver, and 287,000 drachmas.[2] He also commanded vast popular support in Rome, though he lacked the basic ingredients of political power—eloquence, wealth, and family background; the aristocracy viewed him with fear and contempt. For the Roman ruling group, there were many unpalatable details about Marius. His ancestry was modest, he had not been born in Rome, and he was not awed by the senators' social status and family history. He used to taunt the aristocrats that his nobility was carried in the wounds of his body, not on "monuments of the dead nor likeness of other men."[3] The commoners who would come to see him as their champion respected his honesty, as well as his tendency to challenge and rebuke his reputed superiors in society.

Marius's campaign against the Teutones was a model of the Roman art of war in the later stages of the republic. In preparation for the confrontation, which was causing great fear in Rome, this man, who was ambitious, quarrelsome, and fond of war, proceeded to challenge the invaders in a methodical, logical way. He carefully trained his troops both mentally and physically, putting them through long marches and quick races in short bursts and training them to carry their own baggage.[4] When he arrived close to the enemy, first attentions were devoted to defense. He set up a fortified camp near the River Rhone in Gaul. In a precaution typical of the Roman art of war, he made sure that abundant supplies were stored in the camp and that if more were needed they could arrive in a speedy and easy manner. Engineering would help with the latter: The Rhone's estuary into the Mediterranean was silted with mud, sand, and clay, allowing only a slow, difficult journey upstream. Marius built a canal connecting the river with a bay that provided protection from the bad weather and access for large ships.[5]

Upon their arrival the Teutones and their allies, the valiant warriors known as the Celtic Ambrones, set up camp nearby and challenged the Romans to come out of their fortified camp. It was an enticement that the legionnaires could hardly resist. Yet in the best spirit of another Roman characteristic, Marius and his officers were able to hold their troops in check. It was difficult and at times seemed almost impossible, for the legionnaires often desired to leave their posts and respond to the Teutones' attacks against the camp. But Marius intended to get his men accustomed to the savage appearance of their enemy, their war cries, their equipment, and their movements in order to transform "what was only apparently formidable, familiar to their minds from observation."[6]

Finally, after storming the Roman camp unsuccessfully, the Germans decided to bypass Marius and proceed toward the mountain passes. Plutarch puts the Teutones and the Cimbri, who were operating north of the Alps, at 300,000, a number that he insists was less than the one mentioned by other authors.[7] The Teutones' marching column was so long that it took six days to pass the Romans. Thus it became time for Marius to break camp. He followed close, never forgetting, however, to fortify his camp and place it in a strong position at night.[8] The moment for engagement came when they arrived at Aquae Sextiae (Aix-en-Provence) in the proximity of the Alps (see Figure 1.1).

Marius's preparations were again meticulous. The Aquae Sextiae camp was set in a strong position but, strangely, away from a river running near the enemy camp. At the moment of confrontation, it seems Marius wanted to place his troops in a situation wherein their desire to win would be intensified by the need to secure a water source. Actually, access to the water became the incidental trigger for the battle. Taking advantage of the fact that the barbarians were eating or engaged in leisure, Roman servants moved to the river to fill their containers. Once there, they came upon a group of bathing barbarians, who called other tribesmen to their aid. The Ambrones, although heavy with the barely completed dinner and their minds inebriated by wine, rushed to the spot, a move that triggered the legions' Ligurian soldiers to press forward to succor their servants. The clash was harsh and violent with both sides, Ambrones and Ligurians, uttering similar war cries since both claimed a similar descent, likely Celtic. (The Ligurians lived in the area nearby the modern city of Genoa.) When other legionnaires joined the Ligurians, the Ambrones fled toward their camp, their blood and bodies polluting the river water. As they reached the camp, an unusual spectacle awaited both fugitives and pursuers. The barbarian women dashed forth, swords and axes in hand, calling their men traitors and attacking the Romans, sometimes with their bare hands. The struggle ended at night when the Romans withdrew to their camp.[9] It was a scene repeated a year later

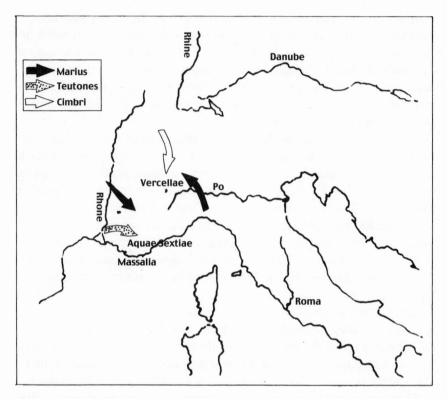

FIGURE 1.1   *Marius Against the Teutones and the Cimbri, 102–101 B.C.*

when Marius confronted the Cimbri at Vercellae. When the women, dressed in black garments, saw their men fleeing from the battlefield and reach for the wagons where they stood, they slew them with their own hands before killing their children and taking finally their own lives.[10]

Marius's men spent the night in "fears and commotions," for the daytime fight had prevented them from fortifying their camp with a palisade or a wall, and the enemy facing them was numerous. Wails, howls, and shouts of grief and of revenge reached them from the enemy camp, mourning the Ambrones, casualties. No attack came during the night, and none the day after.[11] Yet battle was inevitable.

The barbarian camp was also located in a strong position, atop slopes and protected by ravines. In preparation for the confrontation Marius detached

3,000 men to lie in ambush in a wooded area near the enemy camp, ordering them to strike at the enemy's rear if the opportunity arose. Then he made sure that his soldiers were well fed and took a good rest. At daybreak he sent his cavalry on the plain and lined his infantry in front of the Roman camp, which had been set on a hill. It was a clever deployment that used the terrain to the utmost (his soldiers would have the advantage of height over the opponent and secure rear and flanks); the cavalry threatened the enemy flanks, and the men in ambush, when they came out of hiding, would bring the element of surprise to deliver the killing blow.

The Teutones and the remaining Ambrones obliged by rushing uphill, probably deployed in large squares with a depth equal to their front, as the Cimbri would fight at Vercellae.[12] It was enticing for Marius's soldiers to charge downhill, but Marius relied on their discipline so that their desire to fight would not imperil the situation. He sent his officers along the line with specific orders: Do not charge; launch your javelins *(pila)* as the enemy rushes forward, then use your sword *(gladius)* as they come face to face and hit with your heavy shield *(scutum)* to push them back. Those were instructions that he himself carried out, for "he was in better training than any of them, and in daring surpassed them all."[13]

Having rushed uphill, the Teutones must have been out of breath when they came to grips with the Romans. Moreover, their blows and the clash of their shields, originating from the lower ground, must have been weak. In the meantime their large numbers must have been a handicap, for disorder reigned in their rear. This was the moment that the 3,000 Roman troops in ambush had been awaiting, and they hit the enemy's rear. The barbarian array broke up and fled, likely being pursued and cut down by the cavalry deployed in the plain. Counting their dead and prisoners, the tribesmen left some 100,000 people on the battlefield. So many human bones covered the terrain afterward, it was said, the people of nearby Massalia fenced their vineyards with the bones of the fallen.[14] A year later the Cimbri, who had finally come across the Alps, met a similar defeat at Vercellae in northern Italy. About 60,000 fell prisoner; double that number perished on the battlefield. Marius again was the winning general.[15]

Marius's victories became part of Rome's collective memory and were celebrated centuries afterward. And although the clashes at Aquae Sextiae and Vercellae are splendid examples of the way the Romans carried out their brand of war, even more important for the military future of the state was Marius's recruiting reforms, coming about four years before the battle in transalpine Gaul.

Recruiting All Citizens

In 107 B.C. Gaius Marius opened the army to all Roman citizens regardless of their wealth. It was the last, dramatic stage in the troops' proletarization. In the past, at least from the time of Servius Tullius (ca. 580–530 B.C.), the function of soldier had been the prerogative only of those who owned a certain amount of property. Personal assets dictated one's own position in the battle line as well as one's equipment. The division into five classes of different wealth meant that the men of the highest wealth (the first three classes) constituted the heavy infantry, while the remaining two classes (the fourth and fifth) played less crucial roles on the battlefield. The fifth class included citizens who had property valued at least 11,000 *asses* (Roman copper coins). Moreover, each soldier was responsible for buying his own weapons and armor. The richest men of the state manned the cavalry *(equites)*, the rest the infantry.

Marius's recruiting reform would bode ill for the future of the Roman republic, yet it was the logical conclusion to a phenomenon that had begun at least a century earlier, something that Rome's imperialist ventures on increasingly far-flung fields had exacerbated.[16] Rome began to experience recruiting problems in the early stages of the Second Punic War (218–201 B.C.). In the aftermath of the crushing defeats at Trebia (218 B.C.), Trasimene (217 B.C.), and Cannae (216 B.C.), the Senate made the first change to the Servian Constitution probably between 214 B.C. and 212 B.C.[17] The property requirement was lowered from 11,000 to 4,000 *asses*. The war's heavy casualties must have made the new policy necessary, but already a few years earlier, in 217 B.C., the state had recruited slaves as ship rowers. This probably meant that the usual crew, normally made up of *proletarii* or *capite censi* (the poor, people whose only asset was their children) and freedmen, must have been employed in the land army.[18]

What had been a state of emergency around 214 B.C. did not disappear with the end of the conflict against the Carthaginians during the Second Punic War. Rome's expansion, coupled with an intense economic crisis, increased the need for a larger recruitment base, especially after 159 B.C., because many small farmers no longer qualified for even the minimum property requirement. Thus the number of *assidui* (people qualified for military service) became increasingly smaller. The census reveals a decline of 6 percent between 163 B.C. and 135 B.C., a time when Rome's military obligations were becoming more extensive (see Figure 1.2, which depicts Roman provinces around 120 B.C.).[19] It also seems that some sectors of the *assidui* became increasingly reluctant to perform military service. In 168 B.C. the

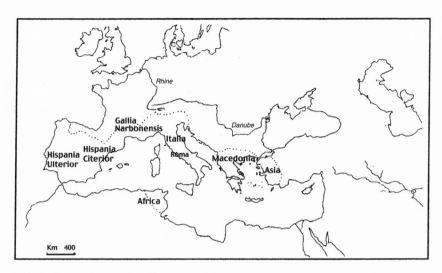

FIGURE 1.2   Roman Provinces, ca. 120 B.C.

government placed a higher military burden upon the allies *(socii)*.[20] Yet already in 151 B.C. it became quite difficult to recruit soldiers for Spain, a battlefield with the reputation of low financial gains and great hardships.[21] In 134 B.C. Scipio Aemilianus was compelled to recruit 4,000 volunteers, many of them his own *clientes* (free men who entrusted their well-being to a powerful patron), for his Spanish campaign. In the years following 133 B.C., the state tried to solve the problem by reducing the property qualification to 1,500 *asses*. The change added about 75,000 *proletarii* to the *assidui*.[22] Yet the difficulty had not been solved.

The destruction of Carthage, and the collapse of Macedonian and Greek power on the opposite shore of the Adriatic Sea and in the Aegean Sea, might cause one to infer that prosperity and internal peace were the hallmarks of the Roman state toward the middle of the second century B.C. On the contrary, several problems, some of them dating from the past, came to a crisis stage. The gap between rich and poor increased. The aristocracy and the equestrian class had reaped most of the benefits from the battlefield. Their vast estates *(latifundia)* became larger and their profits greater; cheap labor was abundant given the influx of slaves as Romans defeated other civilizations on the battlefield. Moreover, the destruction of Carthaginian power, coupled with Roman supremacy in the Aegean, meant that most of the Mediterranean was open to exploitation by the upper levels of Roman society.

The subjugation of other peoples became the root of social displacement, affecting many small farmers and the lower middle class outside Rome, including craftsmen in smaller towns. The introduction of slave labor meant their labor was less valuable, with less demand and lower prices for their products. In the decades before Marius's emergence, it had become increasingly clear that many men could not qualify even for the lowest army level. Even if they could, the necessity of buying one's personal armaments must have increased their financial distress. In other words, what had been the core of the republican armies became smaller and smaller, with the resultant increase in unemployment or underemployment and pauperization. This was a problem that did not seem to touch the Roman plebeians, for the commoners living in the capital continued to enjoy the traditional economic benefits and handouts of the residents of the city.

In the past the problem had been attenuated by having the lower rural and provincial groups share in the profits of war.[23] However, after the conflicts of the first half of the second century B.C., available enemy targets were of limited economic benefit while requiring great military effort. This was especially the case in Spain, where local resistance had not been crushed yet, and of Numidia in Africa. Moreover, internal upheaval in key places like Sicily also limited the revenue flow into the city.

The crisis became serious in the years preceding and following Marius's reform when the Cimbri and the Teutones with their allies wreaked havoc in the territories of the Roman Empire. The two Germanic tribes left Jutland (the mainland of modern-day Denmark) around 115 B.C.[24] For the next few years they seemed unstoppable, defeating a consular army in Noricum in 113 B.C. and another Roman host four years later in the Rhone Valley. But the worst was still to come for in 105 B.C. at Arausio (modern-day Orange) they crushed a large Roman army, inflicting no less than 20,000 casualties. A conservative estimate puts the total Roman dead in all their encounters against these Germanic tribes at some 35,000, the equivalent of seven 5,000-man legions.[25] But even after Arausio, Rome remained safe, for the Germanic tribes chose Spain as their next target. Soon thereafter, however, they retraced their steps, moving toward the Italian peninsula. Marius stopped them in two great battles—the Teutones in 102 B.C. at Aquae Sextiae (Aix-en-Provence) and the Cimbri one year later at Vercellae, near Padua, on the plains of northern Italy.

Total Roman casualties, even before Arausio, had been high, especially if we include the continuous conflicts in the Iberian peninsula and Numidia.

The situation was serious as well because the *socii*, who normally provided half the forces of the Roman legions, were becoming increasingly restless. In exchange for their loyalty they demanded the right of citizenship, something the Romans steadfastly refused.

Thus toward the end of the second century B.C. the problem the Roman state faced was where to find more manpower. The army was at the core of the republic, but Roman society had never been broken into the three Indo-European categories, often hereditary, of military, religious, and economic groups, as was common in similar civilizations. All citizens were eligible to serve, although in practice for the first few centuries of its existence Rome limited duty only to the *assidui*. The minimum property level to qualify for service was not necessarily high, because there were still many small farmers who qualified for the property requirement. Actually the archetype of the Roman soldier was, as Cato expressed in *De agri cultura*, the citizen who was a farmer. The increasing pauperization of the agricultural classes, and hence the inability of the lowest levels to qualify, thwarted this ideal, especially after the failure of the land redistribution schemes supported by Tiberius and Gaius Gracchus. The efforts of both brothers ended in ruin—Tiberius was assassinated in 132 B.C., Gaius ten years later.

The Gracchi reforms, which envisaged the redistribution of public lands to landless citizens, certainly may have been motivated by personal ambition; yet their plan could have solved the recruitment problem by enlarging and strengthening the base of small landowners—the backbone of the Roman army from the very beginning. It would have made the republican order much stronger. The plan's rejection and the resulting violence, during which the Gracchi and their followers were killed by their opponents, spelled disaster for the political and social health of the Roman republic. Tiberius's murder introduced extreme violence to Roman politics.

What Marius did in 107 B.C. was to legalize a process that had been present for about a century and that the Roman ruling class had failed to implement: open up the army to all citizens regardless of their property, arm them at state expense, and recruit not through the *dilectus* (the mandatory levy of the citizens from their tribes) but on a volunteer basis. The new approach did not imply the abolition of the *dilectus*, which remained part of Roman policy, but rather the abolition of the principle that men of property equaled "soldiers" and that the degree of one's property found its equivalent in the individual's position and function on the battlefield. In the past, the *proletarii* (propertyless individuals whose only asset was their children) served in the army only in case the state called a *tumultus*, that is, a general conscription in a situation of dire emergency. Now, instead, they were placed on a par with the rest of the population and could fight side by side with men of property on the battle line.

Later, when the civil war between Marius and Sulla shredded the social fabric of the state, Marius was accused of implementing the reform of 107 B.C. to gain political support from men of property unwilling to serve.[26] Eventually the *capite censi* (all citizens regardless of property; rated by head count, not by property) constituted the bulk of the army after the introduction of the new policy. Thus modern scholar Emilio Gabba is correct to argue that the lack of other volunteers before the new policy's introduction in 107 B.C. must have meant that the social groups that had traditionally monopolized war were no longer willing to shed blood for every enterprise, especially when material rewards might have been minuscule, as in Numidia, where Marius was directed.[27]

There were good reasons for every citizen to be squeamish about enrollment. Polybius says that cavalrymen were required to serve a maximum of ten campaigns; the required number for footmen could be as many as sixteen or twenty.[28] As P.A. Brunt argues, the term "campaigns" should not be necessarily translated as "years," for campaigns, especially in the earlier period of the Roman republic, might last just a few months.[29] Certainly, however, there is no doubt that the success of the Roman state meant that military service must have become more burdensome, especially among the lower-income *assidui*. Campaigns in faraway places could mean neglect and disaster for small farms, with owners returning to lands after years of absence.[30] True, soldiers stationed near their place of residence were granted periods of leave. Such a policy did not make sense, however, when they were stationed far from home, at least in light of the transportation costs. Even less logical for commanders was to substitute reliable veterans possessing knowledge and experience with recruits. Moreover, granting leave and then choosing replacements from Rome could stir political opposition from those people eligible to serve as well as their families. In other words, there was little incentive to send veterans home; it would be expensive and nonsensical politically.

Soldiers' Pay

It seems hard to understand why, at least during the later stages of the republic, generals were able to raise larger and larger armies even though the soldiers' wages were low. Military pay had been introduced much earlier, probably at the beginning of the third century B.C. or at the end of the fourth or, according to some, even earlier—during the long siege of Veii in 412 B.C.[31] But the actual amount of money was miserly. It was well below the wages of a manual laborer, who commanded about twelve *asses* per day in the second century B.C. The soldier's pay was four *asses* in 214 B.C., and it was raised to five later in that century. We have to wait for Caesar, toward the middle of the first century B.C., for the wages to be doubled to ten *asses*.[32]

Merely counting how many *asses* soldiers received, however, misses the point. Their pay was meant to satisfy equipment and subsistence needs, not be a substitute for normal living expenses (although eventually the state, around Marius's time, would pay for equipment). Moreover, in most cases the soldiers were expected to live off the land, and there were other financial rewards to be had besides pay. Soldiers typically could rely on gifts or *donativa* (donatives) from their commanders—for acts of courage and bravery, for distinction on the battlefield, or perhaps as a general reward for a successful campaign. Brunt, for instance, shows that fairly large amounts of money were distributed to the troops during the campaigns of 201–167 B.C. with a peak being reached in 167 B.C. After the defeat of the Macedonian king Perseus the donatives reached 100 *denarii* (silver coins) per footman, 200 per centurion, and 300 per cavalryman. Since the *denarius* was worth ten *asses*, this meant that in one fell swoop footmen, for instance, received the equivalent of 200 days' wages. At the time of their discharge, soldiers would normally receive *praemia* (rewards) in money or, increasingly beginning with Marius, in land allotments. Some soldiers also rounded out their income by acting as suppliers for comrades.[33] But the reality is that the greatest economic rewards were the result of plunder.

The Roman laws of war took for granted that conquered peoples surrendered their freedom and property to Rome. Yet this provision was applied to its fullest only when the enemy strenuously opposed the Roman armies. In that case, land automatically devolved to the state, but disposition of the enemy's movable assets—animals, precious metals, and so on—was left to the discretion of the commander. In some cases greedy generals distributed little among the subordinates; some were outright stingy if they desired to punish the troops (e.g., if they had opposed the general's policies during the campaign). In all cases part of the booty had to go to the treasury to relieve the citizens' war burden. Still, the soldiers almost always received a portion of the booty. According to Polybius, the Romans pillaged in a most orderly fashion, with half of the army, selected evenly from every cohort, keeping guard against potential intruders and the remaining personnel methodically pillaging the enemy city. All the items were then carried to a central location and fairly distributed among the actual pillagers and those soldiers who had remained on guard.

Again, limiting the analysis to the economic benefits does not paint the full picture. War was also a lure for the adventurer or the dreamer who hoped to strike it rich. And simply comparing soldiers' pay to the wages of a manual laborer misses the harsh reality of this preindustrial society. Paid labor was not widespread, so even subsistence wages might have appealed to large segments of the population if they lived outside the walls of Rome, where the *plebs* (commoners) were normally kept at peace by grants and support from the state.

The Equipment of the Roman Soldier

Marius is also credited with a series of equipment changes. The Roman citizens manning the ranks of the *velites* (light infantry) disappeared from the battle line. They were substituted by auxiliaries, that is, non-Roman citizens. The tripartite division of the heavy infantry into *hastati* (first line), *principes* (second line), and *triarii* (third line) was also dropped.[34] Now all Roman citizens fighting in the heavy line were armed in the same manner—a large shield *(scutum)*, a deadly sword *(gladius)*, and one or two javelins *(pila)*, one heavier than the other.

The *scutum* was a curved, oblong shield that was unlike the shield of the Greek hoplite (heavy soldier), as it was used for both defense and offense. Polybius has left us a description that coincides with a sample found at Kasr el-Harit, Egypt, in its main characteristics.[35] According to the Greek historian, it was 75 centimeters wide and 1.2 meters long. It was made up of two wooden sheets glued together and covered first by canvas and then by calfskin. The top and bottom were covered with iron to protect against the cutting blows of the enemy and the wear and tear of resting it on the ground. A metal boss was placed in the center. It was thicker at the center than at the edges, giving it flexibility near the rim and protection in the center[36] against stones, heavy missiles, and spear points.[37] The Romans adopted the *scutum* during the Latin Wars of the fourth century B.C. Before then they must have mainly used a round shield *(clipeus)* in the manner of the Greek hoplite.[38]

The *scutum* was heavy indeed. Peter Connolly, who has constructed a modern replica, confirmed by archaeological finds, puts its weight at about 10 kilograms.[39] Clearly, it could not be kept raised off the ground for long.

Thus logically (and this according to a suggestion Connolly himself put forward) the legionnaire would hold his shield high and straight as he rushed the enemy, hitting down hard with the intent of sending him sprawling to the ground. If that did not work, he would anchor the *scutum* on the ground, using it as protection against enemy blows while he tried to attack with his sword.[40]

Another piece of equipment, the *gladius*, was a short, double-edged sword used for thrusting as well as cutting. Its efficacy and use as a main weapon in the legions set the Roman soldier apart from his contemporaries and those who preceded him. Probably of Spanish origin, the *gladius* seems to have been adopted by the Romans beginning in the early fourth century B.C.[41] The only sample recovered from the republican period dates from 69 B.C. It is 76 centimeters long, including the handle, and 5.7 centimeters wide.[42] The blade probably must have been 50–55 centimeters.[43] It was the ideal weapon for soldiers, like the Romans, who emphasized close-order combat after throwing their *pila*. Moreover, the apparently preferred mode of using it in a thrusting motion made it deadly because of the likelihood of striking an enemy's vital organ. The *gladius*, introduced around the early fourth century B.C., became standard army equipment by the later third or early second centuries. It must have been used during the Macedonian War against Philip, for Plutarch mentions that Macedonian soldiers, on their way to the battlefield at Cynoscephalae (197 B.C.), were horrified upon seeing the types of wounds suffered by their comrades in a previous encounter against the Romans.[44]

The use of the *pilum* went further back in history, although its first description appears in the second century B.C. in a rather confusing testimony by Polybius.[45] The Roman soldier carried two *pila*, one heavier than the other. The light *pilum* was launched at a greater distance from the enemy, soon followed by the heavy weapon before the close, when shield and sword would then come into play. We can reconstruct the *pilum* fairly well on the basis of Polybius's description and from archaeological discoveries. Light and heavy *pila* were composed of two parts—a very long iron section and a wooden shaft. The blade of the light *pilum* was usually attached through a socket, whereas a tang was used for the heavy type. The metal section ended in a barbed blade that was at times flat but more usually polygonal.[46] The weapon's effectiveness, at least in its heavy format, was based on its weight, not velocity.[47] Modern experiments have shown that a *pilum*, thrown from a distance of 5 meters, could pierce 30 millimeters of pinewood or 20 millimeters of ply.[48]

Polybius says that the metal part was 135 centimeters long. The most complete example of the heavy *pilum* found in Spain has a head 60 millimeters long, a shank of 554 millimeters, and a tang of 90 millimeters long and 55 millimeters wide.[49] The metal part of the heavy *pilum* was by Marius's time held to a wooden shaft by two metal rivets. The idea of this construction was to prevent the enemy from throwing back the *pila*, for the metal head would bend or break upon impact even if it missed the target and hit the ground. But it must have worked otherwise. Marius or someone else during his time retained one metal rivet but substituted a wooden pin for the other.[50] Experimentation with the *pilum*'s design did not end there, however. About fifty years later, Julius Caesar tempered only the point of the blade, leaving the base untempered.[51] This meant that the point retained its murderous penetrating capacity while the rest would bend upon impact. If it hit the shield, it would have rendered it unusable; if it hit the ground, the javelin's point would lose its shape and thus could not be thrown back at the Romans. Put simply, the *pilum* would either penetrate flesh or become useless to the enemy. The final stage in the development came during the first two centuries A.D., when the *pilum* became much lighter; a modern reconstruction puts its weight at less than 2 kilograms.[52]

The adoption of identical weapons by the heavy infantry signaled a symbolical and tactical change. In symbolical terms this implied that after the elimination of the *velites* all Roman soldiers were equal. They wore the same weapons and deployed in similar lines. The tactical implications were much more important. In the Second Punic War (218–201 B.C.) the republican armies included legions of Roman citizens, matched by a roughly equivalent number of allies who deployed double the number of *equites* present in the legion. A legion at full strength would include about 4,200 infantry and 300 cavalrymen, the allies 4,200 footmen and 600 horsemen. The Roman infantry was divided into four lines, one of light infantry *(velites)*; the other three were all heavy infantry divided into *hastati* (first line), *principes* (second line), and *triarii* (third line). (See Figure 1.3.) The first two heavy lines were armed with *gladius, pilum,* and *scutum,* the third with spear, *gladius,* and *scutum.* The full complement of each line of *velites, hastati,* and *principes* was about 1,200 each, the *triarii* about 600. Each line had ten maniples that included two centuries (the smallest unit of the Roman army). There were 120 men in the maniples of the *hastati* and *principes* and sixty in those of the *triarii.* It is likely that initially on the battlefield the maniples deployed in a checkerboard fashion, each line a certain distance from the other. The soldiers were organized into cohorts, ten for each legion, not into maniples as in the past.

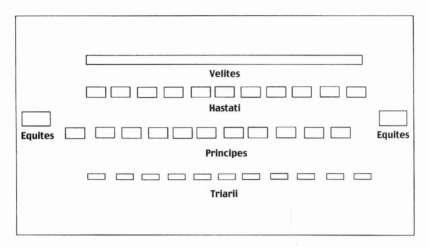

FIGURE 1.3 The Manipular Legion

Unlike the continuous process that must have been typical of Greek armies, the Roman battle system of the middle republic was a process of different stages. First, the *velites* performed the usual task of light infantry, trying to disorganize the enemy or discovering its weak spots. Then the *hastati* moved forward, engaging the enemy first at a certain distance with the *pila* and then at close range with *scutum* and *gladius*. If the enemy held on, the *principes* moved forward for the decisive blow. If this failed, the legionnaires had the possibility of withdrawing from the battlefield under the protection of the *triarii*'s spears. In this arrangement the usual task of the cavalry was to protect the legion's flanks. The adoption of similar weapons for all Roman infantry heralded a change also in the troop deployment—a reform usually associated with Marius but that must have been in the offing for decades before him.

The basic fighting unit of the new army—the cohort—was much larger (see Figure 1.4). It grouped a maniple from each line of the *hastati*, *principes*, and *triarii* into a single unit. This implied that the cohort, about 500–600 men each, had much more weight but less flexibility than the maniple. Still, however, the use of the *pila* and the sword gave the Roman line much more flexibility than the Greek or the Macedonian phalanx. It still remained, as Hans Delbrück mentioned long ago,[53] a phalanx with joints. The ten cohorts of each legion could be deployed in a single line, in two

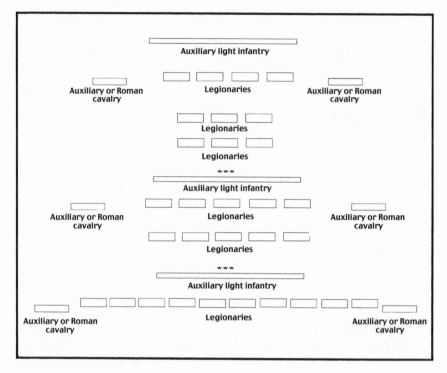

FIGURE 1.4   Formations of the Cohortal Legion

lines, or more likely in three (four cohorts in the first and three each in the other two lines).

It is unclear why the term "cohort" was adopted for the new fighting formation. The name was already in use in the third century B.C. to identify the legion's allied complements. In the second century B.C. it must have become quite common, for Livy mentions it in his description of the Battle of Pydna (168 B.C.)—but again only to refer to the allies.[54] Sometime in the later second century B.C. the term must have become widespread, coexisting with the old terms, but it is only during Caesar's time that the term "cohort" was permanently substituted for the terms of the manipular legion.

The formal adoption of a larger basic fighting unit (the cohort of 500 men) against a smaller unit (the maniple of 120) was probably the result of the defeats experienced against the Cimbri and the Teutones, whose furious charges could be overwhelming during initial fighting.[55] Of course the Romans had already fought against similar tactics—the Italian Celts—and it could be argued that since they had not adopted it at the time there was no reason to do so at the end of the second century B.C. Yet after defeating the Celts with a certain difficulty, the more usual enemies of the Romans— Carthaginians, Greeks, and Macedonians—were better confronted by re- taining the manipular system. Once the Cimbri and the Teutones appeared on the scene, then, it is no surprise that the Romans would experiment with a different system.

Romans always demonstrated the uncanny ability to learn from defeat and to imitate the methods of adversaries if found to be more efficient than their own. For instance, one reaction to their reverses against the men from Jutland and Frisia was to rethink their soldiers' training. The same year as the defeat at Arausio, the consul who had remained in Rome (the other con- sul, Marius, was in Africa) hired the teachers from a gladiator school to im- prove the soldiers' dueling skill.[56] Also, Marius introduced a crucial im- provement in their training. In the manner of Philip of Macedon, the father of Alexander the Great, Marius not only reduced the camp followers but also pushed the troops' physical resilience to the extreme. He cut the size of the baggage train by forcing his soldiers to be self-reliant and carry their equipment—tools and weapons—necessary not just for combat but for se- curity, like building camps and field fortifications. His soldiers were nick- named "Marius's mules."[57] Moreover, he went to great lengths to keep disci- pline intact. There is no better example of this than the treatment of his nephew, an officer named Caius Lusius.

Lusius had developed a strong attraction for one of his younger soldiers, Trebonius, who despite repeated entreaties had refused his commander's homoerotic approaches. Lusius persisted, and one night he summoned the young soldier to his tent. It was an order that Trebonius could not disobey; but when Lusius tried to rape him Trebonius drew the sword and killed his commander. At the trial no one took the stand to defend the soldier, worried that Marius, regardless of the evidence, would punish the killer of his own flesh and blood. But the general, to the surprise of all, listened to Trebonius's tale that he had never prostituted himself to anyone, although many had of- fered great gifts for his sexual favors. It was a defense that Marius accepted graciously. Instead of punishing Trebonius, he granted him the customary crown for bravery and indicated that he had acted nobly and that he stood as an example of the "most noble conduct" to the rest of his soldiers.[58]

The size of the Marian and post-Marian legion has been a matter of con- troversy. It is likely that it averaged some 5,000 men but the total comple-

ment could be higher (6,000) or, more likely, much lower (3,000). The ancient sources confuse the problem because, as Brunt points out, they normally multiply by 5,000 or so whenever they use the term "legion." In other
words, "legion" is equal to 5,000 regardless of actual size.[59] Yet many vari-
ants might have affected a legion's size. Sometimes the commanding general
was unable to raise an adequate complement of soldiers, especially during
the first century B.C.[60] For instance, Lepidus's sixteen new legions in 36 B.C.
were described as being "half-full" *(semiplenae)*.[61] Sometimes disease, hard-
ship, and occasionally desertion thinned the ranks, although the latter must
have been rare. Brunt calculated that only 60 percent of Augustus's soldiers
were present at the time of their discharge.[62] Sometimes it was the result of
casualties. It is likely that heavy casualties had reduced Caesar's legions in 49
B.C. to about 4,000 men each.[63]

Finally, Marius strengthened the legion's sense of identity by adopting the
silver eagle as its symbol.[64] Animal symbols were not new among the Romans or other peoples of the Italian peninsula. For instance, the Hirpini
tribe of the hills near Avellino and Benevento used the wolf as their symbol;
indeed, their name derived from the Samnite term for "wolf" *(hirpus)*. The
same is true of the Celtic tribes of northern Italy. With Marius, however, the
eagle became the legion's predominant symbol. Its adoption in the manner
of a flag or banner strengthened one's allegiance to his unit, much like the
battle flag for later armies. Moreover, it is likely that it was used to convey
signals on the battlefield.

The Making of the Roman Man

Even as the Roman republic was on the road to oblivion, intellectuals constructed an archetype for the ideal Roman male. The construction was a
subtle reworking of older themes that had first appeared in the first half of
the second century B.C. and were based on the "customs of our ancestors"
(mos maiorum). It was an ideal that the great intellectual and political figure
Marcus Tullius Cicero articulated best, but outsiders were influential in
fashioning and spreading the notion. For instance, the Greek Posidonius,
who arrived as the Rhodes ambassador to Rome in 87 B.C., described the
Romans as modest, frugal, law-abiding citizens. They lived a simple life, de-
void of luxuries; they worshiped their gods piously; they respected the
rights of all.[65] It was a portrayal that the Greeks had made for themselves as
to Persians during the great wars of the fifth century B.C.[66]

The *mos maiorum* was a highly idealized version of the community's behavior, existing in Rome at least up to the last stages of the Second Punic War (218–201 B.C.) and vaguely present in earlier times. It became a longing for times past as well as a restatement of proper community behavior, even as the republic waned. It emphasized the hereditary hegemony of the oligarchy and the network of rights, duties, and moral obligations that tied the citizens to the state. Altruism was the key to behavior—the citizen's duty, in Cicero's view *qui, non quid efficere posset in re publica, cogitavit, sed quid facere ipse deberet.* Almost 2,000 years later, U.S. President John F. Kennedy would address the American people with these similar words: "Ask not what your country can do for you—ask what you can do for your country."[67] And the greatest service of any Roman was service to the state, which was inevitably mingled with both political and military life, for Romans saw hardly any distinction between the two.

L. R. Lind argues that the Romans combined civic behavior with moral obligations, something the great families had shown in the past when their stand against all enemies (internal and external) saved not only their own existence but the state as well. They extracted the basis for ideal behavior of present and future generations from the ancients' *exempla virtutis* (acts of courage, patriotism, and selflessness). The *mos maiorum* then became a statement of the key virtues of the citizen. They included glory *(gloria),* greatness of spirit *(magnitudo animi),* praiseworthiness or honorability *(dignitas),* authority *(auctoritas),* seriousness *(gravitas),* public recognition *(honos),* and nobility *(nobilitas).*

The most cherished ideal was glory, which was given to those who had selflessly defended their country with great personal danger and dedication. It could be given to an individual, an army, a clan, a rank of society. It was a recognition that once received could be passed on to one's descendants, thereby becoming a permanent trait of the family. The glory that Scipio Africanus achieved by defeating Hannibal during the Second Punic War forever belonged to succeeding generations of the Scipio clan.

Greatness of spirit was connected with deeds that a family demonstrated by defending and attacking Rome's enemies. It was an ideal connected with action. It was, as Lind says, "warlike animus at its highest level," and it was shown not just for one's own ends but for the republic as a whole. It also included "hope, perseverance, and patience."[68]

Praiseworthiness was again a value connected with the state. The individual possessed it if "he maintained his own lofty interests and fulfilled his own wishes for advancement by advancing the interests of the state." In other words, patriotism and duty to the state were inseparable aspects of that value.[69] The best arena to display this was a mandatory turn in the military, as service therein was the prerequisite for achieving a magistrate's honors. In other words, praiseworthiness, whether gained in the military or in public service, gave authority to the individual's deeds and words and thus enhanced his status among the citizens.

Seriousness was the visual and psychological rendition of the public man. His visual appearance conveyed his values as a man of public weight.[70] Public recognition, or *honos*, was closely connected to glory, but whereas glory acquired an inner meaning and was granted to the individual and his clan forever, *honos* was the public recognition that one had "done his duty and nothing more."[71] As Cicero says, "Where the honor is not public, there can be no desire for glory."[72]

The last virtue was nobility. Although applied originally only to certain families, nobility reflected not only bloodlines but proper moral and political behavior. As Cicero argues about an athlete, "It was never yourself for which you became famous but for your lungs and muscles."[73] It was inevitably connected to a conservative view of life in which anything new meant danger and improper behavior; as such, it became a tenet of the policies of the Roman oligarchy. The term "*novus*" implied disturbance in the normal cycles of civic life. As Lind argues, it stood for revolution in the phrase *novis rebus studere* for the cancellation of debts (a request strongly opposed by the oligarchy), in *novae tabellae*, and for a man without aristocratic roots in *homo novus*.[74]

The bias toward identifying the *mos maiorum* with the oligarchy is clear in all the values making the ideal citizen of the republic. The providers of the *exempla virtutis* (modes of exemplary behavior) were from the great clans. Greatness of spirit was "an exclusively aristocratic trait . . . [indicating] the eager bravery of spirit with which the ruling class of the great families defended Rome or attacked her enemies." Dignity *(dignitas)* was the domain of the aristocracy, not of commoners, for the tools needed to gain it—knowledge of the law, public speaking, leadership on the battlefield—were usually not within the commoner's reach. Authority was usually the reserve of the great clans. A successful general could gain both glory for his clan forever and *honos*, that is, a lifetime of external recognition for his acts; a commoner received financial rewards or prizes *(praemia)*, which were transitory and could not be transferred to future generations.[75]

These values, first articulated by Cato the Censor in the first half of the second century B.C. and then most completely by Cicero in the first century B.C., came when the notion of the republic's decline was being expressed with dates and arguments ranging chronologically from the beginning of the second century B.C. to the destruction of Carthage at the end of the Third Punic War (149–146 B.C.). Like all myths, these values combined reality with characteristics that had existed only in a few individuals and only for a certain time. Although Romans prided themselves on their respect for law, it is also clear that personal interests preceded the law and that the law could be bent to justify actions. The idealization of the past thus must have been a restatement on the justness and efficacy of the hegemony of the ruling class when, beginning with Marius if not with the Gracchi, that hegemony was questioned and challenged. The very existence of the challenge and several other stresses meant that the adoption of the idealization of the past had to be popularized in a way that would represent all Roman citizens, not just the oligarchy. It was so because of political changes, characterized by the fall of the republic under Caesar and the establishment of the Principate under Augustus, and many other stresses that tended to weaken the structure of Roman society.

Foremost was the integration of disadvantaged groups, at least the provincial poor, into the system; they would man, after 107 B.C., the ranks of the Roman legions. Then there was the switch of allegiance from the state to individual generals—whether Marius, Sulla, Sertorius, Pompeius, or Caesar—which meant that the Senate, which embodied the *mos maiorum*, became increasingly irrelevant while the individual became the center of authority. This phenomenon was paralleled by the emergence of individualism, probably the result of Roman contact with the Hellenistic world. Moreover, the very success of the Roman legions created another problem, for a political structure that could efficiently control a small republic was forced to deal with the difficulties of overseeing an ever-expanding empire. Finally, new men—the so-called *novi homines*—not of aristocratic background, appeared on the scene: people like Marius and Cicero.

The emergence of the ideal Roman preceded and followed the army's radical reorganization by Marius. Marius finalized a process that had been ongoing for decades. The most important change was the decision to open the army ranks to all Roman citizens regardless of property held. It was momentous, a decision dictated not by Marius's ambition but by the new needs of the Roman state. However, the accusation that the proletarization of the army heralded new changes in the makeup of the state rested on a more solid foundation. This proletarization became inevitable in the future, although neither Marius nor his opponents nor the aristocracy were aware of the possibility of such a development. Actually, the aristocracy raised no opposition to the new policy, an attitude shared by the other groups that were reluctant to enroll in the army.

The new soldiers had less reason to defend the traditional structure of their society, unlike the men of property of the past. Those men of property, whether large or small landowners, thought they *were* the state and that the state belonged to them—at least in theory. The army of dedicated and loyal amateurs of the past would eventually become the professional army of the future. In the end, the loyalty once pledged to the republic would switch to the generals—upon whom they relied for economic survival.

Notes

1. Plutarch, Marius 11.3.
2. Plutarch, *Marius* 7.2, 14.1–3, 12.4.
3. Plutarch, *Marius* 9.2.
4. Plutarch, *Marius* 13.1.
5. Plutarch, *Marius* 15.1–3.
6. Plutarch, *Marius* 16.1–3.
7. Plutarch, *Marius* 11.2, 8.
8. Plutarch, *Marius* 18.1–2.
9. Plutarch, *Marius* 18.
10. Plutarch, *Marius* 27.2.
11. Plutarch, *Marius* 20.1–3.
12. Plutarch, *Marius* 25.6.
13. Plutarch, *Marius* 20.6.
14. Plutarch, *Marius* 21.1–4.
15. Plutarch, *Marius* 25–27.
16. Emilio Gabba, *Esercito e società nella tarda repubblica romana* (Firenze, 1973), pp. 1–45.
17. Ibid., p. 12.
18. Ibid., pp. 12–13.
19. P. A. Brunt, *Italian Manpower, 225 B.C.–A.D. 14* (Oxford, 1971), pp. 74–75.
20. Ibid., p. 398.
21. Polybius xxxv.4.
22. Gabba, *Esercito*, pp. 24–25.

23. Antonio Santosuosso, *Soldiers, Citizens, and the Symbols of War from Classical Greece to Republican Rome, 500–167 B.C.* (Boulder, 1997), pp. 158–160.

24. They were identified as Celtic by some authors. See, e.g., Lawrence Keppie, *The Making of the Roman Army from Republic to Empire* (Norman, OK, 1998), p. 59. Certainly the Ambrones who fought at Aquae Sextiae must have spoken Celtic. It is more than likely that the rest were Germans.

25. Brunt, *Italian Manpower*, p. 82.

26. On this, see for instance, Sallust, *Bellum Iugurthinum* 86.3.

27. Gabba, *Esercito*,pp. 35–36.

28. Polybius vi.19. This is the usual interpretation of the Greek historian's passage, but the manuscript line on the infantry is uncertain. The text is corrupt.

29. Brunt, *Italian Manpower*, pp. 399–400.

30. Ibid., pp. 309–402.

31. C. Nicolet, *The World of the Citizen in Republican Rome*, tr. P. S. Falla (London, 1980), pp. 115–116.

32. Ibid., p. 116.

33. Ibid., p. 121.

34. On the republican military system before the later second century, see Santosuosso, *Soldiers, Citizens, and the Symbols of War*, pp. 150–157.

35. Polybius VI.23. Cf. M. C. Bishop and J.C.N. Coulson, *Roman Military Equipment from the Punic Wars to the Fall of Rome* (London, 1993), p. 58; Peter Connolly, *Greece and Rome at War* (Englewood Cliffs, NJ, 1981), p. 131.

36. Bishop and Coulson, *Roman Military Equipment*, p. 59.

37. Polybius vi.23.

38. Livy viii.8.

39. Connolly, *Greece and Rome at War*, p. 131.

40. Ibid., p. 233.

41. Leonid Tarassuk and Claude Blair, eds., *The Complete Encyclopedia of Arms and Weapons* (New York, 1982), p. 193.

42. Bishop and Coulson, *Roman Military Equipment*, pp. 53–54.

43. Tarassuk and Blair, p. 193.

44. Livy xxxi.34.4.

45. Polybius vi.23.8.

46. Bishop and Coulson, *Roman Military Equipment*, p. 48; Tarassuk and Blair, p. 367.

47. Bishop and Coulson, *Roman Military Equipment*, p. 48.

48. Ibid., p. 48.

49. Ibid., p. 50. The *pilum* was found in Renieblas, Spain.

50. Plutarch, *Marius* 15.1.

51. G. R. Watson, *The Roman Soldier* (Ithaca, 1969), p. 59.

52. Connolly, *Greece and Rome at War*, p. 233.

53. Hans Delbrück, *History of the Art of War Within the Framework of Political History*, vol. 1, translated by W. J. Renfroe Jr. (London, 1975), p. 275.

54. Livy xlii.31.

55. See Keppie, *The Making of the Roman Army*, pp. 63–64.

56. Valerius Maximus ii.3.2.

57. Plutarch, *Marius* 13.1–2.

58. Plutarch, *Marius* 14.3–5.

59. See Brunt, *Italian Manpower*, esp. pp. 687–693.

60. Ibid., p. 688.

61. Velleius Paterculus ii.80.

62. Brunt, *Italian Manpower*, p. 689.

63. Ibid., p. 690.

64. Keppie, *The Making of the Roman Army*, pp. 67–68.

65. Cf. L. R. Lind, "The Tradition of Roman Moral Conservatism," in *Studies in Latin Literature and Roman History*, edited by Carl Deroux (Bruxelles, 1979), vol. 1, p. 7.

66. Santosuosso, *Soldiers, Citizens, and the Symbols of War*, pp. 74–79.

67. Cf. Lind, "The Tradition of Roman Moral Conservatism," p. 28, n. 38. Cicero's expression is in *Philippic* 1.15.

68. Lind, "The Tradition of Roman Moral Conservatism," p. 20.

69. Ibid., pp. 27–29.

70. Ibid., pp. 34–38.

71. Ibid., p. 41.

72. Cicero, *De lege agraria* 2.91. Cf. Lind, "The Tradition of Roman Moral Conservatism," p. 42.

73. Cicero, *Cato Maior* 27.

74. Lind, "The Tradition of Roman Moral Conservatism," pp. 45–46.

75. Ibid., pp. 14–42.

2

Armies of Pillagers

Frequent riots, party strife, and finally civil wars broke out, during which a few powerful men, to whose influential position most people had lent their support, were attempting to win absolute rule masquerading as champions of the senate or of the people. The terms "good" and "bad" were applied to citizens, not on the yardstick of services rendered or injuries inflicted on the state, since all were equally corrupt; any individual of outstanding wealth and irresistible in his lawlessness was considered "good" because he was the preserver of existing conditions.

Sallust, *The Histories,* i.12

Marius's reform of 107 B.C., unopposed at the time, opened a Pandora's box. For the next sixty years or so the Roman army, which, tradition maintained, was a symbol of honor, bravery, and patriotism, became an emblem of everything that was wrong during the later stages of the Roman republic. On the surface nothing seemed to have changed. The aristocracy, the state's ruling group, still provided the military commanders. The legions' soldiers were still all Roman citizens; most originated from the traditional sources—the countryside and small towns. Yet soon enough the armies were no longer the guardians of the probity and health of the Roman state. Rather, they were armies of pillagers. Only with the rise of Julius Caesar would Rome regain and restore at least the pretense of the old soldierly virtues.

The destruction of the invaders from the north—the Cimbri and Teutones—and the defeat of the Numidians in North Africa (111–104 B.C.) did not bring peace to the republic. The enemy within became the element of destruction, its threat more serious than most any in Rome's past. The republic's own soldiers, with the allies and Italians who had fought side by side with the legions, became the enemy of the people. But the threat did not end there, for the slaves who had strengthened the wealth of the upper classes of the republic rose up in arms to break their legal, social, and economic chains. It was like reliving the bitter nightmares of the Second Punic War. Now, however, most of the enemies at Rome's gates were not only strangers from faraway lands but also people who were familiar in look and character and spoke the same language.

The Social Wars

The troubles began as turmoil within the community of people who normally provided half or more of the Roman troops. Not every subject of the Roman state was treated equally. There were at least five levels in society, each with decreasing rights, duties, and privileges: Romans, Latin tribesmen closely related to the Romans, mainland Italians south of the northern part of the peninsula, the people of the main islands (Sicily and Sardinia), and the Ligurians and the Celts in Cisalpine Italy (that part of the peninsula north of the Rubicon River and south of the Alps; see Figure 2.1). The problem was not the Latins, who shared most of the benefits that war accrued to the commonwealth, or the islanders or even the Celts (both harshly treated) but the Italian tribes of the center and of the south; some, the Samnites, for instance, had been Rome's bitter enemies in the past.

Initially the Italian allies (the so-called *socii*) had provided soldiers that equaled or doubled the Roman contribution (for infantry and cavalry, respectively). According to a recent estimate, they supplied the legions with about 80,000 soldiers against 50,000 Romans in the period 200–179 B.C. and an average of about 54,000 against 45,000 in the decade that followed.[1] Specifically the figures show that 65,000 *socii* against 45,600 Roman legionnaires served in 169 B.C., 76,440 against 58,200 in 168 B.C.[2] Data for the following years, to the turn of the century, are less reliable. P. A. Brunt argues that the complement of allied soldiers increased during the period of the Gracchi, whereas V. Ilari feels it happened after Marius.[3]

The *socii* commitment to the Roman war policy did not end with providing a majority of the soldiers. They were also forced to support their soldiers' pay and food requirements through taxation[4] (Roman citizens were exempted from the tax beginning with the Third Macedonian War, 171–167

FIGURE 2.1   Italy

B.C.).[5] Moreover, the allies' treasury was not replenished with the spoils of
the enemy, as was the case with the Roman public treasury.[6] And when it
came to dividing spoils on the battlefield, the allies were again shortchanged
to the benefit of Roman soldiers. Polybius mentions four cases of the distribution of loot in the period 201–167. In one case at least, in 177 B.C., allies
received only half the booty granted to Roman citizen-soldiers.[7] Four years
later their lots of land in Roman colonies were smaller than those awarded
to Romans. Although allies fought next to Romans on the battle line, the
highest officers were Romans; their own chiefs were not necessarily part of
the war council.[8] It is also likely that the allies' deployment in battle exposed

some to the greatest danger.[9] This seems to have been the case, for instance, in the early stages of the Battle of Pydna. Wulff Alonso argues that this was reflected also in the disposition of the army on the march. The allies, so-called *extraordinarii* (elite troops) led the troops, followed by the allied cavalry. Another group of allied cavalry closed the deployment. The Roman soldiers were safe inside the middle of the marching column.[10] In other words, the *socii* were exposed to the greatest danger points, the front and rear. Inequality was also reflected in food distribution. According to Polybius, allied and Roman footmen received the same quota, but allied cavalry collected only five food rations, not the usual seven plus one and one-third of hay.[11]

At times, Roman individuals and Roman institutions abused the Italians outright. The Senate could intervene in all their major political affairs, and Roman leaders might disregard the rights of Italian citizens. For instance, in 173 B.C. a Roman consul requested food and lodgings from an allied city, Praeneste, which was an illegal action according to custom. Another consul publicly whipped a leading magistrate of another city. One of Scipio Africanus's legates in 205–200 B.C. imposed heavy duties on the citizens of the southern city of Locri in Calabria, breaking the terms of the city's alliance with Rome. And finally, another consul in 174 B.C. stripped the marble from a temple in Crotone, Calabria, for a building in Rome.[12] Another good example of Rome's heavy hand was its suppression of the popular cult of the Bacchanalia, which honored the god Dionysus.

The Bacchanals were of Greek origin. The cult appeared first in Etruria (modern Tuscany), then spread in a more radical form to other parts of central Italy, especially Campania, and throughout the south. Our knowledge of the ritual is fragmentary, but we know that the Italian sect, unlike those in Hellenistic lands, was well organized and open to men and women. In 186 B.C. a man and his mistress revealed to one of the consuls the extent of the cult's membership and the beliefs that a Campanian woman had introduced, which were at variance with the original creed. When the Bacchanals had first spread to Italy, the state raised no opposition, but the Senate was stunned when at the end of an investigation the consuls reported that the cult was widespread and that the Bacchanals challenged many of the state's key values and institutions. Their society was very secretive: It met at night unsupervised by a legally delegated magistrate; its members were tied by an oath that—the senators must have feared—could supersede loyalty to the state; they did not respect property rights, for they forged bogus wills and held property in common; men and women joined together in ritual; there were many supporters in southern areas, traditionally hostile to Rome; the sect emasculated young men of recruiting age and thereby endangered Rome's military supremacy; and its members celebrated with orgies that may have included murder. Clearly most of the accusations cannot have been correct. The most likely worry, then, was the potential for civic disturbance that the Bacchanals represented in Rome and especially in the central and southern towns. Although they had many adherents in Rome—perhaps even a few distinguished Roman families—most supporters were from the allied territories of central and southern Italy and thus represented the lower social classes.

The Senate adopted measures of repression with no input from the commoners (but likely with the approval of the provincial aristocracy, who must have regarded the Bacchanals as a threat to their hegemony). The government's suppression was immediate. The members of the Bacchanals were hunted down, prosecuted, and destroyed in a nightmarish climate. Many were denounced, jailed, and condemned. Some committed suicide in jail. In Rome alone over 7,000 persons were apprehended before the magistrates moved out of the city to eradicate the cult throughout the rest of Italy.[13]

In the end, however, the main reason for the outbreak of the Social War—the confrontation between Rome and the central and southern Italians that began in 90 B.C.—was the issue of citizenship, which Rome had steadfastly refused to grant to the *socii*. Initially, the allies' social and political leaders opposed the grant of citizenship to their people, fearing it would increase the exodus of their commoners to Rome. According to Roman law, any male individual, regardless of origin, acquired citizenship if he was listed in the city's census. If unchecked, such a situation would hurt the interests of the leading citizens of the Italian tribes. The influx of non-Roman natives into the capital must have made it difficult for the allies to fill soldier quotas for the Roman armies, made labor more expensive, and shrunk their taxation basis. In 187, 177, and 172 B.C. Rome expelled from the city all people who had acquired citizenship illegally, probably an ally request.[14] However, the situation changed by the end of that century.

The new attitude of the *socii* was evident indirectly in a series of laws beginning with the older Gracchus to Marius. These failed laws were opposed by the Roman ruling class and supported by the allies. All either extended greater privileges to the non-Romans or granted them citizenship. The tribune Livius Drusus the Younger was the author of the last attempt (91 B.C.). When he paid with his life for his daring proposal (an unknown assassin stabbed him in front of his house), the Italian tribes felt that only force could bring what they wanted. Ironically, the demand for granting citizenship was led by the Italian aristocracy, the same group that in the past had opposed the idea. What had changed was that the allies' ruling class now preferred equality with Rome to independence. In order to achieve more political rights, the allies' leaders were ready to relinquish some of the economic benefits they had defended so strongly in the first half of the second century B.C.[15] They wanted to be part of the empire: "all Italy was now demanding not freedom but a share in government and citizenship."[16]

The allies began their citizenship drive by pressure and persuasion.[17] When that failed, war became the only alternative. Most tribes in central and southern Italy joined together in the Italia confederation—the beginning of a four-year war: "the most warlike and most numerous of the Italian peoples combined against Rome, and came within a little of destroying [Roman] supremacy."[18] Not all joined the insurgents, including the Latini, Etruscans, and Umbrians; and not everybody, even among the fiercest enemies of the Romans like the Samnites, would share the views of their leaders. For instance, in the Hirpini town of Aeclanum (the Hirpini were one of the formidable groups among the Samnites), a leading citizen, Minatius Magius, stood on the Roman side.[19] Others, like the citizens of Naples and Heraclea, with cherished Greek roots, preferred to retain their ancient independent status rather than enjoy Roman citizenship.[20] War continued until the Romans finally concluded they were in the wrong, and by 88 B.C. Rome extended citizenship to most people of peninsular Italy south of the Po River.[21] From then on, there was no distinction between a Roman and an allied soldier. In the long run this was beneficial to the army's strength; in the short run it added to the confusion and fratricidal war between the armies of Marius and those of Sulla.

The Face of the New Soldier

The immediate cause of the civil war that pitted Marius against Sulla in the later stages of the Social War was the rivalry over who should lead the campaign against Mithridates, the king of Pontus, in Asia Minor. Mithridates had successfully challenged Rome's hegemony not only in Asia Minor but in the Near East and Greece. The matter was of great urgency to the Senate and appealed to the men of arms, for the region was wealthy with the prospect of riches. The rivalry between the two leaders dated from much earlier, sometimes the result of childish pique and contests.[22] It had begun during the Numidian War (111–104 B.C.)—Sulla had served under Marius—and continued during the Social War. It was not just a matter of mutual dislike; they held opposing views as to the republic and the political and social roles of the Roman people and their subjects. Eventually Sulla would stand for an aristocratic view of the state as defined by Servius Tullius and, generally, for the aristocratic and wealthier citizens of Rome. Marius would become the symbol of the popular faction, championing the interests of the commoners and new citizens—that is, the old *socii*. In reality, however, the motivations of the leaders and their supporters were more complex, and their opposing interests were never clear-cut. In the end they would symbolize all that was wrong in the late Roman republic.

History would judge Marius more with abuse than praise. He was, they said, a man of sordid origin whose ambition almost destroyed Rome; a disloyal individual who had betrayed his patrons; a man who had stained his hands with the blood of Roman citizens. Actually, he was from a good provincial family, although not from the traditional Roman upper classes; his personal behavior was not uncommon at the time; and his reform of 107 B.C. made official what had existed in practice and seemed at the time to be an excellent solution. Moreover, he did not start the massacres of other Romans: The opponents and supporters of the Gracchi began that process some three decades earlier. Born in Arpinum, a small hill town in the Apennine Mountains southeast of Rome, around 157 B.C., Marius belonged to a family that had recently gained the equestrian class. His marriage to a member of the Julii made him part of one of Rome's oldest families. The Julii were aristocrats who claimed the goddess Venus as their ancestor.

The Greek historian Appian of Alexandria (ca. A.D. 90–160) chose sharp words to describe the climate created by Marius's rivalry with Sulla: "Hitherto the murders and seditions had been internal and fragmentary. Afterward the chiefs of factions assailed each other with great armies, according to the usage of war, and their country lay as a prize between them."[23] He continues: "The seditions proceeded from strife and contention to murder, and from murder to open war."[24] One's own kind and kin became the enemy. The targets were not only individuals and political groups but also the most revered institutions of the state—the elected and the religious magistrates: "There was no restraint upon violence either from the sense of shame, or regard for law, institutions, or country."[25] It was an environment where all factions became masters of evil. This was the time when even a high religious authority such as Jupiter's priest, Lucius Merula, who had also been chosen as one of two consuls at the time, saw no alternative but suicide to escape the revenge of Marius's men. After removing his conical hat *(fla-*

men), which he always wore as a symbol of his priestly duties, he cut his veins.[26] The other consul, Octavius, suffered a similar end even though his enemies, Marius and Cinna, had sworn that he would suffer no harm. As Marius's men stormed the city, Octavius refused to leave. He withdrew to the Janiculum, one of Rome's hills, with the aristocracy and the rest of the army and waited for the arrival of his enemies. His soldiers and friends urged him to escape and brought him a horse, but he refused. He waited in the robes of his office, seating on the curule chair, as his status warranted, and surrounded by the lictors (attendants of the magistrate), again a symbol of his dignity. Such symbols of authority did not stop Marius's soldiers: They cut off his head and displayed it in the Forum in front of the rostra (the traditional speaker's platform), "the first head of a consul that was so exposed."[27]

These were the most prominent victims of the bloodbath that Marius orchestrated in 87 B.C. after his return from Africa, where he had run to save his life. At the time, Sulla was in Asia Minor, on the eastern Mediterranean, fighting Mithridates. Appian describes Marius then as an old, savage man with revenge on his mind yet commanding a devoted following. But Octavius's head was not the only one displayed in the Forum. Many senators suffered a similar fate. "Neither reverence to the gods," comments Appian, "nor the indignation of men, nor the fear of odium for their acts existed any longer among [Marius's supporters]. After committing savage deeds they turned to godless sights. They killed remorselessly and severed the necks of men already dead, and they paraded their horrors before the public eye, either to inspire fear and terror, or for a godless spectacle."[28] The executed men were not spared the ultimate offense: Forbidden proper burial, the bodies were left in the open to poison the air and be torn to pieces by dogs and birds.[29]

Marius's bodyguard, a group of former slaves known as Bardyiae, distinguished itself in this gruesome task of retribution. They would kill on Marius's direct order—or even an indirect order. For instance, when Marius entered the city but refused to acknowledge the greetings of a senator and a former praetor (magistrate), the Bardyiae moved forward and slaughtered them. From then on, they interpreted Marius's failure to return a personal greeting as an order to kill.[30] The Bardyiae also entered the houses of purported enemies, butchering the heads of the household and raping the children and women. These cruel acts so disgusted Cinna, a Marius ally, that he and another Roman, Sertorius, surprised the Bardyiae while they slept and slaughtered them.[31]

Marius did not let old friendships stand in the way of revenge. His former colleague in the victorious campaign against the Cimbri, Lutatius Catulus, paid with his life. In answering those who pleaded for Catulus, Marius simply stated, "He must die"; Catulus then locked himself in a room, charcoal burning in the fireplace, and the poisonous fumes took his life.[32] Even when Marius won the consulship for a record seventh time, he never stopped this behavior, for he ordered a Roman citizen to be pushed to his death from the top of the Tarpeian Rock, the traditional place and mode of execution in Rome. The execution was a daring challenge not only to old Roman customs but to destiny itself, for the Romans believed that such an act committed during the election was a sign of the evil that would fall upon Marius, his supporters, and Rome.[33]

Yet Marius's massacres paled in comparison to Sulla's later actions. Unlike Marius, whose physical appearance—wild and forceful—hinted at hard and cruel behavior, Sulla was a man of great physical appeal, with piercing blue eyes and golden hair; he liked good company, good wine, and lustful women and men. His favorite companions were actors. Only later in life did his appearance begin to change, when red blotches covered his face, regarded as a symbol of the disintegration of his soul.[34]

Most of the central issues of the civil wars began with the failure of the Gracchi programs, but they transformed into a spiral of violence when Sulla, leading the soldiers of the republic, marched on Rome to foil the Marius faction's attempt to deprive Sulla of his leadership in the war against Mithridates. It was an action that Sulla's soldiers supported, for "they were eager for the war . . . because it promised much plunder, and they feared that Marius would enlist other soldiers instead of themselves."[35] Marius and his followers fled the city. Eventually he was proscribed and escaped death by seeking refuge in North Africa, from which, as already explained, he would return in 87 B.C. to punish his enemies.[36]

It was inevitable that Sulla would seek revenge after Marius returned from Africa and conducted his awful campaign against his enemies. Marius died in 86 B.C. while Sulla was still across the sea. Two years later Sulla was back on Italian soil. Appian opens the events to come with phrases that remind the reader of Xerxes' march against Athens as described by Herodotus. "Mysterious terrors came upon many, both in public and in private throughout Italy."[37] Ancient oracles were remembered. Abominable events took place: a mule foaled; a woman gave birth to a viper; an earthquake destroyed some of Rome's temples; the Capitol, which the ancient kings had built centuries earlier, was destroyed by fire of unknown origin. Those events were a frightful foreshadower of Sulla's return—massacres, the conquest of Italy and Rome, the introduction of new constitutional laws.[38] In Sulla's mind there was "destruction, death, confiscation, and wholesale extermination" against those who had supported Marius. According to Appian, 50,000 men of both sides were killed in the fighting over control of the capital city.[39]

Sulla's massacres in Rome were horrific, much worse than those committed by Marius and his men. They began with the butchering of 6,000 Samnites who again had unsuccessfully tried to revolt against Rome. He had them lined up in the circus just as he was speaking to the Senate, not very far from the prisoners. In the surreal atmosphere, his tone of voice was calm, his face without expression; from outside, the cries of the Samnites, who were methodically massacred, reached the ears of the senators. When the senators turned their heads toward the cries, Sulla calmly remarked that they were criminals receiving their just punishment.[40]

Sulla made lists of his enemies. The first list, according to one source, included 80 men; the next day there were 220 more, another 220 on the third.[41] Appian's figures list 40 senators and 1,600 members of the equestrian class (the richest citizens) initially and then more in the next few days.[42] The unfortunate were hunted down like wild dogs—in their houses, in the streets, even in temples, where one could have sought asylum in the past. Once caught, they were thrown into the streets from their windows or dragged in the open to Sulla's feet. At the same time spies were everywhere to search for the quarry.[43] The bodies were thrown into the River Tiber in disregard of the most sacred rituals: "It was now the custom not to bury the dead,"[44] just like Marius had done.

The climate of treachery, violence, abuse, and trampled rights toward fellow-citizens did not end with Sulla's death in 79 B.C., even though the final tally of his tenure included, according to Appian, the deaths of more than 100,000 young men in war, 90 senators, 15 consuls, and 2,600 equestrians.[45] War would continue during the subsequent decades in Italy and elsewhere, especially Spain. It ended in 31 B.C., when Octavian finally defeated Marcus Antonius and Cleopatra in the Battle of Actium off the western coast of Greece.

The civil wars were not just a stage for wholesale murder; they were the conduit for the final disintegration of the Roman armies. The new armies had become the symbol of abuse, treachery, and disorder. The sense of discipline that separated the Roman soldier from his Greek and Macedonian counterpart eroded to the point that even loyalty to the general was put at risk if the latter was not forthcoming with the booty. The list of military and civil authorities murdered by soldiers or civilians is extensive. At the end of the Social War, a group of Roman citizens, enraged by a proposal to revive a law against usury, surrounded the drafter, a praetor, while he was offering sacrifices to the gods. They stoned him, and when he sought refuge in a tavern, they cut his throat.[46] The consul Quintus Pompeius suffered a similar end: Instructed by the Senate to take command of the army, he was murdered by a group of hostile soldiers the moment he began to take over his duties.[47] In 84 B.C. trouble developed when a group of soldiers unwilling to take arms against Sulla angrily surrounded another consul, L. Cornelius Cinna, during a troop assembly. Violence erupted suddenly after a lictor, trying to clear the path for the consul, hit a soldier. One of the assembled then hit the lictor, and Cinna immediately ordered an arrest, which prompted the crowd to stone the consul to death.[48]

The goals of most soldiers became twofold: to associate with the winner and to reap the highest economic benefits possible. Loyalty became a game of musical chairs, as in the case of the so-called Fimbriani, the men commanded by L. Valerius Flaccus. In 86 B.C. they switched allegiance to Gaius Flavius Fimbria after Fimbria murdered their commander. Sent from Rome as Flaccus's legate, Fimbria had been at odds with him, as he was unwilling to use all means possible to defeat the cities loyal to Mithridates and did not allow the indiscriminate pillage of the Greek cities.[49] When Sulla, an enemy of Fimbria, emerged as the winner against Mithridates and marched against Fimbria, the legions abandoned their commander in his tent and swore allegiance to Sulla. Fimbria, alone and desperate, committed suicide. In the 70s B.C. the Fimbriani were under another commander, Lucius Lucullus, whom they abandoned in 67 B.C. to accept the leadership of Pompeius Magnus. The Fimbriani are the best-known example of this behavior, surely one of many. Similar treachery was exhibited by the army under L. Scipio, a descendant of the great Scipio Africanus; it passed wholesale to Sulla's side.[50] It could happen even in the heat of battle, as it did during the Battle of Sacred Lake when the left wing of the Marian army threw down its standards and joined Sulla's battle line.[51] Five more cohorts did the same soon after that encounter.[52] When 10,000 of Marius's faction died in another clash, 6,000 survivors deserted and the rest of the army disintegrated; a legion of Lucanians (a tribe from southern Italy) also deserted upon hearing of that defeat.[53] Such disloyalty could be demonstrated by hardened auxiliaries like the Celtiberian horsemen, people from the middle Ebro Valley and the eastern Meseta region of Spain, whom Sulla met on the banks of the River Glanis. When Sulla killed fifty of them, 270 immediately passed to his side while the enemy general massacred the rest for the cowardice and treachery of their compatriots.[54]

Most historians thus agree that the armies of the late Roman republic switched allegiance from the state to their generals. And this is correct, insofar as we realize that fidelity even to a man like Sulla could be transparent, changing suddenly if the general was unable to provide financial gains. Plunder, looting, and pillaging were the legionnaires' goals. Roman armies, like all people of the ancient world, normally saw economic gain as a powerful motivation for war. The new twist demonstrated by the late Roman armies was that the desire to acquire that which belonged to others became the dominant cause of conflict against *anybody*. As for Sulla, his leadership both in the Social War and in the civil wars became a litany of plunder, often followed by massacre. The action against the Hirpini town of Aeclanum, for instance, was probably Sulla's most notorious episode in the war against the allies. When Sulla arrived at the city walls, the inhabitants begged for some delay to consider whether to surrender their town peacefully. (They hoped that an army of Lucanians would come to their rescue.) Sulla gave them one hour and in the meantime piled bundles of wood around the walls. He set them on fire after an hour, forcing Aeclanum to a quick surrender. Under normal circumstances the treatment of the Hirpini would have been lenient. Instead, probably because of his lifelong animosity toward the Samnites and because Aeclanum was prosperous, Sulla allowed his soldiers to plunder the city. His explanation was that "it had not been delivered up voluntarily but under necessity."[55]

And in Asia, upon realizing that his soldiers did not approve of the peace terms with Mithridates (the king's indemnity was not high enough), he defeated the Roman general Fimbria, who had stirred trouble against him, then forced the Asian cities that had sided with Mithridates to pay 20,000 talents (each Attic silver talent was worth 6,000 *denarii* and, if gold, 60,000 *denarii*).[56] Also, during the first stages of his confrontation with Marius, Sulla argued with his soldiers that his appointment against Mithridates promised "much plunder."[57] When in 82 B.C. he finally conquered Praeneste (modern Palestrina), a city about 37 kilometers southeast of Rome, he allowed his soldiers to loot the town, for it was "extremely rich."[58] Disappointment, however, awaited his troops when they moved to nearby Norba. Its citizens, despairing of their destiny, closed the gates of the town, set the city afire, and committed collective suicide, either by their own hand, by falling against swords held by fellow citizens, or by hanging.[59] In Appian's summary of Sulla's treatment of enemies during the civil wars, Sulla established colonies of his troops in the lands of the defeated, confiscated their lands and houses, and divided them among his soldiers.[60]

Another example of the importance of pillage in the relationship between a general with his forces was Sulla's plunder of the sacred treasuries of Greece in Epidaurus and Olympia. He did so to reward and motivate his soldiers for the forthcoming attack against Athens and Piraeus. He even broke a large silver jar into pieces so that the baggage animals could carry it. In his recounting this deed, Plutarch is horrified, because the jar was the last remaining royal gift in the sanctuary.[61] No one had ever behaved in such a manner; not Titus Quinctius Flamininus, the winner of Cynoscephalae in 197 B.C. over Philip V of Macedonia; not Aemilius Paulus, who defeated Philip's son, Perseus, at Pydna about twenty-nine years later. But these times were different. In the past, the troops were disciplined, and their generals kept their expenses within certain limits and maintained some independence from their soldiers. But Plutarch describes how the picture had changed. The new generals rose to the top through violence against their own kind; they were compelled to combine the skills of a military leader with those of a manipulator; they gained support from troops by lavishing them with money; the whole country was up for sale. And of all the generals, none was worse than Sulla. "In order to corrupt and win over to himself the soldiers of other generals, he gave his own troops a good time and spent money lavishly on them. He was thus at the same time encouraging the evils both of treachery and of debauchery."[62]

Plunder was foremost in the minds of the soldiers and their commanders; it strengthened loyalty to the commander, not to the state. Still, plunder also represented the road to enrichment for the commander himself. The troops' ties to the leader were also strengthened by the grants of lands that most veterans came to expect at the end of service. That process had begun much earlier; for instance, Curius Dentatus, consul in 290 B.C., rewarded the soldiers with grants of land.[63] But it became widespread from Marius's time onward. Establishing new colonies among the defeated was a way of securing Roman control over enemy territory, but it was also a reward for serving the republic. It became a necessity when the poor were allowed into the army. Land grants ensured soldiers' loyalty; established, especially through colonies, a network of Roman enclaves in erstwhile enemy territories; and ensured the psychological and social allegiance of the soldiers for the present and future.[64] According to Appian's comments on Sulla's grant distribution, in Rome he freed 10,000 slaves of his vanquished enemies and granted them

Roman citizenship so that the former slaves, now plebeians, would be "always ready to obey his commands." He also distributed to his twenty-three legions "a great deal of land in the various communities . . . some of which was public property and some taken from the communities by way of fine."[65] Land grants thus became the best way to forestall troops' potential disloyalty once they left the army ranks. Julius Caesar openly favored land distribution: Money could be squandered, making the soldier poor and a threat to society; land made him a respectable, obedient, lawful member of the state.[66] At this stage the land grants, which seem to have been, for simple soldiers, between 25 and 65.66 *iugera* (but higher for officers) according to the type of soil,[67] did not make the veteran wealthy but probably were enough to provide for his family.

The new soldier after 107 B.C. was an element of disorder not only on the battlefield but also in politics and society. He was violent, untrustworthy, and eager to fight any enemy, whether from outside or within the republic. He shared the fascination with violence that characterized the Romans of the early republic. He became a "pillager."[68] Rome's sense of destiny—which had been the "religion" of past armies and would return with Julius Caesar and then Augustus—was no longer part of the soldiers' psychological makeup. Surely the late republican recruits and leaders were no different in appearance: The core of the armies still came from farms and small towns, and the commanders were still members of the old families. But in the past the ideal and practice of the legionnaire was to return to his home fields, to lead a sober lifestyle in his native region. After 107 B.C., most of the recruits had little or nothing to which they could return. Their meager fields, indeed if they owned land at all, were insignificant compared to the prizes of war, and their pay hardly guaranteed any savings even when coupled with the standard gifts and awards. Thus they had to make their years of service count, and their goal became the *praeda*—the loot. They were single-minded in their pursuit, and their commanders were forced to fulfill such desires in order to ensure their loyalty. This military world, once an allegiance to Rome, now centered on esprit de corps in the legion. The enemy was not necessarily the people on the far shore of the Adriatic or on the northern shores of Africa or on the Iberian fields. The enemy's face could be a neighbor loyal to another commander.

The Roman soldier thus became a pillager within a rapacious army, putting his own life in jeopardy only if the potential loot justified the risk. The annihilation of the enemy, part of the old Roman credo, was not paramount if the loot appeared too small or was more attractive elsewhere.

These armies were not even class-conscious, for in the end their motivation was personal gain. The republic was in a sad state. Those individuals who were better off killed one another, and the mainstay of Roman power and stability—the army—became itself an element of disorder and cynicism.

Spartacus and the Slave Revolt

The civil wars were not the sole problem plaguing the Roman commonwealth in the first century B.C. For three years (73–71 B.C.), a slave revolt blossomed from a few dozen to probably about 150,000 men.[69] No soldiers were then in Italy to keep internal order; thousands were on the move in faraway fields—Spain, Macedonia, and along the eastern Mediterranean.[70] The only positive aspect of the revolt was that the poorer elements of Roman society, except for a few individuals, never shared unity of intent and commonality of ideals and goals with the slaves—a menacing alliance of this nature could not happen considering the ideological biases of the time.

As the historian Lucius Annaeus writes, "The common soldiers being *slaves* and their leaders being *gladiators*—the former men of the *humblest* and latter men of the *worse*, class—added insult to the injury which they inflicted upon Rome."[71] In Roman society, as in most Indo-European groups, a person with freedom *(libertas)* was an individual who was not a slave. This meant that any freeman, regardless of social condition, thought himself far superior to any slave. Being a slave meant one was property, an animal.[72] Slaves could be sold, given away, tortured, killed, left as inheritance, and forced to mate with another when so ordered.

Especially for slaves residing in Rome, the harshness of their legal position was often not applied, because some were used for more important tasks than simply physical labor, including commerce, industry, and education. Some were set free by their owners, and many worked side by side with freemen seemingly without differentiation. Moreover, the condition of the slaves must be seen from the Romans' perspective: In society, even citizens (e.g., those in debt) and family dependents could be treated harshly. The head of the extended family *(paterfamilias)* had the power of life and death.

The color of the human skin was no cause for discrimination among Romans. They drew slaves from across Europe and the Mediterranean, especially Celts, Germans, Thracians (roughly in modern Bulgaria), eastern Mediterraneans, and North Africans. Generally, it was understood that no Roman citizen or peninsular Italian south of Gallia Cisalpina (northern Italy) should be enslaved. This had not always been so in the past, when many defeated Italians from the central and southern regions had been forced into slavery.[73]

P. A. Brunt believes that in A.D. 14, about a century after the slave revolt, 2–3 million slaves were in Italy, mostly engaged in rural work. The peninsula's free population, excluding Gallia Cisalpina, was about 4 million, with 500,000–600,000 within Rome.[74] This means that in the first century A.D. there were about two or three slaves for every four Roman citizens.

Normally slaves challenged their Roman masters not through open violence but rather by running away. Still, serious revolts were not uncommon. Two especially serious revolts occurred toward the end of the second century B.C. (137–133 and 104–101), both in Sicily. But no other was more dangerous than the rebellion led by Spartacus in 73 B.C. The initial upheaval was greeted with disbelief and ridicule, but soon enough people came to fear that Rome itself would succumb to the slaves.

The historical evidence regarding this revolt is sparse and contradictory. It comes mainly from Appian, Florus, and Plutarch's biography of Crassus, the person who eventually extinguished the rebellion. The main leader, Spartacus, was a Thracian who had served in the Roman army as an auxiliary and then deserted to become a bandit.[75] When caught, he had been sold as a gladiator.[76]

The revolt began in a gladiatorial school in Capua, an important city near Naples. A group of about 200 gladiators, mainly Thracians and Celts, resentful of their owner's inhumane treatment, tried to escape. Fewer than half seem to have succeeded.[77] Seeking safety, they took refuge on nearby Mount Vesuvius, where other slaves and even some freemen joined them.[78] Thus far their flight followed the routine for runaway slaves, but these were professional fighters, and their leader, Spartacus, was clever indeed. He defeated all soldiers sent against him over the next three years, the first being rather limited detachments, then even some consular armies.

As the rebel army grew, it ravaged the surrounding countryside, first in southern Italy, then toward the center; finally it moved toward the Alps until it reached the territories of Mutina (modern Modena). The goal was to cross the mountain range and seek refuge in native lands. But their successes against the Roman forces sent to stop them near Mutina became their own greatest enemy. They decided to continue ravaging the Italian territories, probably against Spartacus's advice.[79] The evidence is ambiguous on this point, but it seems that the slaves, after defeating two consular forces, felt they could conquer Rome and turned around instead of proceeding straight toward the passes and eventual freedom.[80]

By now Rome's apprehension and fear were high, and the Senate entrusted the new consul, Marcus Crassus, to stop the rebels. Crassus was a wealthy man with intense political ambition. Later he would become one of the three men in control of the republic, the other two being Pompeius and Julius Caesar. He also had a competent military mind, at least in this instance (later he led the Roman army to an enormous disaster against the Parthians at Carrhae in 53 B.C.). For the moment, however, his military decisions were justifiable. When the soldiers of two legions behaved cowardly against Spartacus, he struck terror in his soldiers' hearts by ordering a decimation, that is, some of the offenders were executed in front of the whole army—an ancient practice rarely used by this time.[81]

Crassus pursued the slave army, and although in the end Spartacus escaped by seeking refuge again in southern Italy, Crassus must have stopped the Thracian's drive toward Rome. When Spartacus reached the tip of the peninsula, at first he tried to reach an agreement with some pirates to carry his army across the strait into Sicily, where, he must have reasoned, it would have been easier to thwart the Romans dogging him. After the pirates apparently took his money and left surreptitiously, he camped near the tip of the peninsula. Crassus soon cornered him there.[82]

Crassus must have feared his opponent, for instead of forcing a decisive battle he tried to close all avenues of escape. He built a wall from sea to sea with a ditch 4.5 meters wide and 4.5 meters deep.[83] But Spartacus was able to break out. During a wintry night, with snow falling on the ground, the slave forces fled, covering sections of the ditch with bundles of wood. Again Crassus pursued. Time was in the Romans' favor, for two other armies answered Crassus's call for reinforcements; from the north Pompeius had returned from Spain, and from the east Lucullus[84] was in Thrace but may conceivably have disembarked at Brundisium when he arrived in Italy.

Spartacus must have realized then his best option was to defeat the enemies in detail. He had already defeated two consular armies in the north, and his army was still dangerous—but not unbeatable. Overconfidence had been a pitfall among the ranks. And Spartacus, usually clever on the battlefield itself, lacked a clear strategic aim. The slaves had wavered between various goals—to escape from their masters, to cross the Alps, to attack Rome, to move to Sicily. Even at this moment Spartacus seemed to have two different goals: to defeat his enemy in detail, and to move into Samnium, a region located in the Apennine Mountains of central-southern Italy that held a notorious hatred toward the Romans.[85] Samnium represented the first step in escaping toward northern Italy again. By then, however, the slave army's strength was sapped, probably due to divided goals and loyalty. Moreover, despite their numerous defeats, the Romans had been able to slaughter many opponents caught away from the main army—a group of Germans,[86] a large force of 20,000–30,000 under a Gallic commander in Apulia,[87] and thousands more as rebel groups became separated from Spartacus during his attempted foray into Samnium.[88]

Although Crassus never relented in his pursuit, he had been reluctant to engage the enemy outright in a pitched battle. Now he, too, wanted a definitive resolution. He had ten legions under his command and felt that his request for reinforcements was a mistake, for now he would be forced to share his victory with Pompeius and probably with Lucullus.[89] Thus he moved forward to engage Spartacus but was cautious, first digging a defensive ditch before his men. Spartacus, probably overconfident but more likely fearing that other Romans would soon join the fight, decided to attack. There would be no escape in this encounter. The Thracian fell on the battlefield (his body was never found), and the slaughter was so great that the Romans found it impossible to count the victims. The few survivors made a desperate attempt to escape by splitting into four groups; some were hunted down by Crassus's men, and some encountered Pompeius's forces, hurrying toward the battlefield.[90] Six thousand survivors were crucified at the side of the road from Capua to Rome.[91] In all, probably 60,000 slaves were killed;[92] among the Romans, 1,000 were killed.[93]

Persistence, a continuous supply of recruits, and engineering (building trenches, a ditch, a wall) had once again been the winning formula for the Romans. Still, victory had its price: three years of devastation, especially in southern Italy,[94] 40,000–50,000 additional young men recruited from the countryside to fight the rebellion, and increasing pirate raids on the Italian coast, less defended now than in the past. Soon after Spartacus's defeat the pirates pillaged the city of Caieta near Naples and captured the grain fleet at Ostia, a few kilometers from Rome.[95] All this was on top of the heavy casualties of the war—about 150,000[96] among the slaves and thousands of Romans. The conflict probably displaced many people, rebel survivors and poor peasants alike, who must have resorted to banditry, the only alternative in poor preindustrial societies. It was not until 36 B.C. that the state was able to mount an effective campaign against brigandage,[97] although one is left to wonder how efficiently. Brigandage remained an endemic problem of the Italian center and south until about one hundred and thirty years ago.

Caesar's Soldiers

Western civilization has usually looked at the fall of the Roman republic from our viewpoint as the Renaissance's classical heirs and in the guise of

Cicero's children in the sense that the republican writer influenced with his biases and style generation after generation of western Europeans. Moreover, in a twisted chain of events the forced association of regimes like fascism with imperial Rome reinforced our contentious relationship with Caesar and his period. In reality, Caesar did not treacherously kill the Roman republic. The traditional ideas, beliefs, and values had been dead for decades; they were recalled with nostalgia only by those who benefited from the status quo or the ever-present turmoil. Caesar merely crushed what had become a phantasm of the past, the vicious maker of disorder and bloodshed. As the children of modern democracy we may carry an inherent hostility toward this destroyer of democratic institutions. Despite crushing the traditional structure of the Roman state, Caesar's actions revitalized the strength of the Roman republic as an imperial power.

Julius Caesar and Pompeius opened the last stages of the civil wars. Caesar would emerge the victor, combining shrewdness with concern for his soldiers and demonstrating his conviction that the old system was self-destructive. He achieved his goal logically and coldly—at times deceitfully—but always for the benefit of those who had suffered the most under Sulla. As one of his enemies said, Caesar was the only one who "undertook the overthrow of the state when sober."[98]

Caesar, according to Svetonius, was a tall man, fair of complexion, with "shapely limbs, a somewhat full face, and keen black eyes."[99] He was born in 100 B.C. to a family, the Iulii, that claimed a most illustrious ancestry, a hero like Aeneas and a goddess like Venus. However, it was not this connection that influenced Caesar's career initially; rather it was the fact that his aunt had married Marius. After spending some time in the eastern Mediterranean mainly for education, Caesar returned to Rome. He began a career highlighted by marriage alliances and political appointments, but he remained perpetually on the brink of collapse due to his heavy expenses to gain the favor of the crowd and to secure election to offices. Eventually the greatest influence in his life was his clever manipulation of his two rivals to power, Marcus Licinius Crassus and Gnaeus Pompeius Magnus. Insolvency remained his major recurring problem, but it was forestalled by his military service in Spain and then by his appointment to Gaul, a treasure house that financed his rise to enormous power. His relentless warfare in the area secured Gaul for Rome, immense treasure to him and his soldiers, and legions that could "storm the heavens."[100] The price paid by the Gauls was enormous: destroyed cities, massive casualties, displaced populations, confiscated treasuries of the sacred—all for Rome's benefit. Plutarch mentions that a million Gauls were killed during the wars against Caesar.[101]

The Gallic campaign was just the beginning of more turmoil. When Crassus was killed during a disastrous campaign against the Parthians, only one major contender, Pompeius, remained to challenge Caesar's conquest of power. After long and fruitless negotiations Caesar crossed the Rubicon River, the symbolic dividing line between Gallia Cisalpina and Rome, and marched on the capital. He pursued Pompeius relentlessly until he defeated him at Pharsalus (48 B.C.). He continued operations in Africa and Spain to mop up the remaining centers of opposition. The civil war stopped momentarily with Julius Caesar's assassination (44 B.C.) at the hands of dreamers bent on restoring the old republican values. It restarted first with the punishment of Caesar's assassins, then in the struggle for power between Octavian—Caesar's great-nephew and heir—and Caesar's lieutenant, Marcus Antonius, and his lover Cleopatra, queen of Egypt (who earlier had been Caesar's lover). This, too, was resolved. In 31 B.C. in the Battle of Actium off the Greek coast, Octavian's fleet defeated his rivals. A year later Antonius, then Cleopatra, committed suicide.

Caesar understood his soldiers as few did, with the probable exception of Marius. He shared with them the glories, the rewards, but also the toils and miseries of military life.[102] He was a master of the psychology of his subordinates, using clever actions through the authority of his office and memories of past rewards and promises of future ones. He was also able to play on more subtle motivations, reminding troops of the importance of personal honor—an approach that the previous leaders of the Roman civil wars had ignored or, more likely, been unable to stir.[103]

In battle he shared the same risks as his troops. When the encounter's outcome was doubtful, he would send away the horses that he and the rest of his officers rode, showing that he, like the rest, could not escape from the enemy blows and that he was ready to die with them.[104] Once, while crossing a wild and woody place during a storm, Caesar insisted that his weakest man rest in the only covered place that they found, a hut. He and the rest slept on the bare ground.[105] He often appealed in the name of the interest of all, making the troops feel not like a host of mere pillagers but an army of citizens and thus pillars of the state. He used his own funds to add another legion to his army, rewarding the new recruits, who were Gauls, with Roman citizenship.[106] Ample and continuous financial prizes were showered on his troops.[107] He enriched them during his first tenure as a leader in the Iberian peninsula,[108] and he gave them much more when he went to Gaul. He doubled their pay, distributed generous quantities of grain when plentiful, then gave each soldier a slave from the defeated enemies.[109] The veterans, at the time of his triumphs in Rome, received 24,000 *sesterces* (small silver coins worth about one-quarter of the *denarius*) each above the 2,000 he had given them at the beginning of the civil strife, in addition to probably the most cherished gift of all—land.[110] He allowed frequent pillage to meet the needs of his war machine, plundering, contrary to custom, those towns of the Lusitanians that had opened their gates peacefully to him. The shrines and temples of the Gallic gods and more often Gallic towns fell prey to his legionnaires more for the sake of plunder than any other reason.[111]

He accumulated so much gold that it was sold in Italy at the low rate of 3,000 *sesterces* per pound. Nothing stood in his way if he needed funds for war or reward. Not even the treasure of Jupiter in Rome was safe: He took 3,000 pounds of gold, placing there an equivalent weight in bronze before leaving for a campaign in the eastern Mediterranean. Peace or alliances were often measured by the reward the state and his army would receive—6,000 *talents*, for instance, from the king of Egypt, Ptolemy,[112] and 4 million *sesterces* per year as tribute from the Gauls.[113]

The fruits of war and Caesar's easy manner of command and deep concern for soldiers made his army again the disciplined war machine that in the past had conquered the Italian peninsula and then the Mediterranean. The soldiers who fought well were treated with respect and kindness. After a great victory he relieved them of their duties so they could celebrate as they liked. He did not address them as "soldiers" *(milites)* but used the more flattering term "comrades" *(commilitones)* and showered them with precious gifts.[114] But his mild approach to discipline could change to harsh punishment when the situation required it. Deserters and mutineers found little compassion in Caesar's heart.[115] In Africa in 46 B.C. he did not hesitate to discipline five officers in order to restore, as he said, the discipline of old—three for having achieved their rank by favor, not merit; one for being mutinous and disloyal; the other for having transported his household slaves and supplies instead of soldiers in his crossing from Italy to Africa.[116]

Caesar's behavior strengthened his troops' loyalty and their esprit de corps. At times this brotherhood included the soldiers of enemy leaders; it was not unusual for Caesar to free his enemies after defeating them on the battlefield. Later he even supported some who were running for public office.[117] When on the Pharsalus battlefield his troops were intent on slaughtering Pompeius's soldiers, he cried out to spare their fellow-citizens.[118]

In the past even the strongest leaders—Sulla, for instance—sometimes had to follow what the soldiers wanted, not what was practical and beneficial in the long run. Caesar, in contrast, was the absolute voice of authority in his army. His legionnaires would follow him anywhere, for he knew best what was good for all.[119] At the onset of Caesar's confrontation with Pompeius, every centurion in his legions paid a horseman from his own allowance; other soldiers offered to serve Caesar without pay and rations, the task of feeding them taken over by their better-off comrades. There were few desertions from Caesar's army. If taken prisoner, his soldiers were willing to die rather than switch allegiance.[120] When Caesar's opponent during the civil war in Africa offered to spare the life of a captured officer of Caesar's army, the officer plunged his sword into his own body, remarking that "it was the custom with Caesar's soldiers not to receive but to offer mercy."[121]

Maintaining Caesar as a symbol, these legionnaires, under his successor Augustus, would share goals that were beneficial to the commonwealth. They were the defenders of a popular view of the state against the oligarchic structures of the past and of an Italo-Roman army not just in fact but in ideology. They felt that Caesar's behavior had broken Rome's discriminatory practices, especially in regard to land grants. In other words, Caesar's followers believed that the legions had to be the tool not just of Rome but of all Italy. Soon this privilege enveloped all Roman citizens, whether they lived south of the Rubicon River or in colonies anywhere. The army of Caesar's Gallic wars was an array of men that could be called a national army.[122] In the soldiers' view they manned the body that best represented the state and its values. They internalized the attitude of the early republican times, now applied to all citizens, not just to the men of property.

Typology of Warfare in the Last Days of the Republic

The Roman civil wars were different from conflicts past and future (except those in the aftermath of Nero's death).[123] The first obvious characteristic was the nature of the enemies: They were not outsiders, as in the past, but one's own kin or new Roman citizens. Rarely did the army play an independent and direct political role during the initial years of the civil wars. In most cases it expressed civilian wishes and aims, but its leadership remained in the hands of the ruling class. Although a different case can be made for Marius, Sulla and the rest were tied to the political elite by ideology and blood. They were military men engaged in the pursuit of political careers. This is no surprise, for civilian concerns blended with military ones. Any ambitious Roman had to be a soldier before qualifying for high political office. Cicero, for instance, a man not known for his military inclinations, felt compelled to admit that running for political office required at least one year of military service.[124]

The leaders were the war managers; they decided when to fight and against whom. The soldiers would obey as long as the commander's choice promised material benefit. In other words, a leader had to take care of the legions' material greed if he wanted to gain or keep supremacy in the political arena. This was precisely the case when Sulla marched against Rome in 88 B.C.

Veterans—that is, individuals who had chosen the army as their profession—were the core of the armies, but the rank and file were civilians with limited battlefield experience. They should not be seen, however, as poor soldiers. Their background (most were farmers and peasants), their place of birth (especially the Samnite lands and central Italy), their long and bloody experience in the Social War, and the violent tenor of their environment must have made them well suited for the soldier's profession, considering as well the likelihood of material reward at the end of their term of service.

The profession of arms and the troops' proletarization tended to separate the soldiers from the civilian population. One of the results was the civilians' dislike, even hatred, toward the army. This us-versus-them mentality, the sense of camaraderie (typical of soldiers in any period), and the conviction that material prospects were tied to mutual behavior and their leader's loyalty strengthened their esprit de corps and made them, at times, close to the soldiers fighting for another man. It is no surprise, then, that in the end the troops themselves would support the cause of internal peace. A striking example of this attitude is seen in the reaction of men under Octavian, Caesar's heir, at Perusia (modern Perugia) in 41 B.C. As the legionnaires of Octavian's enemy, Lucius, moved forward to surrender, Octavian's own men came forward to embrace them, weeping for joy. They had realized that Octavian was ready to punish those who had served under Lucius against him.[125]

By this time an important change had taken place. Caesar, assassinated a few years earlier, had changed the army from a pawn in the hands of others—a body of pillagers with allegiance only to those who placed gold in their hands—into a group of men equivalent almost to a political party. The soldiers were the heirs of Caesar's legacy. The army became "the guardian and guarantor of a kind of posthumous Caesarism."[126] Naturally the soldiers' political awareness remained tied to their own interests and the defense of their privileges. And the actions of Caesar's soldiers should not be interpreted as something completely new, for other armies in the Roman civil wars did likewise. In 108 B.C., for instance, Marius's soldiers in Africa had supported their commander's candidacy to the consulate by urging their kin in Rome to vote for him.[127] Now, however, the political awareness of Caesar's army would turn into the rule, not the exception, as it had been in 108 B.C.[128]

It was so until Augustus decided that all power had to rest with the emperor and his family.

Notes

1. Fernando Wulff Alonso, *Romanos e Itálicos en la Baja República: Estudios sobre sus relaciones entre la Segunda Guerra Púnica y la Guerra Social (201–91 B.C.)* (Bruxelles, 1991), p. 143. Alonso's conclusions summarize the views presented by P. A. Brunt, *Italian Manpower, 225 BC–A.D 14* (Oxford, 1971), p. 681; Virgilio Ilari, *Gli italici nelle strutture militari romane* (Milano, 1974), p. 137.

2. Wulff Alonso, *Romanos e Itálicos en la Baja República*, p. 144.

3. Brunt, *Italian Manpower*, pp. 684–685; Ilari, *Gli italici nelle strutture militari romane*, p. 166ff.

4. Wulff Alonso, *Romanos e Itálicos en la Baja República*, pp. 148–150.

5. Jean-Michel David, *The Roman Conquest of Italy*, translated by A. Neville (Bodmin, 1997), pp. 140–141.

6. Wulff Alonso, *Romanos e Itálicos en la Baja República*, p. 149.

7. Polybius xl.43, 7; xli.7.3; xlv.43.7; xli.13.8.

8. Wulff Alonso, *Romanos e Itálicos en la Baja República*, pp. 146–147.

9. Ibid., pp. 151–153.

10. Ibid., p. 152.

11. Ibid., p. 150, from Polybius vi.39, 13–14.

12. Livy xxix.3, xli.8, xliii.10.3. See also P. A. Brunt, *The Fall of the Roman Republic and Related Essays* (Oxford, 1988), pp. 95–96; David, *The Roman Conquest of Italy*, p. 143.

13. See R. A. Baumann, "The Suppressions of the Bacchanals: Five Questions," *Historia* 39 (1990): 335–348; Livy xxxix.14.3–18.9; Cicero, *De legibus* 2.37. For the Senate decree read A.H.M. Jones, *A History of Rome Through the Fifth Century*, vol. 1: *The Republic* (New York, 1964), pp. 84–85.

14. Brunt, *The Fall of the Roman Republic*, pp. 75–100.

15. See the argument in ibid., pp. 95ff.

16. Justin xxxvi, quoted in Brunt, *The Fall of the Roman Republic*, p. 103.

17. Ibid., p. 101.

18. Plutarch, *Marius* 32.3.

19. Velleius Paterculus ii.16.
20. Brunt, *The Fall of the Roman Republic*, p. 105.
21. The key laws were the lex Calpurnia of 90 B.C., which granted citizenship to the loyal allies who had distinguished themselves on the battlefield; the lex Julia (also 90 B.C.), which granted citizenship to all the Latins and to the allies who had not taken arms against Rome; the lex Plautia-Papiria (89 B.C.), which granted citizenship to any individual resident of any allied city after contacting the Roman praetor within ten months' time; and the lex Pompeia (also 89 B.C.), which granted citizenship to all residents of the Latin colonies that had been established in Cisalpine Gaul.
22. Plutarch, *Sulla* 4.
23. Appian i.7.55.
24. Ibid., i.7.60.
25. Ibid., i.7.60.
26. Ibid., i.8.65.
27. Ibid., i.8.71.
28. Ibid., i.8.71.
29. Ibid., i.8.73.
30. Plutarch, *Marius* 43.
31. Ibid., 44.
32. Ibid., 44.
33. Ibid., 45.
34. Plutarch, *Sulla* 1, 5.
35. Appian i.7.57.
36. Ibid., i. 7–59–62.
37. Ibid., i.9.83.
38. Ibid., i.9.83.
39. Ibid., i.9.82.
40. Plutarch, *Sulla* 30.
41. Ibid., 31.
42. Appian i.11.95.
43. Ibid., i.11.95.
44. Ibid., i.10.88.
45. Ibid., i.12.103.
46. Ibid., i.6.54. Asellio was the praetor's name.
47. Ibid., i.7.62.
48. Ibid., i.9.78.
49. Ruggero F. Rossi, *Dai Gracchi a Silla* (Bologna, 1980), p. 329.
50. Appian i.10.85.

51. Ibid., i.10.87.

52. Ibid., i.10.88.

53. Ibid., i.10.91.

54. Ibid., i.10.89.

55. Ibid., i.6.51.

56. Plutarch, *Sulla* 24.

57. Appian, i.7.57.

58. Appian i.10.94.

59. Ibid., i.10.94.

60. Ibid., i.11.96.

61. The whole episode and comments are based on Plutarch's statements; *Sulla* 12.

62. Ibid., 12.

63. Jacques Harmand, *L'armée et le soldat à Rome de 107 à 50 avant notre ère* (Paris, 1967), p. 470.

64. Harmand, *L'armée et le soldat à Rome*, pp. 471–472.

65. Appian i.11.100.

66. See Brunt, *The Fall of the Roman Republic*, pp. 270–271.

67. Ibid., pp. 271–272.

68. Harmand, in Jean-Paul Brisson (ed.), *Problèmes de la guerre à Rome* (Paris-La Haye, 1969), p. 63.

69. Brunt, *The Fall of the Roman Republic*, pp. 287–288; also see p. 122.

70. Ibid., p. 79.

71. Florus ii.8.20; emphasis added.

72. On "libertas in the Republic," see Brunt, *The Fall of the Roman Republic*, pp. 281–350. On slavery, see Alan Watson, *The Law of Persons in the Later Roman Republic* (Oxford, 1967), pp. 158–200.

73. See the list of captives enslaved by Rome in the period 297–293 B.C. in S. Oakley, "The Roman Conquest of Italy," in *War and Society in the Roman World*, edited by John Rich and Graham Shipley (London, 1993), p. 25.

74. Brunt, *The Fall of the Roman Republic*, pp. 241–242.

75. Florus ii.8.8. The other two leaders were Gauls named Crixus and Oenomaus (ibid., ii.8.3).

76. Appian i.14.116.

77. 78 in Plutarch (*Crassus* 8.2); about 70 in Appian (i.14.116); 64 in Velleius (ii.30.5); a little more than 30 in Florus (ii.8.3).

78. Appian i.14.116; Plutarch, *Crassus* 9.3.

79. Plutarch, *Crassus* 9.6.

80. Appian i.14.117.

81. Plutarch, *Crassus* 10.2–3; Appian i.14.118.

82. Plutarch, *Crassus* 10.3–4.

83. Ibid., 10.5–6.

84. Possibly Lucullus; ibid., 11.2.

85. Appian i.14.119.

86. Plutarch, *Crassus* 9.7.

87. It is 30,000 in Appian (i.14.117); 20,000 in Livy (*Fragments* xcvi).

88. It is 12,000 in Appian (i.14.119); 35,000 in Livy (*Fragments* xcvii).

89. Brunt, *The Fall of the Roman Republic*, p. 450.

90. Plutarch, *Crassus* 11.5–8.

91. Appian i.14.120.

92. Livy, *Fragments* xcvii.

93. Appian i.14.120.

94. Florus ii.8.5.

95. Brunt, *The Fall of the Roman Republic*, pp. 288–289.

96. Ibid., p. 107.

97. Ibid., pp. 108–109.

98. Svetonius, *Divus Iulius* 53.

99. Ibid., 45.

100. Caesar, *De bello hispaniensi* 42.7.

101. Plutarch, *Caesar* 15.5.

102. Ibid., 17.1.

103. On this and what follows, cf. Harmand, in Brisson, *Problèmes de la guerre à Rome*, pp. 70–73; and C. Nicolet, *The World of the Citizen in Republican Rome*, translated by P. S. Falla (London, 1980), pp. 134ff.

104. Svetonius, *Divus Iulius* 59. This behavior is also reported in Plutarch, *Caesar* 18.3.

105. Svetonius, *Divus Iulius* 72; Plutarch, *Caesar* 17.11.

106. Svetonius, *Divus Iulius* 24.2.

107. Plutarch, *Caesar* 17.1.

108. Ibid., 12.4, 15.4.

109. Svetonius, *Divus Iulius* 26.3.

110. Ibid., 28.1.

111. Ibid., 1–3.

112. Ibid., 53.3.

113. Ibid., 24.1.

114. Ibid., 57.1–2.

115. Ibid., 57.1.

116. Caesar, *De bello Africo* 54.

117. Svetonius, *Divus Iulius* 73–75.

118. Ibid., 75.2.

119. Plutarch, *Caesar* 16.1.

120. Svetonius, *Divus Iulius* 58.1.

121. Plutarch, *Caesar,* 16.9.

122. Harmand, in Brisson, *Problèmes de la guerre à Rome*, p. 71.

123. Nicolet's comments have been very helpful in the formulation of the following section; see *The World of the Citizen in Republican Rome*, pp. 137–148.

124. Ibid., p. 136.

125. Appian, *The Civil Wars* 5.46.

126. Nicolet, *The World of the Citizen in Republican Rome*, p. 139.

127. Sallust, *Bellum Iugurthinum* 65.4–5; Plutarch, *Marius* 7.4.

128. Cf. the comments in L. Perelli, *Il movimento popolare nell'ultimo secolo della repubblica* (Torino, 1982), pp. 237–239.

3

Julius Caesar: Thoughts and Actions of a Commander

[Caesar] joined battle not only after planning his movements in advance but on a sudden opportunity, often immediately at the end of a march, and sometimes in the foulest weather, when one would least expect him to make a move.

Svetonius, ***Divus Iulius*** 70

Caesar lacked Hannibal's cunning and Alexander the Great's sense of destiny yet probably understood the social, psychological, and practical implications of warfare as well as any of the great leaders of the ancient world. His practical military training before he moved into Gaul had been minimal. It included a fascinating encounter with pirates as a young man, a short participation in the so-called Third Mithridatic War (74–63 B.C.), and the office of legate in the Roman war against the pirates in 74 B.C. Also, a few years before his appointment to the Gallic territories he had tasted warfare firsthand as praetor and propraetor in Spain (61–60 B.C.). And as Luigi Loreto suggests, we should also consider Caesar's theoretical and literary preparation, that is, his reading and analysis of military matters in works by the likes of Polybius, Cato, Posidonius, and probably Thucydides.[1] The problem, however, is not whether Caesar's war experience was extensive before he engaged in the Gallic adventure; rather it is whether his actual achievements on the battlefield (whether in Gaul or during the Roman civil wars) were innovative, effective, and original. It is on that score that Caesar the military man must be judged.

The Conquest of Gaul

In 62 B.C., after a short stint in the Third War, Gaius Iulius Caesar (100–44 B.C.) was appointed praetor and propraetor to Spain. He returned to Rome in 60 B.C. and one year later won the consulate. Upon his return from Spain, in a series of clever political maneuvers, he formed a political alliance with Pompeius and Crassus, the Roman republic's most powerful individuals. One term of their agreement was to grant Caesar a five-year control of the affairs in Cisalpine Gaul (northern Italy) and Illyricum (the region from the Adriatic Sea to the Danube); the Senate added Transalpine Gaul. This appointment would transform Caesar into a most powerful political leader and an exceptional commander of troops.

Gaul (see Figure 3.1) included four main regions: Gallia Transalpina or Narbonensis (southern France), Aquitania (the region bordered by the Pyrenees on the east, the Garonne on the south and west, and the Bay of Biscay on the north), Lugdunensis (the lands from the Garonne to the Rhine), and Belgica (the area east of the Seine and north of the Marne up to the Rhine). The Gallic Celts were separated from the three other Celtic-dominated areas in continental Europe—the Iberian peninsula, northern Italy (Gallia Cisalpina), and the strip of land from the Rhine to the Black Sea along the banks of the Danube. In fact, the Gallic Celts seemed to have a closer ethnic relationship with Celts living in southern Britain. At the time of Caesar's appointment, only the Narbonensis, the territories from Lake Geneva to the Pyrenees along the Mediterranean coast, was under Roman control. It had been made into a province in 128 B.C. initially to protect Roman trade with Spain.

Gaul's predominant culture was Gallic, but the region also included other Celtic groups, as well as Ligurians and Iberians in the southern areas and in Aquitania and German-speaking peoples in the northeast. Gaul possessed rich agricultural soil, hosted a sophisticated civilization, including centers of skillful iron manufacture, and commanded the tin route originating in the British Isles. Their coins were of silver and gold. Some 10 million people lived there at the time of Caesar's conquest, but unlike Iberian Celts, who divided into small clans, Gallic Celts organized into larger tribal groups based on the leadership of aristocratic houses. Initially, the Arvernians were the dominant house, but by 58 B.C. supremacy had passed to the Aedui, Roman friends who occupied the Burgundian lands and were in perpetual conflict with the Arvernians.[2]

Caesar's initial move into Gaul was motivated by the migrations of the Helvetii, a Celtic population living near Lake Constance and Lake Geneva,

FIGURE 3.1   *Gaul*

whose move might open the door to hostile pressure from Germanic tribes. In combination with other tribes, they prepared for their migration for two years. Finally, during the spring of 68 B.C. they asked Rome's permission to cross the Rhine and continue their trek through the Narbonensis. Rome refused, and so the Helvetii and their allies, numbering about 250,000, chose a more northern route; Caesar then defeated them near the Aeduan capital, Bibracte (near modern-day Toulon-sur-Arroux).[3] He forced most of the survivors back to their lands as a barrier against the Germanic tribes.

Caesar realized that Roman hegemony in the Narbonensis and elsewhere in Gaul was endangered not so much by the Celts but by Germanic expansion on the Rhine's right bank. Also worrisome were German Suebians, who had settled, since 71 B.C., in Aeduan territory under the leadership of their king, Ariovistus, a clever and courageous man. When the Aedui begged Rome to expel the Suebians, Caesar, after preliminary but unsuccessful negotiations with Ariovistus, met the German king in a pitched battle, probably near modern-day Belfort, in September 58 B.C. Caesar won again, and the survivors crossed the Rhine again except for a tribe that eventually was absorbed by the Celtic population.

The year 57 B.C. brought new campaigns and new successes against Belgians and more Celtic populations, but Caesar barely escaped an ambush near the River Sambre as his legionnaires were setting up camp. A year later, in the spring of 56 B.C., the target was Aquitania and control over that part of Gaul located on the Atlantic coast. Again Caesar emerged the victor. In the following two years he became concerned with the safety of the frontiers reached during the previous campaign. On the northeast a likely threat came from two Germanic tribes, the Usipetes and the Tencteri, originally from Westphalia. After moving into traditional Gallic lands they asked permission to settle in the area. Caesar struck first, mounting a daring land-sea operation in the region of the Batavians on the lower Rhine; then, under the pretext that some Usipetes had sought refuge among the Germanic Sicambri, Caesar built a bridge on the Rhine near modern-day Neuwied. The Romans crossed to the other bank, campaigning for about two weeks before returning to the left bank. That same year, 55 B.C., Caesar also crossed the English Channel, embarking from a place west of Calais and landing on the Kent coastline. He returned to Gaul after two or three weeks, achieving little success. He invaded Britain again in 54 B.C., achieving more tangible yet transitory successes. (Under Claudius, who was emperor during A.D. 41–54, the Romans finally conquered the island.) In 54 B.C. Caesar also defeated, after many dangerous moments, the Eburones (a Belgian tribe, probably a combination of Germans and Celts), who, led by their chief, Ambiorix, caused much distress and casualties to the Roman legions posted between the Meuse and the Rhine. One year after that, in 53 B.C., Caesar built another bridge crossing the Rhine near Neuwied and campaigned briefly in German territory.

But that year closed with ominous signs for the Romans. The problems originated in Rome itself, not in Gaul; and Caesar, worried about the events in the capital, spent most of the winter of 53–52 B.C. back in Rome. Yet before spring he was back in the Narbonensis, worried that most of the Gallic tribes had united under a young leader whose intent seemed to be to remove Rome's supremacy in their land. That leader was a young Arvernian aristocrat named Vercingetorix.

Caesar mistakenly thought that he could still control the situation before facing Vercingetorix, and he punished some of those who had rebelled. He was generally successful except Gergovia, the Arvenian capital, which withstood a siege; Caesar finally had to withdraw after suffering heavy casualties. News of Caesar's setback at Gergovia convinced the Aedui—the only major tribe that had not allied with Vercingetorix's forces—to join the insurgency. By this time Caesar's situation was critical, as he was stranded with his legions in the center of Gaul, apparently with only two tribes, the Remi and the Lingones, who remained loyal to him. He had only 50,000 men, was short of cavalry (the best troops among his opponents), and was in danger of having his safety and lines of communication to the south cut off. He reinforced his cavalry by hiring German horsemen, who brought their own foot skirmishers to fight with them; prudently, he moved south. At least 50,000 warriors (Caesar mentions 80,000) were now on his trail, and Vercingetorix could recruit many more.[4]

The Gallic chieftain's plan at this stage was to avoid a pitched battle against the superior Roman infantry while harassing Caesar with his cavalry. He almost succeeded in ambushing the Romans nearby Vingeanne, deploying his soldiers on the flanks and in front of the marching Roman column. Caesar unexpectedly escaped the trap, and a final charge from his hired German cavalry routed the enemy. Vercingetorix withdrew to the fortified town of Alesia (Alise-Sainte-Reine in the Côte-d'Or near Dijon), which stood on a plateau 150 meters high, 1,500 long, and 1,000 wide on about 240 acres (see Figure 3.2). In his typical fashion, Caesar immediately exploited the adversary's weakness, stopping his march to safety and moving on Alesia to lay siege. Near the walls of Alesia the two opposing cavalries came to blows; again the Romans prevailed.

Vercingetorix, his food supplies running short, sent a call to the rest of Gaul for aid. About six weeks later, according to Caesar, some 258,000 warriors marched against him. Caesar faced three problems: how to keep his troops supplied longer than Vercingetorix's warriors in Alesia, how to blunt an attack coming from Alesia once the enemy relief forces arrived, and how to meet a combined assault by troops coming from the rest of Gaul and those still in Alesia. He solved the supply problem by gathering most of the resources available in the area. Toward the end, as the besieged Gauls starved, the Romans had ample food supplies. The threat from Alesia itself was met by building a fortified line about 16 kilometers long with ramparts,

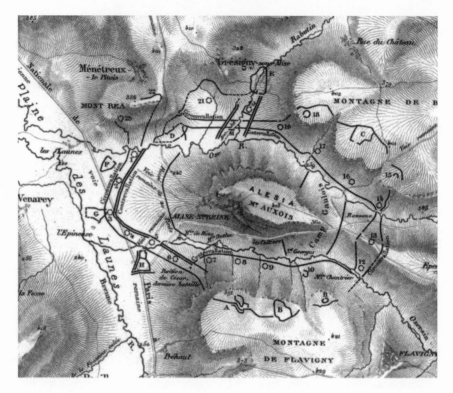

FIGURE 3.2   Alesia, 52 B.C.

palisades, and towers, all defended by trenches and booby traps of iron obstacles and sharpened wooden sticks, their location hidden by branches. The
threat from the outside was faced with a corresponding line of fortification
similar to the line facing Alesia, its circumference being about 28 kilometers.
His troops were stationed at intervals between the two fortification lines,
which must have been an engineering marvel greater even than his two
bridges across the Rhine. Six weeks later, the campaign ended with victories
against those in Alesia as well as their relief forces. About two years later, in
50 B.C., the whole of Gaul had fallen into Roman hands. Caesar and his lieu-
tenants carried out several mop-up operations after Alesia, sometimes with
great ruthlessness. In 50 B.C., for instance, the people of Uxellodunum
(modern-day Puech d'Issolu) had their hands lopped off for their resistance
of the Romans.

War According to Caesar:
Psychological, Strategic, and Tactical Concepts

Caesar began his Gallic adventure with four legions. By the time he ended he had raised four more on his own, and then two more, for a total of ten. In the process he conquered a large, wealthy area that would provide Rome with lands, gold, and soldiers to fight its wars. His conquest had not been a deliberate policy of the Roman Senate and people. Actually war, as conceived by Caesar, was in opposition to the normal Roman concept of "just war," which could be waged only against people threatening the state's security, to right a wrong, or at times to civilize barbarians. The Gauls spoke a different language than the Romans, but by Caesar's time few would have called them "barbarians," as the Romans were wont to do with many other peoples. Moreover, Caesar's action was at variance with the policy of the highest organ of the state, the Senate. As Christian Meier argues, his decision was "an enormity even by contemporary standards."[5] The truth, however, is probably different.

Rome lived on war from the very beginning of its founding, although in appearance it tried to follow guidelines set by just laws. In reality Rome had always been externally aggressive, quick to pursue economic benefit from others, often using security as rationale. What Caesar did in Gaul and elsewhere was to approach the problem realistically, presented rather candidly in *De bello gallico*, his "memoirs." The Gauls, he often states, were proud people who wished to remain free. And the Senate wanted them to remain so. But Caesar thought differently. In reality, Gallic pride and their belief in freedom were dangerous to Rome—meaning the particular interests of Caesar and his men. Thus the Gauls had to be subjugated.[6]

The direct beneficiaries of Gallic subjugation would, of course, be Caesar and his men—but this also included Rome. As one of his adversaries, the German Ariovistus, stated, it is the right of war that winners dictate as they please to the conquered even if with a certain scorn; he added that the Romans used this practice in the past, but no longer.[7] Still it was Caesar who placed these words into his enemy's mouth, surely to indicate how wrong any Roman was to criticize his aggression. Rome's destiny was to conquer and dominate other peoples. This meant that the conqueror owned everything that belonged to the enemy, even their bodies. What Caesar does not say, however, is that a pre–civil war general would have followed the Senate's orders; now, Caesar made the decision and carried it out regardless of opinions in Rome. It was the logical conclusion to decades of civil turmoil and fratricidal bloodshed, for power had left the Senate and the people of Rome and fallen into the hands of the powerful. The end of the Roman republic was symbolized later, in 49 B.C., when Caesar crossed the Rubicon. In reality Rome had fallen earlier, on the fields of Gaul. The gold and successes reaped by the armies in Gaul killed definitively an institution that had been withering at least since 88 B.C., when Sulla marched on Rome.

Unlike Cicero, who argued that the scope of war was the search for peace, Caesar looked at the problem in a more realistic vein.[8] War was meant to conquer other peoples and establish Roman rule. The end result was to enrich those in the field and the citizens back home. At times, then, war was naked aggression, pure and simple. In 60 B.C., while a praetor in the Iberian peninsula, Caesar justified his attack on the Lusitanians as an attempt to stifle the brigandage ravaging their land; soon thereafter, it was clear that the casus belli was an invention of Caesar's making. He ordered the tribes to move from their rugged terrain to the plains, aware that they would never do so and that their refusal would give him reason to attack.[9] When the German Ariovistus moved into Gallic lands, Caesar showed that he had no other recourse than to attack him; otherwise the obligations that he and the Senate had taken to defend the friendly Aedui, the German's target, would not have been fulfilled.[10] Ariovistus's action, Caesar stated, was a major threat to Rome, when in reality it involved a few Gallic tribes and an arrogant but rather minor barbarian.[11] He based his action against the Belgae, a dangerous tribe in northern Gaul, on the assumption that they were preparing to attack the Romans.[12] On this issue, Caesar's action was based on evidence that he could manipulate.[13] Even the campaign against the two German tribes, the Usipetes and Tencteri, showed again that Caesar was the aggressor, more so than the Germans on the other side of the Rhine. The Germans did not take the first step toward war, but Caesar exploited their natural tendency for aggressiveness.[14]

These two tribes had crossed the Rhine near the sea under pressure from the Suebi, an expanding, more powerful German tribe. An incident was created when a small cavalry detachment harassed a small body of Romans. Caesar, probably worried that this small action would lead to larger conflict, fell upon the tribes unexpectedly, slaughtering men, women, and children. He stated that 430,000 Germans perished while the Romans suffered but a few wounded.[15] Caesar did not hide the fact that he wanted war and that punishment was extreme. It is clear, however, that for Caesar the Germans represented a threat to his control over Gaul and that he needed a firm, ruthless action to strengthen that recently conquered area.[16] At odds with our modern perspective (or even Cicero's), such ruthlessness was faithful to a Roman tenet: conquer and destroy the enemy if peaceful subjugation was not possible.

Caesar meticulously examined the strategic moves necessary for victory. He sought to place his main body in a central position from which he could dash out according to circumstances; to defeat the enemy in detail if faced by a numerically superior foe; to lash out at the target and thereby spread terror physically and psychologically; to retain the initiative; and finally, once intelligence on the enemy had been received and evaluated, to strike with speed.

This strategic view started with the assumption that there should be no internal threat to Rome's supremacy in the territory under control. Also, frontiers should be totally safe. In the long run this meant controlling all of Gaul, as well as containment and deterrence on the Germanic border, identified as the Rhine for historical, ethnic, and geographical reasons, although Celtic influence spanned both banks in most parts.[17] His two expeditions to Britain illustrate the identical viewpoint.

Yet sometimes Caesar failed to apply these strategic concepts, as at the onset of the Alesia campaign, when he and his legions found themselves stranded in Gaul with their lines of communication to the south threatened or cut off. Sometimes his own success on the battlefield tended to strip his normally careful control of the environment. His speed *(celeritas)* in pursuit of a specific goal or to inflict a decisive blow (Alesia again comes to mind) could place his soldiers in grave danger. But generally Caesar was keenly conscious that it was imperative to hold locations essential for security, to provide enough supplies to his men, to limit the possibilities of treason, to secure safe forays into enemy lands, and generally to defend his lines of communication. There is evidence of this approach in the conquest of Gaul and during the civil war, for instance, in holding Vesontio (Besançon), which combined a strong physical position, and abundance in food and weapon supplies, with access to the Saône Valley; and in Noviodunum (Nevers), which was located in a key position on the banks of the Loire; and in Avaricum (Bourges), a well-fortified city "situated in a most fertile district."[18] Early in the civil war against Pompeius, he immediately moved toward occupying the harbor at Brundisium (Brindisi), which served as a point of escape from Italy, a place of embarkation for Greece, and a landing spot for troops from the east. As Caesar put it, whoever held Brundisium "might more easily control the whole Adriatic from the extremities of Italy and the shores of Greece and so carry on war from either side."[19]

What Caesar intended most times was to spread his troops in such a way that his contingents could intervene and support one another. For instance, while operating in northern France he concentrated the main forces in Brittany and Normandy, but he also placed covering troops on his flanks, sending them left, in Aquitaine, and right, along the lower Rhine. Moreover, he divided the main theater of operations into three subsectors, deploying three legions in Normandy, taking personal control in Armorica (the region on his left), and placing the fleet under independent command.[20] Once he concluded that a forceful confrontation was feasible, Caesar's main goal was to bring the most pressure to bear on the enemy as possible. The army's central position allowed him to bring all his forces into action and, if the occasion appeared, to defeat the enemy in detail. He faced this very situation against Ariovistus: Not only were the German leader's men already across the Rhine in Gallic lands; 100 additional Suebian tribes had gathered on the river's banks, ready to cross. Thus it was mandatory to approach Ariovistus with forced marches "for fear that . . . if the new company of Suebians joined the old forces of Ariovistus . . . resistance might be more difficult."[21] But normally Caesar tried to retain the initiative, which meant to attack even before the enemy formulated its offensive and spread terror psychologically and physically—in other words, deterrence.

People, beginning from Caesar's time, have usually praised him for his *celeritas*, his quickness of action at both the strategic and tactical levels. The emphasis on this characteristic tends to obscure the laborious intelligence-gathering that preceded his campaigns. Luigi Loreto argues that Caesar's process of information typically went through three phases. The first was prior to the campaign; the second when he set his troops' goals before moving into action; and the third during the campaign.[22] Caesar's intelligence-gathering was thus in continuous flux, which meant that he could devise campaigns or change plans during any stage of the operation on the basis of the reports received.[23]

There was practically no source that Caesar ignored. He wanted to know everything possible on the target he had chosen—land, terrain, inhabitants, whether they were warlike or not, rich or poor, how they lived, what their behavior had been in the immediate and remote past. Sometimes his intelligence-gathering began by perusing literary sources. Sometimes he sent a subordinate, and sometimes he personally surveyed the area.[24] There were other methods—questioning prisoners, traders, neighboring tribes friendly to Rome, his own officers, his cavalry, and the special units known as *exploratores* (a body of scouts) and *speculatores* (spies). When Ariovistus continually avoided any pitched battle, Caesar interrogated a few German prisoners caught during a skirmish. When they revealed that Ariovistus would not dare attack before a new moon in obedience to a divination, he deployed his army the next morning and compelled Ariovistus to engage when the Romans must have fought with the psychological edge.[25] And in 54 B.C., as a confrontation against a Gallic tribe was becoming more and more serious, a legate, besieged by the enemy, sent Caesar dispatches explaining the dangers the legate was facing. Caesar reacted by advancing to relieve his troops. The Gauls, facing a threat from another front, abandoned the siege.[26] And when he was organizing his second expedition against the Germans, Caesar ordered a friendly tribe from across the Rhine to send scouts into the territories of the Suebians, Caesar's specific target, and to gather information on their movements.[27] In preparing his attack against the Belgae, Caesar instructed nearby Gallic tribes to keep him updated on the Belgaes' movements before moving against them.[28]

Rumors also played a role in Caesar's intelligence scheme. Initially "frequent rumors" had put him on guard as to the Belgaes' intentions.[29] Another time he paid special attention to a peculiar Gallic way of spreading information on the eve of the great revolt under Vercingetorix: "whenever any event of greater note or importance occurs, the Gauls shout it abroad through fields and districts and then others take it up in turn and pass it on to their next neighbors." The deed being relayed that night was the massacre of Roman traders.[30]

Caesar skillfully used sections of his legions for intelligence purposes.[31] His cavalry fulfilled the normal tasks—pursuing the enemy, harassing a retreating host, skirmishing, defending the lines of communication; but it also scouted, accumulated information, evaluated other sources, and so on. One of his two units specifically organized for intelligence-gathering, the *exploratores*, seemed to have operated at a certain distance from the main army, usually 15–36 kilometers ahead (about one day's ride). They were positioned at river crossings, guarded fords, gathered rumors and information, surveyed the terrain, discovered ambushes, chose campsites, made sure the area was safe, and found out the plans of the enemy.[32] The other intelligence body, the *speculatores*, instead were people entrusted with spying missions and infiltration of enemy camps.[33] *Exploratores* and *speculatores* were used in Gaul and during the civil wars.

Amazing even today are Caesar's extensive efforts to gather information and its careful sifting once it reached him (but not always, as in Britain). For instance, when Caesar realized that the Belgae were abandoning their camp at night, he delayed his strike; then, once convinced of the certainty of the reports, he moved to the attack.[34] And when he was relayed all the movements of the Helvetii trying to cross the Saône, he fell quickly upon them.[35] Caesar's Herculean intelligence efforts gave him a great advantage over his opponents. They turned territory unfamiliar to his soldiers into familiar territory; allowed him to strike the weakest point of the enemy defense; and made possible the development of a coherent strategy that he could always change in the field as new details surfaced.[36]

A typical example of Caesar's care in gathering intelligence is his first invasion of Britain, although in the end, despite his efforts, the information was not detailed enough and the invasion failed.

After his first foray across the Rhine, Caesar decided to move into Britain, an island outpost of which the Romans knew practically nothing. The invasion fit Caesar's strategic and tactical mind-set: Because the Britons had sent help to the Gauls against the Romans, a preemptive strike was necessary; his presence on the island would strike terror among the natives, who inevitably would be reluctant to help the Gauls again; and he could gather useful information on the character of the inhabitants and the terrain, harbors, and suitable spots for landing.[37] Although Caesar realized that winter was nearing and that cold weather would limit the expedition's duration, he thought that the venture could be effective.

Reviewing literary sources, a normal first step for Caesar, provided nothing about the island. Some sources even maintained that Britain did not exist. Traders, the only ones to have journeyed there, knew little or were unwilling to cooperate with the Romans. Thus Caesar sent a subordinate on a warship to scout while he moved his army to the coast nearest Britain, perhaps Boulogne or, more likely, Sangatte and Wissant, west of Calais.[38] Caesar's intent was praiseworthy, but his orders were somewhat lacking. The ship was not entrusted to actually land and make observations as to the interior terrain and people, only to scout the coast. This would not be enough. But Caesar eventually landed on the island, his boats damaged by the tides; he had to retreat soon thereafter. He would make certain that the next expedition would be better prepared.[39]

This first "invasion" of Britain points out the strengths and weaknesses in Caesar's approach to war. One could say that one of his greatest traits as a general—*celeritas*—became a burden. In his haste to launch the invasion before winter, his preparation was haphazard. His instructions to the scout—"return to him at once"—were not conducive to providing proper intelligence on the island, even on a good landing spot.[40] In fact when Caesar reached the British shore he found steep heights, with enemies assembled atop.[41] This plus the channel's capricious nature made the disembarkation difficult indeed.[42]

In Gaul, the main external threat (at least in Caesar's mind) came from across the Rhine despite the fact that this natural dividing line between the Germans and Gauls provided a formidable obstacle to his armies. But for Caesar the river alone was not enough to stop the Germans: It had not stopped Ariovistus at the head of 15,000 warriors,[43] and it had not prevented a much larger force of Usipetes and Tincteri from crossing the Rhine near the sea.[44] Caesar would eventually aim at establishing a cordon sanitaire across the river—deterring the Germans from helping the rebels or moving into Gaul's more fertile lands—and resisting more strenuously the expansion of the Germanic tribes, which had placed the Romans in danger time and again.

After the annihilation of the Usipetes and Tincteri, Caesar approached the problem in the typical manner—a preemptive strike. His motivation was clear: to spread fear among tribes on the far bank and to show that there was no place to hide for an enemy of Rome.[45] The casus belli was created when the Usipetes and Tincteri cavalries, which escaped destruction, sought refuge with the German Sugambri tribe across the river. Caesar demanded that the Sugambri surrender these men, but they maintained that Roman control ended at the Rhine. Likely, this was the answer Caesar wanted— meaning he could undertake a "just" war. And not all opposed him. At least one German tribe sent hostages and promised men and boats to cross the Rhine as evidence of its good faith. But Caesar felt that it did not fit the dignity of the Romans to land in other people's boats, and such a crossing would not strike terror among the enemies. The result was the construction of a bridge. It took Caesar ten days to build what must have been a technological marvel. He then moved into enemy territory, destroyed their crops, burned their villages, received homage from other tribes, and then returned across the river.[46]

This entire campaign well illustrates Caesar's system for waging war, not to mention several Roman tenets—speedy decisions, preemptive strikes, combining physical and psychological terror, the emphasis on the dignity of the Roman people, and finally the distinctive combination of the sword and the shovel, that is, the power of arms, technological expertise, and heavy labor. Viewed from a different angle, Caesar's foray into German territory looks also like the medieval *chevauchée*—a raid to intimidate your opponents, demonstrate the power of your soldiers, and convince those sitting on the fence to support your side.

As Caesar would later realize, however, a single strike against the Germans was not enough. According to Caesar, the reason for crossing again into Germany was twofold: to punish Germanic tribes helping the Gauls, and to prevent the Gallic leaders from seeking refuge among the Germans. He built a second bridge close to the first location, and as he crossed into Germany the same tribes that had earlier given up hostages reconfirmed their loyalty. The Suebians were Caesar's target, but this time he could not come to grips with them. Because they had no riches to defend, they withdrew from the Roman army, seeking refuge in an immense forest. Caesar decided to withdraw. He was worried about the corn supply and the turmoil in Gaul. He destroyed the section of the bridge on the German side to protect his rear, erected a high tower on the left bank—the Gallic end of the Rhine—and posted a garrison of twelve cohorts, some 5,760 men.[47] This expedition again illustrates the sheer strength of the Roman army and its uncanny ability to overcome the most taxing obstacles of terrain. But it also illustrates a weakness when confronted by a relatively poor people: The Germans, unlike the Gauls, had no major urban center that Roman soldiers could advance on, take, and devastate, and their reliance on agriculture was not an immediate, crucial concern, because they hunted as well.

Caesar's mode of attack, put simply, was to conquer either by violence or by psychological persuasion: seize the initiative, striking before the enemy attacks; manipulate people and the environment to your advantage; reward those who, cowed by fear, follow your goals; strike terror among those who do not peacefully accept your aim. Caesar saw this as a three-step process marked by a disciplined and strong Roman army; the memory of recent victory to shake the enemy's confidence; and the majesty of his office and previous achievements to weaken the opponents' resolve.[48] His weapons were legions that, as he claimed, could storm the heavens with or without him.[49]

Rome would not rest until all enemies were subjugated or destroyed. For those who physically challenged the Roman administration or did not fulfill treaties they had signed, punishment was total destruction. Deterrence did not always imply an immediate violent strike but rather the manipulation of a variety of methods, depending on the target and the environment. Force was the prerequisite not just to protect the borders of the empire but to peacefully administer the territories just conquered and to project the power of the Roman legions across the borders. The idea was to establish an area around the empire where inhabitants feared the Roman legions and would not conceive of helping the empire's internal enemies.

But violence and the threat of violence were not the only tools for deterrence under Caesar. Deterrence could be achieved by manipulating the mind of the opponent. Here, together with the use of the sword, Caesar tended to project the image of clemency. This was never used with outsiders, who were not subject to Rome, but with those already incorporated into the empire and who constituted, for the moment at least, a minimal threat to Roman supremacy. This could include granting tribes a favorable alliance (e.g., the Gallic Aedui), supporting chiefs as friends of Rome, planting spies, or manipulating old wounds among various tribes.[50] The alternative for such "friends" was utter horror, well demonstrated by the Roman legions in the near past.

Caesar's psychological strategy was so effective because it fit hand in glove with the tactical power of the legions and his consummate leadership ability. J.F.C. Fuller, a modern-era scholar who harbors many doubts about Caesar as strategist, nevertheless believes that Caesar's total self-confidence made him "one of the greatest fighting generals of the Classical age."[51] Rapid decisions and implementation on the battlefield were just the beginning; a host of other gifts made him virtually invincible. His defeats and setbacks were less than a handful—Gergovia and Dyrrachium and the setbacks at the Sambre, the ambush near Dijon, and the encounters at Ruspina and Munda; in most, he eventually would attain victory.[52] But his conviction that the plan, once conceived, must be carried out with the utmost urgency gave him a great edge. As Fuller argues, Caesar did not rely on numerical superiority but on surprising the enemy with his celerity and audacity: "By surprising his opponent he caught him off-guard, and got him so thoroughly rattled that either he refused his challenge to fight and in consequence lost prestige, or, should he respond, was morally half-beaten before the engagement took place."[53]

Caesar's quick transition from planning to operation gave him an added advantage. It allowed him to surprise the enemy and, at times, achieve numerical superiority on the battlefield. Speed is a major leitmotiv in Caesar's writings on the Gallic wars and the civil war.[54] And he virtually wrote the book on *celeritas*.[55] For instance, as soon he received news that the Suebians were on the banks of the Rhine ready to reinforce Ariovistus, Caesar moved to attack.[56] Speed was "the only means to the general safety" when two Gallic tribes assaulted the troops of his legates.[57] In an earlier situation, in the words of one of his legates, if the Gauls joined forces with the Germans "the

sole chance of safety lay in speedy action."[58] When he defeated Vercingetorix's cavalry near Vingeanne during the Alesia campaign, he did not seek
safety by moving south but pursued the Gauls, from hunted to hunter.[59]
When at the Rubicon he realized the disarray of the Pompeian forces, Caesar, after a wrenching internal debate on the political gravity of his action,
forcefully struck despite having only one legion, as "he was accustomed to
rely upon the terror caused by the celerity and audacity of his movements,
rather than on the magnitude of his preparations."[60] And soon enough he
would move on Brundisium, where he had not enough transport, not
enough troops, and not enough warm weather; still, he judged that he had
to cross the Adriatic after Pompeius, for "the most potent thing in war is un-
expectedness"; Pompeius would have expected him instead to retire to winter quarters.[61] And during the dangerous turmoil caused by Ambiorix, the
Eburones leader, the Gallic tribe of the Senones, which had joined the revolt, surrendered immediately when the legions' speed surprised them before they could seek refuge in their strongholds.[62]

There were still other qualities that made Caesar a great tactician: an aggressive posture even in defense; a tendency to pursue and annihilate a defeated enemy; a charismatic influence over the troops; the exploitation of
the opponent's psychology; the ability to make changes even in the heat of
battle (difficult especially in ancient times); diversification of his tactical approach; *coup d'oeil*, that is, the ability to grasp immediately every facet of the
battle, even the need to join fighting in the front line when the army was on
the verge of defeat (e.g., the Sambre) or when the moment had arrived to
move in for the kill. Yet Caesar did not always aim for the total destruction
of his foes. He was a master at balancing terror with leniency. Especially
during the civil war he seemed to have been sincerely bothered by the constant carnage. In 49 B.C., during the early stages of the civil war, he put it
thus: "By moderation we can win all hearts and secure a lasting victory. . . .
This is a new way of conquering, to strengthen one's position by kindness
and generosity."[63] In Gaul he forgave the Senones when they sided with Ambiorix yet did not hesitate, when the town of Uxellodunum fell, to bring the
harshest punishment to those who had raised weapons against him: Caesar
cut off their hands as a daily reminder of the penalty befalling "evildoers."[64]

Loreto rightly argues that we cannot characterize Caesar's way of waging
a battle as being typically his own, unlike the other great leaders of antiquity—Alexander, Hannibal, Scipio. Fuller argues otherwise, finding that
Caesar, aware that the rear was the weakest point in the enemy line, "whenever opportunity offered . . . combined a rear attack, or threat of one, with

his frontal attack."[65] But Fuller merely utters a truism that any leader from any period would try to follow. Striking the enemy's rear was a long-standing practice among the ancients, as Marathon (490 B.C.) shows. What distinguished Caesar is that his tenets for battle tended to vary according to the enemy, the circumstances, and the terrain. Yet we can discern several traits wherein tactics and strategy blended together through Caesar's actions: the demoralization of the enemy before the actual engagement; the personal surveying of the terrain; reliance on heavy infantry; the massive and disciplined impact of the legionnaires (e.g., against the Gauls); the minimal role played by light infantry; the quick exploitation of favorable opportunities (e.g., the closing stages of Alesia); the tendency to totally destroy the enemy; and the inspiration provided by his personal intervention on the front line.

Sometimes Caesar's physical location on the battlefield reminds one of the attitude held by most leaders of antiquity, especially among the Greeks and the Macedonians. The Romans, beginning probably with Scipio Africanus, had adopted a more logical position for the commander; he stood not in the thick of battle but in a location where he could make rapid calculations to exploit victory or avoid defeat. And there is no doubt that at times Caesar took up such a prudent position, lest it become impossible to understand how plans could be changed quickly as the thousands battled. Yet often we find him next to his troops, exposing his life to danger. Caesar was indeed a gambler, although one who carefully hedged his bet: If he stepped into the fight, the decision was taken either by necessity or by the certainty that the risk was limited and the promise of reward great.

At the Sambre, for instance, Caesar's army was caught totally unprepared while making camp; the cavalry was off foraging. The Gauls emerged suddenly from the forest on the other side of the river, routing the cavalry, then quickly crossing the water. They ran uphill against the Roman troops, who were entrenching the camp. Disorder followed, and although the Romans pushed back the Gauls on the left and pursued them across the river, the right remained in deep trouble. The 12th Legion, on the right, was closely packed together, with little space to fight. Many of its centurions had been wounded or killed, and the *primipilus* (the centurion of the first cohort) was wounded so many times that he could no longer stand upright.

Caesar rushed forward, grabbed a shield from one of the soldiers in the rear, and moved to where the fray was heaviest (the first line); calling on the names of the centurions still standing, he encouraged the men to widen their spaces so that they could use the swords. He gave hope where previously there had been despair. In the end the legion that had defeated the enemy on the left returned from across the river, and the two legions that had been protecting the baggage advanced from the rear; thus Caesar obtained victory.[66] Caesar's energetic reaction and splendid example of bravery had saved the day.

At Alesia, in contrast, he led the final attack as the enemy was ready to crumble. Caesar sent part of the cavalry outside the fortifications, to strike the Gauls in the rear; he hurried with more horsemen and legionnaires toward the front. When the soldiers there realized that Caesar himself was coming (they knew from the color of his cloak), they fought with greater energy. The legionnaires dropped their *pila* and advanced with swords in hand. At this moment, the cavalry appeared on the enemy's rear. The Gauls fled, pursued by the horsemen. This marked the end of Caesar's greatest triumph in battle.[67]

The Matter of Logistics

The Romans enjoyed success on the battlefield from the third century B.C. to the third century A.D. They lost battles to be sure, but in the end they won wars; only the Rhine in the west and the Parthians in the Near East stopped their advance toward world supremacy. The skills of generals like Caesar and those of clever emperors like Augustus and Trajan help explain the Romans' record of success. But there were other reasons: the clever combination of technology and warfare and, as Polybius says, the "inexhaustible supplies of provisions and men."[68] "Gaius Caesar," according to Frontinus, "used to say that he followed the same policy towards the enemy as did many doctors when dealing with physical ailments, namely that of conquering the foe by hunger rather than by steel."[69]

As for Roman logistics, Jonathan P. Roth correctly argues that the Romans used supplies not just to feed their troops but as a strategic and tactical weapon. Their mastery of the supply system was essential to ongoing military success.[70] Once in the field there were three methods to meet the supply needs of the men: keeping communication to your supply line safe; requisitioning on the spot; and foraging and living off the land. The Romans used a mixed approach.[71] They employed all three elements, relying on what was most effective given the situation.

Xerxes' invasion of Greece in 480 B.C. may have required the largest supply effort. But in the end the Persian invasion attempt failed, with supply difficulties being instrumental to the final defeat.[72] The Romans were much more successful. They were able to satisfy the needs of thousands of men by both sea and land. They investigated the problem at the beginning of every campaign, large and small. It was unusual if they engaged in hostile action before solving the details. The highest priority was food, and when the army carried it they made sure it was located in the safest position possible (i.e., in the center of the marching soldiers). At least from the time of the Jewish historian Josephus (first century A.D.), military servants in charge of the supply train would have had some training as soldiers. The Romans at the end of their march every day built a fortified camp, which served not only as protection for the troops—a place of last refuge in defeat—but also as a tactical base for provisions. When foraging parties were sent out, special armed soldiers would go with them and move to the sources of supply by different routes and at different times of the day.[73] Starting with Marius, the Romans may have reduced the amount of supplies that moved with the army, for the non-combatants who transported them reduced the troops' freedom of movement. Yet they must have paid great care to establishing safe lines of communication when combatants were forced to carry their own provisions.

The Romans were convinced, and rightly so, that soldiers should be well fed when moving to strike the enemy. They must have remembered the disaster at the Battle of Trebia in 218 B.C. against Hannibal. Building up energy and stamina through nutrition must have been compulsory for warriors who undertook short but tiring bursts of activity. The Romans cooked their meals in groups of eight and ate together, strengthening the sense of camaraderie, essential for making good fighting soldiers.[74] Moreover, the attention to logistics was seen as another tool to bring the enemy to defeat. Whenever possible the Romans cut off the enemy supply line, thereby forcing him to do battle or to surrender. They would prevent the enemy's animals from foraging so that they would starve (it is no surprise that, besides asking for relief from the other Gallic tribes, Vercingetorix, when under siege, would send all his cavalry away from Alesia); they shut out the enemy from the sources of water, which could become a disaster for men and animals. Sieges especially required good supply lines, for the preferred method of defeat was starvation, not storming the walls.

At first glance, Caesar's actions in regard to logistical problems and lines of communication are puzzling. In describing the actions of probably his best lieutenant—Publius Licinius Crassus, the son of Marcus Lucinius Crassus, whom the Parthians killed—Caesar clearly demonstrates an understanding of the importance of logistics: The enemy decided to close the roads and cut off the supplies so that they could "secure victory without bloodshed." And later, when the Romans gave the impression that they were retiring for logistical needs (they lacked corn) and were slowed down by their packs (*impedimenta*, i.e., the supplies that each soldier carried), the enemy became convinced they should strike the Romans, for their "spirit would be weaker." It did not work; Crassus decided to attack instead of protecting his line of communication.[75] And Caesar's Alesia campaign is a good illustration of how Caesar understood the requirements of logistics.

Yet Caesar often faced dire logistical problems on the battlefield—inadequate food, obstruction of the lines of communication, poor foraging spots (indeed, in the civil war in Africa he was forced to feed algae to the horses).[76] Caesar's understanding of logistics, like that of Rome in general, was based on the assumption that the terrain would provide more than enough—a realistic conclusion in a place like Gaul. Moreover, one must evaluate Caesar's problem with his lines of communication as a consequence of his own success. His speed and decisive use of the killing blow may have overstretched even the most carefully laid plan. Thus Caesar's genius is evident both in his successes and his failures.

But all his brilliance on the battlefield was not enough to save Caesar from the assassins' daggers on the Ides of March in the year 44 B.C.

Notes

1. Luigi Loreto, "Pensare la guerra in Cesare: Teoria e Prassi," in *La cultura in Cesare*, edited by Diego Poli (Roma, 1993), pp. 242–244.
2. André Piganiol, *Le conquiste dei romani*, translated by Filippo Coarelli (Milano, 1997), pp. 433–447.
3. It was 150,000 Helvetii and 100,000 other Celts according to Piganiol, *Le conquiste dei romani*, p. 437.
4. The estimate by Piganiol is 50,000, *Le conquiste dei romani*, p. 442.
5. Cf. Christian Meier, *Caesar*, translated by D. McLintock (London, 1995), pp. 254–264.
6. Ibid., p. 258.
7. Caesar, *De bello Gallico* i.36; cf. Loreto, "Pensare la guerra in Cesare, " pp. 262–263.
8. Cicero, *De officiis* i.11.35.
9. Dio xxxvii.52.1 and 3.
10. Caesar, *De bello Gallico* i.43.
11. Meier, *Caesar*, p. 242.
12. Caesar, *De bello Gallico* ii.1.
13. Loreto, "Pensare la guerra in Cesare," pp. 266–267.

14. Caesar, *De bello Gallico* iv.7.

15. Ibid., iv.4–15.

16. Meier, *Caesar*, p. 279.

17. Loreto, "Pensare la guerra in Cesare," pp. 273–274.

18. Cf. ibid., pp. 276–277; Caesar, *De bello Gallico* i.38, vii.55, vii.14.

19. Caesar, *De bello civili* i.25.

20. Loreto, "Pensare la guerra in Cesare," p. 288.

21. Caesar, *De bello Gallico* i.37.

22. Loreto, "Pensare la guerra in Cesare," pp. 280–282.

23. Amiram Ezov, "The 'Missing Dimension' of C. Julius Caesar," *Historia* 45 (1996): 64–94, 68–69.

24. Caesar, *De bello Gallico* iv.20–21.

25. Ibid., i.50. On the interrogation of prisoners, see i.22.

26. The legate was Quintus Cicero, the tribe the Nervi; Caesar, *De bello Gallico* v.45–49.

27. Ibid., vi.9. The Ubii were the tribe entrusted with scouting. They had already given Caesar hostages during the previous expedition, and now he made sure of their loyalty by compelling them to give him more hostages and their cattle and food supplies in a specific location.

28. Ibid., ii.2.

29. Ibid., ii.1.

30. Ibid., vii.3.

31. On what follows, see Ezov, "The 'Missing Dimension' of C. Julius Caesar," pp. 64–94.

32. Ibid., pp. 72–77.

33. Ibid., p. 83.

34. Caesar, *De bello Gallico* ii.12; cf. Ezov, "The 'Missing Dimension' of C. Julius Caesar," pp. 84–85.

35. Caesar, *De bello Gallico* i,12; cf. Ezov, "The 'Missing Dimension' of C. Julius Caesar," p. 85.

36. Ezov, "The 'Missing Dimension' of C. Julius Caesar," p. 69.

37. Caesar, *De bello Gallico* iv.20.

38. Piganiol, *Le conquiste dei Romani*, p. 440.

39. Caesar, *De bello Gallico* iv.20–30.

40. Ibid., iv.21.

41. Ibid., iv.23.

42. Ibid., iv.24–25.

43. Ibid., i.31.

44. Ibid., iv.1.

45. Ibid., iv.16.

46. Ibid., iv.16–19.

47. Ibid., vi.9–10, 29.

48. Loreto, "Pensare la guerra in Cesare," pp. 249–250.

49. Caesar *De bello hispaniensi* 42.7.

50. Loreto, "Pensare la guerra in Cesare," p. 261.

51. J.F.C. Fuller, *Julius Caesar: Man, Soldier, and Tyrant* (London, 1965), p. 324.

52. Ibid., p. 324.

53. Ibid., p. 321.

54. R. Lecrompe, *César, De Bello Gallico. Index Verborum. Documents pour servir à l'enseignement de la langue latine* (Hildsheim, 1968), p. 34. In *De bello Gallico* he uses twenty times the concept of celerity—once in Book One, six times in Book Two, twice each in Book Three and Book Four, three in Book Five, and six in Book Six.

55. See Loreto, "Pensare la guerra in Cesare," 293.

56. Caesar, *De bello Gallico* i.37.

57. Ibid., v.48.

58. Caesar attributes these words to his legate Quintus Titurius Sabinus; *De bello Gallico* v.29.

59. Ibid., vi.67.

60. Appian ii.5.35.

61. Appian ii.8.54.

62. Caesar, *De bello Gallico* vi.4.

63. Cicero, *Ad Att.* ix.7c.

64. Caesar, *De bello Gallico* viii.44.

65. Fuller, *Julius Caesar*, pp. 322–323.

66. Caesar, *De bello Gallico* ii.18–27.

67. Ibid., vii.88.

68. Polybius iii.98.8.

69. Frontinus, *Strategemata* iv.7.1.

70. Jonathan P. Roth, *The Logistics of the Roman Army at War, 264 B.C.–A.D. 235* (Leiden, 1999), p. 325.

71. Ibid., p. 331.

72. Antonio Santosuosso, *Soldiers, Citizens, and the Symbols of War from Classical Greece to Republican Rome, 500–167 B.C.* (Boulder, 1997), pp. 72–74.

73. Roth, *The Logistics of the Roman Army*, pp. 326–333.

74. Ibid., pp. 328, 330.

75. Caesar, *De bello Gallico* iii.24.

76. See the arguments in Loreto, "Pensare la guerra in Cesare," pp. 282–288, 293.

4

Of Gods, Military Leaders, and Politicians

The family of my aunt Julia is descended by her mother from the kings, and on her father's side is akin to the immortal Gods; for the Marcii Reges (her mother's family name) go back to Ancus Marcius, and the Julii, the family of which ours is a branch, to Venus. Our stock therefore has at once the sanctity of kings, whose power is supreme among mortal men, and the claim to reverence which attaches to the Gods, who hold sway over kings themselves.

Caesar, on the family ancestry; quoted from
a eulogy for his aunt in Svetonius, *Divus Iulius* vi.1

Caesar's demise was the ultimate symbol of the way that politics, warfare, and religion had blended in the ancient world. Beginning with the Renaissance, Western civilization has tended to separate these elements and, as time has passed, to discard war as a crucial element within our understanding of society. But war defined ancient Rome; no social or political aspect was divorced from events on the battlefield or the leaders and soldiers associated with these glories. Like a mirror of shifting images, war reflected both the strengths and weaknesses of Roman society.

Murder as a Religious Sacrifice

It was late in the day—the fifth hour—on March 15, the Ides of March, in the year 44 B.C. when Caesar left his house to go to the Senate.[1] He had hesitated long before doing so. His wife, Calpurnia, had begged him in vain not to venture there. Inexplicable events had happened during the night. The door of their bedroom had opened suddenly and violently, Calpurnia dreamed she was holding her husband's corpse in her arms, and Caesar himself had dreamed that he was flying over the clouds,[2] grasping the hand of Jupiter, king of the gods.[3] It was the conclusion of a series of portents foreshadowing the coming of evil. The day before a little bird, a king-bird, had entered the hall of Caesar's old enemy, Pompeius, holding a laurel sprig (a sign of glory or, more likely in this case, of prophecy). The king-bird (an obvious symbol for Caesar himself) had been pursued by birds of his own kind (other Romans) and torn to pieces.[4] Caesar, at dinner with friends the night before, had chosen sudden death as his preferred form of dying during a discussion.[5]

But Decimius Brutus, whom Caesar considered a friend, arrived and convinced him not to disappoint the Senate, which was in session and awaiting his arrival.[6] Just as Caesar stepped out of the house, an image, set in the vestibule, fell to the ground and broke into many fragments. This image was of Caesar.[7] He had barely left the house when a friend rushed in with urgent information—news of the plot. He was too late, as Caesar had already left.[8] In the street Caesar confidently addressed a soothsayer and jeered that he was still alive. The soothsayer, who earlier had warned Caesar to beware the Ides of March, retorted that the day had not yet passed.[9] The traditional sacrifice performed before entering the Senate again bode ill. Despite being redone many times, the result was the same—a sign of death, the soothsayer said.[10] But Caesar disregarded the omens and entered the Senate, encouraged by those who would soon murder him in the chamber.

The conspirators numbered more than sixty[11] and delayed before acting, so it is surprising that Caesar had not detected the plot.[12] The conspirators surrounded him near the statue of Pompeius, his old enemy, a symbol of the republic's freedom. First they pretended to plead for a favor, then pulled the toga from Caesar's shoulders—the agreed signal.[13] The conspirators struck from all sides. Caesar, after a wild attempt at defense,[14] realized that his time had come. He fell to the foot of Pompeius's statue,[15] covered his face with the toga, and died. He received twenty-three wounds, but only one—the second near his breast—was lethal.[16] Among his assassins there was an idealistic and arrogant heir of a great family, Marcus Iunius Brutus, whom Caesar had loved like a son. It is said that when Brutus plunged with his dagger, Caesar quietly murmured, "You too, my son?"[17]

But the very process that some of the conspirators sought to prevent—that is, the end of the republic—could not be stopped. Instead Rome was plunged into yet another cycle of civil wars that ended only with the victory of Octavian Augustus over Marcus Antonius. Still, Caesar's death would soon be interpreted as the beginning of a new glorious period—the years of imperial Rome—and he was officially elevated from mortal to divine status.

The deification process had begun during Caesar's lifetime; his death accelerated it. There are many strange events surrounding his murder. One is the fact that it reflected the founding stories of other Mediterranean civilizations, wherein mortal beings, killed in the most violent manner, were then resurrected to divine status, the creators of a new glorious era—Osiris in the Egypt of the pharaohs, Dionysus among the Greek gods; Caesar's death even foreshadowed the life of Jesus Christ.[18] Osiris was a human king, killed and cut into pieces by his brother Seth, who then scattered his remains to all corners of the land. Osiris's sister-wife, Isis, piously recomposed his body after a long search. Horus, conceived and born from Isis and Osiris after the recomposition of his body, avenged his father's death, killing Seth after many dangerous contests. Osiris's death stood for a disturbance in the harmony of the earth cosmically (death was introduced into the world) and politically (Egypt was divided into two kingdoms). It stood for evil's defeat of good. But Horus's avenging role reestablished the supremacy of good over evil, reintroduced order where there was chaos, and returned political union to the land. He became the midday sun; his father, now deified, was the sun of the night and the ruler of the world of the dead.[19]

The Osiris myth is echoed in one version of the life of Dionysus, wherein he, a mortal being, is cut into pieces by the Titans and resurrected and deified by Jupiter (Zeus), becoming the symbol of ecstasy and the expectation of the afterlife. He was, as a Greek writer would say, both "most terrible and sweet to mortals."[20] The life and death of Jesus Christ would be a familiar story to civilizations in the Mediterranean. Christ, the son of God, became a human being in order to save the world, and he would be killed in the most atrocious way, only to be resurrected as God and founder of a new glorious era.

Caesar's sacrifice was the beginning of a new era—imperial Rome—and his life story followed this Mediterranean model. Caesar claimed ancestry from Aeneas, the Trojan conceived by the union of Anchises with the goddess Venus; he was given divine honors during his lifetime; he would be violently cut down by men he trusted, benefited, even loved; and finally his heir, Gaius Octavius Thurinus (Octavian Augustus), a grandnephew whom Caesar adopted as a son, would represent the beginning of a new and glorious age.

The Symbols of Political Power

It would be inaccurate to assert that Caesar began his ascent to power and glory with a well-orchestrated plan for achieving supremacy in Rome. Still, there is no doubt that he was keenly aware of just how to capitalize on any action that could increase his prestige. This is clear early in his political career, in 69 B.C.—long before his successes in Gaul—during the funeral of his first wife, Cornelia, and that of his aunt Iulia, wife of the great Marius. Roman funerals were understood as an occasion to honor both the deceased and the greatness of the *gens* (family). Funerals were held for the living more so than the dead.[21]

According to Svetonius, in eulogy Caesar spoke the words that are quoted at the beginning of this chapter. This eulogy was obviously a restatement of the greatness of his family, for Venus was claimed to be the origin of his people. The goddess had given birth to Aeneas, the mythical hero who had escaped the burning of Troy to seek refuge in Italy. There his son Ascanius (Iulius), the founder of the Iulii family, founded Alba Longa (nearby modern-day Castelgandolfo). After Rome destroyed that city some families, including the Iulii, migrated to Rome.

Aeneas was a powerful symbol indeed, justifying the struggle against Carthage (Aeneas had abandoned the Carthaginian queen, Dido, in escaping to Italy), as well as Roman dominance over the Greeks who had destroyed Troy—Aeneas's own city. Moreover, Aeneas could be considered indirectly to be among the founders of Roman civilization, and he was tied to the gods through birth.

Caesar's eulogy also made clear that Iulia's mother, his own grandmother, descended from one of the "good" kings of ancient Rome—Ancus Marcius. He was good in the sense that Romans distinguished between their good kings (i.e., those of Roman ancestry like Romulus, Marcius, and Numa Pompilius) and the bad (i.e., those of Etruscan origin like the Tarquinii); Servius was located somewhere between.[22]

Finally, his aunt Iulia's funeral prompted Caesar to make his first attempt at becoming the leader of the popular party that in the past had followed Marius. Sulla had been dead for about twenty years by this time, but his followers still controlled Rome. Caesar tried to change this situation using a mixture of idealism, practicality, and astuteness. In Iulia's funeral procession Caesar displayed, besides the images of other members of the family, the image of his deceased uncle Marius, who had been Iulia's husband. Displaying images of relatives was common, but displaying Marius's image was daring and dangerous, because the state had forbidden it. Thus Caesar's action was a deliberate challenge to some of the powerful Roman families that had sided with Sulla. His action was criticized but not punished. Four years later, in 65 B.C., he would surreptitiously place Marius's images in Rome's temples, and he again survived the attack of Sulla's faction and became the spokesman and leader of Marius's party, which favored his conduct.[23]

Caesar's successes grew, and eventually his own ambition, the adulation from supporters, and grudging respect from enemies rocketed him toward the ultimate honor: the achievement of divine attributes while alive and, finally, his apotheosis as god after death. Deification served a high political goal. In the past, as Stefan Weinstock argues, the pagan gods had been the symbol of an authority that the passage of time could not weaken.[24] If one remained merely a magistrate, then one's power was retained only during the tenure in office. Deification was the tool to make mortal power immortal.

How to Deify a Leader

Except for the disputed divinity of the Spartan leader Lisander on the island of Samos in the fourth century, the process of deification in the Greek world began with Alexander the Great in the late fourth century B.C. Up until then, the typical way to celebrate great men was to elevate them to the status of hero, that is, in a category of exceptional human beings somewhere between mortals and gods.[25] The practice of the hero cult, influenced by contact with Persia and then Egypt, resulted in the emergence of a new idea: The ruler, or the successful general, could or sometimes should be granted divine status.[26] It was an idea adopted by the Hellenistic kings, that is, monarchs of Macedonian and Greek descent who controlled the lands of the Mediterranean and Near East after Alexander; the Romans eventually defeated these men. Although the policy of mortal deification was not applied consistently in every location, the Hellenistic monarchs were typically granted divine status while alive; temples were dedicated to their honor, their statues were placed near those depicting the gods, and at times special priests were appointed for their worship. The most celebrated example is the Ptolemaic dynasty (Cleopatra's forebears) in Egypt, but the Hellenistic Seleucids and the rulers in the Near East are good illustrations as well.

There had been no such tradition among the Romans, although they offered private, not public, sacrifices to deceased individuals *(Di manes* or *Di parentum)* or to the ancestors collectively *(Lares)*; they also thought that there was an almost independent spirit *(genius)* for the individuals and for the state as a whole. Thus in the fourth century B.C., in imitation of the Greeks, Romans conferred divine status upon some of the great heroes of the past, specifically Romulus, the founder of the city; Lucius Iunius Brutus, who in 510 B.C. had expelled the last king of Rome, Tarquinius Superbus, and ended the monarchy; and Marcus Furius Camillus, the hero of many battles in the early part of the fourth century B.C. Later, divine status seems to have been granted to Scipio Africanus, the victor in the Second Punic War. Divine honors were also contemplated for Marius and then Sulla.[27] But it was Iulius Caesar who best established the pattern, which was then inherited, imitated, and refined by the subsequent imperial dynasties.

Caesar's deification followed two phases. In the first, attempts were made while he was alive to identify him with a deity; in the second, the cult of Divus Iulius (Caesar the God) was officially established in 42 B.C., two years after his assassination. Caesar was keenly aware of the importance of symbolism. He had demonstrated this not only in the eulogy for his aunt Iulia but also in his continuous reference to his ancestress, Venus, and his descent from the ancient kings. This idea was conveyed through Caesar's speeches, actions, and outward behavior. For instance, after his conquest of Gaul and the defeat of Pompeius, he began to wear red boots, symbolic of his associations with the kings of Alba Longa, the city near Rome whose foundation was linked to his mythical ancestor Ascanius (Iulius), the son of Aeneas.[28] Caesar wore the laurel crown, the symbol of military triumph, whenever he ventured out in public—to hide his baldness, he used to say, but also to remind Romans of his victories. The imagery of military success was a device known well by Caesar; when he began to display Marius's image, no mention was made of the civil wars or his uncle's triumph in Numidia but rather of the victories over Rome's most serious threat—the Cimbri and Teutones.[29]

Caesar's masterful use of symbolism found concrete affirmation in the process that led to his divinity. Caesar again and again emphasized his family's relationship to Venus. It was Venus who by special grace had given his face the "bloom of youth"; Caesar carried her sculpted image on the ring he always wore; he invoked her name in the moments of highest peril;[30] and the goddess of love had given him his good looks.[31] As his power grew and his opponents were defeated, Caesar was transformed into a living symbol of all the virtues that Romans held dear. He was the greatest conqueror (*triumphator*), as his lavish triumph of 46 B.C. showed. He was the deliverer (*liberator*) of his city, as he was pictured in one of two statues erected in his honor, one wearing the grass wreath (*corona obsidionalis*), the other the oak wreath *(corona civica)* as the savior of his country. He was the new founder and father of his fatherland *(parens patriae)*, as Romulus, the founder of Rome, had been. He was the citizen who combined military bravery *(virtus)*, clemency *(clementia*, or kindness toward both fellow-citizens and enemies), obedience of the laws of war *(iustitia)*, and respect for the gods *(pietas)*. He was Jupiter Julius, that is, he enjoyed a special relationship with the king of the gods.[32] He was allowed to ride on horseback in the city, a privilege enjoyed only by kings; he offered the spoils of war *(spolia opima)* on the altar of Jupiter Ferentius, as Romulus had done and as only a general who had killed the enemy commander in battle could do; his face was etched on coins; he was instructed to build a new Senate house that was called, after Caesar's name, Julian; a month (July) was renamed after his family; a gilded chair and the attire of kings were granted to him; his house could have a pediment on its front, that is, the visual symbol of temples and royal residences; a public sacrifice was voted in honor of his birthday; a temple was built to Concordia Nova to celebrate his endeavor in bringing civil discord to an end; statues of his likeness were placed in all the temples in Rome; prayers had to be offered to him; a quadrennial festival and games in his honor were established together with a third college of priests as overseers; and Marcus Antonius was indicated as his personal priest *(flamen)*.[33]

Most of the honors that the Senate granted Caesar were proper for gods. However, although the evidence is controversial, the Senate never granted him outright divine status while he was alive (indeed, the evidence points to the contrary).[34] But the connection between the invincible leader, the gods, and the political master of the state had been made. This is not surprising in the Roman context, because separation of the sacred from the profane was a later development of Western civilization (arguably during the Enlightenment and, in any case, not before the Reformation). And the ancient world from the beginning of recorded history automatically associated political, legislative, and military successes to the gods—whether the Egyptian Amon, the Assyrian Assur, the Jewish Jaweh, or Jesus Christ. Moreover, contacts with the East and Rome's own imperialistic success were changing its dominion so drastically that new governmental structures became necessary when power fell from an oligarchy into the hands of an individual. Put simply, the authority of a leader and his descendants would be made safer and more effective if the office was invested with sacral authority. This approach had been successful for millennia in Egypt, and it was the norm in the Hellenistic kingdoms that the Romans had conquered and in the civilizations they respected, unlike the "barbarian" peoples across the Alps.[35]

Caesar's murder in 44 B.C. arrested the process of deification but did not stop it outright. Two days later, on March 17, the Senate convened in a secular version of the Judgment of the Dead to decide whether Caesar had to be punished or rewarded. Friends of the conspirators (the murderers had left the city) demanded that Caesar be declared a tyrant, denied a funeral, and his body thrown into the Tiber. But Marcus Antonius's view prevailed: Caesar's actions had benefited the state and the Roman people; if he were a tyrant, then all his actions should be considered illegal. Antonius had even more ammunition to defend Caesar's memory when, at the funeral, he read Caesar's will, where his love and concern for the common people and his veterans were revealed. The funeral, probably held five days after the murder, almost ended in a riot. Antonius read the will and then, uncovering Caesar's body, which was in an open coffin, raised his bloody robe on a spear. During the lamentations a member of one of the two choruses, acting as the murdered man, listed all the benefits that Caesar had given his assassins, ending with the poignant words of a popular tragedy, "Have I saved them that they might murder me?" At the same time, a mechanical device turned a waxen image of Caesar and depicted the twenty-three wounds that he had suffered. Then the crowd, instead of proceeding toward the place where Caesar's pyre had been set at Campus Martius (where his daughter Iulia's funeral had taken place), moved on to the temple of Jupiter on the Capitol. There they tried to burn Caesar's body in the room *(cella)* where the statue of the god stood. Prevented by the priests from doing so, they improvised a pyre in the Forum and cremated Caesar's body there; soldiers and citizens, men and women, threw weapons, robes, and jewels into the fire in his honor.[36]

For a time thereafter, a tug-of-war ensued between Caesar's supporters and detractors. According to Weinstock's reconstruction of the events, Caesar's supporters built an altar in his honor; his enemies destroyed it together with all the statues that had been erected in his honor during his lifetime; a new altar, and probably a column, were then erected so that people could continue making sacrifices to Caesar.[37] And then the campaign to bring justice to the assassins was carried out across the Mediterranean. It ended in 42 B.C. when Brutus's head was returned to Rome to be thrown at the feet of Caesar's statue.[38]

In the aftermath of Caesar's death many portents, as was typical in the ancient world, were reported—earthquakes, thunderstorms, and floods damaging the habitations of the gods. But the most striking event was the appearance of a comet. Comets were usually considered to be signs of evil, but not in this case. This comet (which in fact arrived after Caesar's death) was interpreted as a sign that Caesar's divinity was real, for Romans believed that cremation freed the spirit from the body and that the residence of the gods was the sky. The comet thus became the symbol of Caesar's apotheosis: Caesar had joined his fellow gods in the heavens. Later, Augustus would place a star on all the statues of Caesar as a sign of his divinity.[39]

The official consecration came in early January 42 B.C. when the Senate proclaimed the murdered man a god.[40] The Senate apparently ratified again some of the honors previously granted, as well as some new ones appropriate to a divinity, like a temple in the Forum where Caesar had been cremated, the right of asylum for any citizen seeking safety there, statues, a divine name (Divus Iulius), a personal priest for his worship, coins representing Caesar as a god, an annual celebration of his birthday, and the injunction that from then on all victories of the Roman generals should be regarded as being Caesar's own victories.[41]

Yet civil discord continued within the walls of Rome.

Notes

1. Svetonius, *Divus Iulius* lxxxi.3–4.
2. Ibid., lxxxi.3.
3. Dio xliv.17.1.
4. Svetonius, *Divus Iulius* lxxxi.3.
5. Appian ii.16.115.
6. Svetonius, *Divus Iulius* lxxxi.4; Dio xliv.18.1–2.
7. Dio xliv.18.2–3.
8. Appian ii.16.116.
9. Dio xliv.18.4.
10. Appian ii.16.116.
11. Svetonius, *Divus Iulius* lxxx.4.
12. Dio xliv.15.1–2.
13. Svetonius, *Divus Iulius* lxxxii.1–2; Dio xliv.3–4.
14. This is what Plutarch says but not the other sources; Plutarch, *Caesar* lxvi.10.
15. Ibid., lxvi.12.
16. Svetonius, *Divus Iulius* lxxxii.3.
17. Ibid., lxxxii.3; Dio xliv.19.5.
18. See the following articles in Diego Poli, ed., *La cultura in Cesare* (Roma, 1993), especially Ileana Chirassi Colombo, "Il mestiere di Dio ed i suoi rischi (Riflessioni in chiave storico-religiosa intorno a Sig 760)," pp. 397–427; but also Gior-

gio Bonamente, "La scomparsa del nome di Cesare dagli elenchi dei divi," pp. 707–731; Giuseppe Flammini, "L'apoteosi di Cesare tra mito e realtà: Ovid., *Met.*, 15, 745–851," pp. 733–749.

19. For an introduction to Egyptian religion, see Leonard H. Lesko, "Death and Afterlife in Ancient Egypt," in *Civilizations of the Ancient Near East*, edited by Jack M. Sasson (New York, 1995), vol. 3.

20. Euripides, *Bacchantes* 81. For an introduction, see the excellent entry "Dionysus" by Albert Henrichs in *The Oxford Classical Dictionary*, edited by Simon Hornblower and Antony Spawforth (Oxford, 1996), pp. 479–482.

21. Bruce Lincoln, "La politica di mito e rito nel funerale di Iulia: Cesare debutta nella sua carriera," in Poli, ed., *La cultura in Cesare*, pp. 390–391.

22. Lincoln, "La politica di mito," pp. 388–389.

23. On both actions by Caesar, see Plutarch, *Caesar* iv.2 and vi.1–7.

24. Stefan Weinstock, *Divus Julius* (Oxford, 1971), p. 413.

25. For an introduction to Alexander's deification, see Antonio Santosuosso, *Soldiers, Citizens, and the Symbols of War from Classical Greece to Republican Rome, 500–167 B.C.* (Boulder, 1997), pp. 143–147.

26. Ibid., p. 146.

27. For an introduction, see ibid., pp. 198–200.

28. Dio xliii.43.2.

29. Plutarch, *Caesar* vi.2.

30. Dio xliii.43.3–4.

31. Weinstock, *Divus Iulius*, p. 25.

32. See the detailed analysis of these qualities and honors in ibid.

33. Dio xliv.4–6.

34. Ibid., xliv.7.1.

35. E. Badian, *Roman Imperialism in the Late Republic* (Ithaca, 1968), pp. 10–123.

36. Weinstock, *Divus Iulius*, pp. 346–355.

37. Ibid., pp. 364–367. For a different interpretation of these episodes, see Cornelia Cogrossi, "Pietà popolare e divinizzazione nel culto di Cesare nel 44 a.C.," in *Religione e politica nel mondo antico*, edited by Maria Sordi (Milano, 1981), pp. 141–160.

38. Svetonius, *Divus Augustus* xiii.1.

39. Weinstock, *Divus Iulius*, pp. 370–384.

40. Ibid., p. 386.

41. Ibid., pp. 386–398.

5

"My Soldiers, My Army, My Fleet"

Wars, both civil and foreign, I [Augustus] undertook throughout the world, on sea and land, and when victorious I spared all citizens who sued for pardon. The foreign nations which could with safety be pardoned I preferred to save rather than to destroy. The number of Roman citizens who bound themselves to me by military oath was about 500,000. Of these I settled in colonies or sent back into their own towns, after their term of service, something more than 300,000, and to all I assigned lands, or gave money as a reward for military service.

Res Gestae Divi Augusti 3

Making his case to the Roman Senate in 43 B.C., the head of the soldiers' delegation was a centurion named Cornelius. He stood before the senators as spokesman for Octavian, who had just led his legions against Rome "as if it were that of an enemy." Cornelius's request was simple and clear: Octavian and his soldiers demanded that Octavian be made a consul. When the Senate hesitated, Cornelius threw back his cloak, pointed to the hilt of his sword, and said, "This will make him consul, if you do not."[1] Octavian was barely twenty years old at the time. His great-uncle, Iulius Caesar, who had adopted him as a son, had been murdered the year before by those who thought their action could rescue the republic from the tyranny of one person. They were wrong: The republic had become a corpse, the Senate a powerless relic of the past—as Cornelius's insolence demonstrated.

At first glance, Octavian must have seemed an unlikely successor. He was born at Velitrae (modern-day Velletri), a town south of Rome in the Alban

Hills. His father, originally a member of the equestrian order, was a "new man" *(novus homo)*, that is, a person lacking a distinguished family ancestry and only of recent social and political importance. Octavian's mother, the daughter of Caesar's sister Iulia, belonged, however, to the Iulii, a family of great distinction.[2] Even physically Octavian did not share the dashing personality of his uncle. Svetonius describes him as handsome and graceful in all stages of his life, with a sweet and calm attitude and eyes that reflected his divine power. Yet the historian also conveys a less attractive picture: Octavian took little care of his slightly curly and partially golden hair (several barbers cut his hair at the same time); he lost the sight of his left eye later in life; his eyebrows met; his nose projected a little at the top and then bent; he was short of stature; his body was covered with spots and birthmarks; he limped because his left hip, thigh, and leg were not very strong; the forefinger of his right hand was so weak that he could hardly write in cold weather; and he endured pain while urinating until he finally passed kidney stones.[3] In other words, this was not the portrayal of a warrior; it was weak in comparison to his physically strong and politically powerful competitor, Marcus Antonius.[4]

But it was Octavian, not Marcus Antonius, who would become the undisputed master of Rome, his powers greater than any man before, his dignity hereditary, his state's hegemony over the known world more extensive than any in history. It was he—Augustus—who would become the first emperor of an empire that would shape the world even after it fell to Germanic peoples after centuries of supremacy.

The Emperor's Men

About fifteen years before he died, Augustus wrote his political will *(Res Gestae)*, which he deposited with the Vestal Virgins; a copy, chiseled on the walls of a Roman temple in Asia Minor, has been found. The document refers strangely to Rome's armed forces: The army was no longer the army of the Roman people *(populi Romani exercitus)* but the army of the emperor. The adjectives *meus, mea,* and *mei* dominate: *milites mei* (my soldiers), *exercitus meus* (my army), *classis mea* (my fleet).[5] But these were not the useless boasts often found in other monarchs' declarations. Augustus in fact reshaped Rome's military apparatus, thereby strengthening the supremacy of the emperor as commander in chief and honing professionalization in the new army. As Svetonius writes, Augustus "made many changes and innovations in the army, besides reviving some usages of former times."[6]

Rome's land forces included five different types during the Principate (the term usually used to identify Augustus's reign and the period of Roman history up to the third century A.D.). The forces included the legions, the praetorian guard, the *cohortes urbanae*, the *vigiles*, and the auxiliaries. The disputants for power during the civil wars had increased the legions to an unyielding, inefficient, and costly number. At the time of the Battle of Actium in 31 B.C. there were at least 51 legions, probably 60, active in the territories of the Roman Empire.[7] Augustus reduced them to 28 on the basis of a rational scheme of strategic deployment or, more likely, to relieve the empire's financial burden and to establish a climate of peace and prosperity.[8] After the disaster in the Teutoburg Forest in A.D. 9, when Germanic tribes managed to destroy three legions, the number of legions remained at 25 until Claudius's reign (41–54), when their strength was brought up to about 30. Under Septimius Severus (193–211), the number was raised to 33.[9]

The legions became a standing army of professionals,[10] deployed—except for the garrison in Rome—at the frontiers and in the most dangerous areas of the empire. Each legion was given a permanent identification, a number, and a name (III Augusta or IIII Macedonica, for example), and sometimes a nickname.[11] At full strength the legion included 4,800 legionnaires and 120 cavalrymen. The footmen were divided into ten cohorts of six centuries, each cohort being 480 soldiers. Around the middle of the first century A.D. the first cohort was reorganized into five large centuries for a total of 960 soldiers, double the strength of the other cohorts.[12]

The mandatory qualifications for enrollment remained the same—Roman citizenship and certain physical requirements. According to a fourth-century writer, Vegetius, who based his views on the practices of the past, the potential soldier had to be visually healthy with alert eyes, an erect head, a broad chest, muscular shoulders, strong arms, long fingers, a small waist, slim buttocks, and strong more than fleshy feet and legs. The evidence on height is ambiguous: "Brave soldiers are more valuable than tall ones," says Vegetius, but he also mentions that the cavalrymen's height was normally between 1.68 meters (5 Roman feet, 8 inches) and 1.73 meters (5 Roman feet, 10 inches), rather tall for the time.[13] However, another source from the year 367 places the requirement, apparently for all recruits, at 1.60 meters (5 Roman feet, 5 inches).[14] Vegetius's indications seem unrealistic or, at best, applicable only to the Roman armies of his own time, the Late Empire, when cavalry recruits were drawn from taller peoples like the Celts and Germans. The required height of the early Roman armies, when manned by Italian stock, must have been shorter, as evidenced by Caesar's comments that the Celts mocked the Romans' short stature and by contemporary references to the Germans' large size, which implies that Romans must have been shorter by comparison.

Certain social groups of men were automatically excluded from military duties: slaves, those who had been deported or condemned to fight animals in the circus, adulterers, those convicted of other crimes in public jury courts, those still engaged in court disputes, and deserters who wanted to switch from one section of the army to another.[15] If the applicant did not fall into any of those categories and had proved citizenship, he became a recruit *(tiro)* for a four-month period, during which time he remained in a fluctuating status, neither civilian nor soldier. At this stage, before he was allowed to join a legion, he went through a twofold process: His name was included in a special list *(in numeros referri)*, where his origin and class were identified; then he was given a metal tablet *(signaculum)* that he carried on his neck as a symbol of belonging to the army. The third stage, taking an oath to the gods and the emperor *(iusiurandum* or *sacramentum)*, may have occurred at this stage or later, when he officially became a soldier.[16]

The recruit, and then as soldier, followed a rigorous training regimen throughout his service. As Josephus, the Jewish priest and historian of the war against Judaea, described it, the Roman soldiers never took "a holiday from training"; "each soldier practices battle drill every day with great enthusiasm just as it were in battle . . . and their training maneuvers are battles without bloodshed, and their battles maneuvers with bloodshed."[17] The emperors were personally concerned that training be kept at a high level at all times.[18]

The intensive training must be one reason why the Roman soldiers won contests of stamina against larger, stronger peoples. There was little or no gap in the technology among the opponents, and so physical stamina must have been a crucial factor. Thus if the Romans survived the first onslaught against the Celts, they usually emerged the winner thanks to their discipline in training.

Augustus also introduced other changes: "He restricted all the soldiery everywhere to a fixed scale of pay and allowances, designating the duration of their service and the rewards on its completion according to each man's rank, in order to keep them from being tempted to revolution after their discharge either by age or poverty."[19] In 13 B.C. he upped the normal period of service to sixteen (it had been reduced to six during the civil wars);[20] in A.D. 5 he raised it to twenty years.[21] In most cases veterans were not disbanded after the official expiration of their service but were kept active or on reserve status for another four or five years.[22] The legionnaires stationed in Spain, for instance, were discharged only after twenty-five years of service, according to Patrick Le Roux.[23] In other words, life in the army was a career choice that lasted for much of one's adulthood.

Augustus also established urban forces within Rome or nearby. Lawrence Keppie calculates that 6,000 (not counting the *vigiles*) were stationed directly in the city under the control of the emperor.[24] The most important element was the praetorian guard, founded in 27 B.C. Originally the praetorians had acted as a small bodyguard for the praetor, the chief magistrate when the consuls were absent from Rome. Later they were associated with guarding the army commander, whose tent was called *praetorium*. The praetorians, which now constituted the emperor's personal bodyguard, performed a dual role: They were the elite troops when the emperor led the army in battle, and they were the enforcers of his political power at home. Later in imperial history they became the makers of emperors. They were disbanded by Emperor Constantine in 312.[25]

The praetorians, like the legionnaires, were bound to a fixed term of service—twelve years (later raised to sixteen).[26] Initially they were grouped into nine cohorts, each 500–1,000 strong (500 according to Yann Le Bohec on the basis of archeological evidence), probably 80 percent footmen and 20 percent cavalry. Later the number of praetorian cohorts varied between nine and sixteen until Domitian (A.D. 81–96) settled on ten. Their numerical strength also varied, from 500 to 1,000. Later, in A.D. 69, Emperor Vitellius set their strength for good at 1,000 per cohort.[27] Under Augustus, three of the nine cohorts were stationed in the city in civilian clothes; the other six were stationed and housed in towns near Rome. This limited number within the city, as well as their civilian dress, were in deference to the tradition that soldiers should not be stationed within the capital. Later, however, beginning with Tiberius (A.D. 14–37), they camped on the Roman outskirts, just outside the old walls built by Servius, one of Rome's ancient kings.[28]

Praetorian recruits were drawn mainly from the Italian population, at least until Emperor Septimius Severus (A.D. 193–211) disbanded them in 193 for conspiring against the two previous emperors; he reconstituted them using the frontier legions.[29] Augustus's personal guard included, in addition to the praetorians, 100 Germans—the Batavians—momentarily disbanded after Varus's defeat in A.D. 9 and then reconstituted before A.D. 14. Later 300 men were added—the so-called *exploratores* and the personal cavalry of the emperor *(equites singulares Augusti)*.[30]

In A.D. 13 Augustus added three urban cohorts *(cohortes urbanae)* of 500 men each, a number that later varied between 500 and 1,500. Unlike the praetorians, the emperor's personal guard, the *cohortes urbanae* were a policing body within Rome that remained under the emperor's control.[31] In A.D. 6 Augustus established a body of firemen *(vigiles)*, drawn from the humbler sectors of Rome's population. Organized into seven cohorts, they were the nocturnal police but, most important of all, they were the firefighters. Eventually the *vigiles*, at least by the beginning of the third century and perhaps earlier, were, like the praetorians, considered to be military forces.[32]

Beyond the urban forces, large auxiliaries supported the legions throughout the empire. The auxiliaries were normally non-Italian and non-Romans, although occasionally we find Roman citizens among them. They were recruited on a volunteer basis but at times were probably forced into service from the conquered tribes or from those on the borders, like the Celts, Moors, Germans, and even Parthians. Initially they were summoned and discharged on an ad hoc basis, but Augustus incorporated them as permanent bodies.[33]

On the battlefield the auxiliaries performed different roles than the legionnaires and cavalrymen. They operated in units of 500 men *(ala)* if cavalry and 480 *(cohors)* if infantry. They were also combined into mixed units of horsemen and footmen (something Caesar had introduced during the campaign against Alesia when he hired German cavalry, who brought their own footmen to fight in support). Later, the numerical strength of both horsemen and footmen was raised to 800–1,000, although some were kept at 500. The *numerus*, the term mostly used at this time, indicated a body of troops that was neither legion nor *ala* nor *cohors*.[34]

According to Tacitus's description of a Roman triumph in A.D. 69, the auxiliary infantry was grouped according to their ethnic origin or by the type of weapon they deployed. They occupied the last position during a triumphal parade, which opened with the eagles and the various emblems of the legions, followed by those of the cavalry, and then by the legionnaires, and finally the auxiliary infantry. In other words, the legions were the most important troops of the Roman army in terms of prestige and military efficiency, whereas the auxiliaries brought up the rear.[35] In any case, the practice of grouping units by ethnicity seems to have been discontinued over time. A similar change took place with the auxiliaries' command structure. Initially the commanders may have been members of their own tribe, but eventually they were supplanted by Roman citizens.[36]

The Roman land army had a paper strength of about 260,000 men in A.D. 23, about nine years after Augustus's death. About 10,000 were located in or near Rome, with 125,000 legionnaires manning the frontiers with 125,000 auxiliaries. To this we must add 40,000 sailors who plied the waters of Mare Nostrum (literally "Our Sea," i.e., the Mediterranean).[37] After the defeat of the Hellenistic powers all the lands on Mediterranean shores recognized Rome's supremacy; thus there was no power to challenge its supremacy on the seas. Pirates, a dangerous element during the years of the republic (they even captured the young Caesar), were never wiped out completely, but from Augustus onward the threat of piracy was minimal. The Roman fleet was located in two main ports, Misene, near the bay of Naples, and Ravenna, located on the Adriatic. Augustus had experimented with two other locations, one in Provence, the Forum Iulii (Fréjus), and one near Naples, the Portus Iulius. Theoretically the fleet based in Misene was to operate in the western Mediterranean while the fleet at Ravenna took care of the eastern sector.

Thus the total number of Roman forces at land and at sea was roughly 300,000—rather small for such a large empire with dangerous frontiers in Britain, Germany, the Danube region, and Syria. Yet this would serve well enough for the first two centuries A.D., although the empire barely survived a near-simultaneous attack along most of its borders in the third century. Yet it is testimony to the resilience of this security scheme that the Roman Empire would survive two centuries beyond this in the west before succumbing to hostile forces and for another millennium in the Byzantine Empire in the east. Considering that the actual number of soldiers who could be deployed on the various battlefields was actually rather low, this is a remarkable accomplishment indeed.[38] Attrition alone—especially in legions far from Rome where local recruiting opportunities were limited—would invariably reduce the rosters (e.g., Caesar in Gaul). However, Augustus's streamlining and his reorganization of the empire may have eased the problem of keeping the legions at full strength. But even in normal circumstances it must have been difficult to maintain the 5,000-man figure, especially because the legionnaires' duties were not limited to the battlefield. During a lull in fighting or in times of peace, the legionnaires may have worked the agricultural lands, manufactured weapons and armor, mined minerals, and constructed and maintained buildings and roads. Even during wartime, at least some would have been assigned administrative and police duties.[39]

Commanders and the Rank and File

The legion's command structure was fashioned like a pyramid that reflected
the social structure of the Roman state. The soldiers were ranked in declining terms of social order, from top to bottom. The commoners manned the
rank and file (i.e., the base of the pyramid); the higher positions were reserved for the higher social classes; the senatorial aristocrats and the equestrians, with the aristocrats, held the prime posts. For instance, the legate's
post—that is, the legion's commander, the top of the pyramid—was given
to a senator. The candidate's qualifications required a civilian magistracy,
the praetorship, and then service in the lower officers' cadres as a tribune
during his early twenties.[40] These rather stringent qualifications maintained
the aristocracy's prestige and provided an expert military leader; but they
also prevented the appointee from gaining too much power (the legate's
post was limited to two terms for a maximum of six years).

The two highest social orders—aristocrats and equestrians—were reflected in the next command positions, the six military tribunes. One, the
tribunus laticlavius (his toga had a large purple border to indicate his status
as senator), the legion's second in command, trained the troops, performed
a legal role, and acted as adviser to the legate. He became the legion's commander when the legate was absent. Each of the other five tribunes, *tribuni
angusticlavi* (their togas had a thinner purple border, the sign of the equestrian order), were given command over two cohorts. The third in command
was the prefect of camp (not one of the tribunes), whose duties included logistics, siege operations, choosing the proper ground to set up camp, and
organizing defense operations when needed.[41] The choice of officers reflected Augustus's social concerns, for the hierarchy had to remain in the
hands of the highest social orders, aristocrats and equestrians, with the
equestrians as tribunes being trained as substitutes for the aristocracy. The
equestrians also came to monopolize the auxiliaries' highest command
posts, replacing the practice of using tribal leaders. The cavalry reflected the
legionnaires' command structure.

It is often said today that the Roman generals were mediocre and that the
great commander—Scipio Africanus, Caesar, Trajan—was rare.[42] This is not
accurate, for the leadership of the Roman armies (whether republican or
imperial) was normally good and often outstanding. The backbone of the
Roman legions remained the centurions, who were drawn from the lower
levels of society but also from the equestrians. One could rise to the position
of centurion in at least four ways: direct admission from the equestrian or-

der; promotion through the ranks after many years of service; after a career of service as an auxiliary officer; and after serving a stint in the praetorian guard. (We know of at least one promotion from the *vigiles*, the other urban contingent.)[43]

Each legion had fifty-nine centurions. Each centurion was in command of a century, which meant that each cohort had six centurions, one per century. The first cohort had one less, because that unit maintained only five centuries. Service in the first cohort was the most prestigious. Its centurions seem to have ranked ahead of the other fifty-four. The highest rank was held by the *primipilus*, who was the chief centurion of the legion and commanded the first century of the first cohort. Centurions in the first cohort received about ten times the wages of legionnaires and about double the wages of centurions in the other cohorts. The centurions were the administrators of their centuries, disciplined and trained the units, and led their men into battle.[44] They were the linchpins during hand-to-hand combat, which meant they often suffered (during the siege of Gergovia at least forty-six of Caesar's centurions died in a single assault).[45]

Recruitment and Social Status

Keeping legions at full strength (not counting times of emergency) meant recruiting some 6,000–7,000 new troops every year by Augustus's time, about 240 men for each legion,[46] or as many as 18, 000 if we include troops stationed in and near Rome and the fleet.[47] This is a rather small number considering the extent of the empire, and some point out that the attrition level must have been higher. Looking at legions stationed in the Iberian peninsula, for instance, Le Roux argues that each legion needed 360 men each year (that is, if the figures were identical elsewhere) or about 9,000 recruits total.[48] Augustus and later emperors found it increasingly difficult to fill this quota using the traditional recruiting pools.

Italy still remained the preferred area in case of emergency and provided the majority of the recruits under Augustus, most coming from northern Italy; central and southern Italy filled the ranks in Rome, which offered more prestige, better conditions, and higher pay.[49] Over time, however, fewer and fewer Italians enrolled in the legions. Records in which the place of origin is given or can be inferred show 215 Italians against 134 non-Italians under Augustus, 124 against 136 under the Claudii (the next dynasty—A.D. 41–68), 83 against 299 by Trajan's period (99), and 37 against 2,019 during Hadrian's reign (117–138) to the end of the third century.[50] These figures, according to Jacques Harmand, would translate to 65 percent in the first half of the first century A.D., 49 percent under Claudius and Nero, 22 percent during the rest of the first century, and only 1 percent from Hadrian onward.[51] Such conclusions, however, are tentative at best, for only roughly 3,000 documents (epigraphic inscriptions) cover three centuries (first through third) during which some 2 million legionnaires were active.[52]

Italians continued to supply the praetorian guard and the urban units within Rome. Even when Septimius Severus disbanded the old guard in 193 for meddling in the imperial succession, several new praetorians, born in the colonies, must have been of Italian origin.. Yet according to A. Passerini, praetorians born in Italy had constituted 86.3 percent of the praetorians during the first and second centuries; there were none after Septimius's reform.[53]

The dramatic decrease in Italian recruits seems less so if we realize that people of distant Italian background still constituted most of the units, for even after Augustus recruits were drawn from the western part of the empire, that is, from the colonies settled by Roman citizens. It is still not understood, however, why more and more Italians shied away from military service. Reliance on non-Italians was not a deliberate policy of the emperor, but once it began it became unstoppable. Giovanni Forni offers several reasons that help explain this phenomenon. The praetorian guard and the urban units employed some 10,000 men. Life in Italy, especially in Rome and the other major cities, must have been much more attractive (nearness to one's birthplace, family, friends, etc.) compared to the wild places and primitive lifestyles on the frontiers, especially in the west. Moreover, it was in the emperor's interest not to force mandatory conscription at the gates of the Roman Empire, for it may have prompted an inevitable resistance from the population and thus civil disorder. Also, drawing young, energetic forces away from Italy would have handicapped the peninsula's economic life especially in a period of decreased demography.[54] Forni also suggests, on the basis of Tacitus, that a certain amount of cynicism toward military service must have spread among the Italian population after the cruel years of the civil wars. Afterward, the long period of peace might have softened their hearts.[55]

But things must have looked rather different to citizens living in the colonies and to indigenous populations in the west. The promise of pay and prestige must have made military service an attractive option. It typically meant automatic Roman citizenship, membership in the ruling group, and opportunities for their children.[56] Forni identifies two main areas for recruiting non-Italians during the imperial period. He draws a north-south line cutting Moesia (the region from modern Serbia to the Black Sea) in two, continuing south with Dalmatia and proconsular Africa (the area from modern Algeria to the western edge of Cyrenaica) on the west but leaving Epirus and Cyrenaica on the east. The west, which included most of western Europe and North Africa, spoke mainly Latin; Greek was the most common form of language in the east.[57] Initially legionnaires of direct Italian origin were common on both frontiers. However, unlike the western frontier, which provided few indigenous legionnaires, the presence of indigenous legionnaires in the east is apparent from the beginning of the Roman Empire. Asia Minor (modern Turkey) provided most of the recruits on the Euphrates frontier, as well as troops from Pannonia (the region south of the Danube and including most of the former republics of Yugoslavia) to North Africa and Alexandria.[58] Unlike in the west, there were few Roman colonies in the east, and the Hellenistic states already possessed a sophisticated military structure that the Romans inherited and could mold to their needs.

The armies of the first century, deployed in the main western areas—Spain, Britain, and Germany—included, besides many Italians, people from Spain, Gaul (mainly Gallia Narbonensis), North Africa, Dalmatia, and Pannonia.[59] Although the evidence is ambiguous, many must have come from Italian colonies settled in those lands, although Roman authorities must have recruited local people from the beginning. One case in point is the V Alaudae, a legion formed with Celts in 52 B.C. During the Claudian emperors (A.D. 41–68) we find, for the first time, soldiers from the Mediterranean area from Italy to Provence together with men from Britain, Aquitaine, and Noricum (the region east of the Alps south of the Danube). But the greatest increase originated from Spain and southern France (Gallia Narbonensis), the reverse of what happened under the Flavian emperors (A.D. 69–96). At that stage the recruits from Spain and southern Gallia decreased as more soldiers came from the other Gallic regions, Noricum, North Africa, and Numidia. Also at this time, we find the first German legionnaires.[60]

Thus except in case of emergency, recruiting during the second and more so the third centuries A.D. targeted the areas in which the legions were located, and many new troops came from neighboring localities. For instance, one finds many Thracians in Lower Moesia serving in their land of origin. As we move into the third century the recruiting area was even smaller, limited to the immediate vicinity.[61]

The social origin of the legionnaires is even more difficult to identify. The army remained aristocratic at the command level even after Augustus; commoners and people from the lower rungs of the social ladder manned the rank and file. The centurions seem to have had a middle-class background, although many also came from the ranks and thus the lower classes. They originated mainly in Italy, but by the second century A.D. the ratio of Italians declined, and we find many from western colonies and some from the east.[62] This is one of the likely conclusions that can be drawn from the inscriptions found at Haida, a place between modern Algeria and Tunisia, corresponding to ancient Ammaedara.[63]

Safely, then, we can assume that many recruits followed in their fathers' footsteps, especially in the legions far from Rome.[64] Their social standing is debatable, but not in the sense that many came from the lower classes or from rural ancestry. They must have been poor relatively speaking—but not at the bottom of the social scale. Although they lived outside Italy, they must have been able to boast Italian roots or had absorbed the values and cultural milieu of Roman civilization.[65]

Discipline, Pay, and Rewards

One of the problems Augustus faced was how to prevent successful generals from using their armies independently of and against the central authority, as many had done against the Senate during the civil wars. The key, he realized, was maintaining control over the provinces and their economic and military resources; his power, like the supremacy of the later emperors, rested on his ability to pay his soldiers.[66] Thus he had to remain the main recipient of imperial resources so as to curb the ambitions and independence of the upper social orders. But that did not deprive aristocrats and equestrians of their outward dignity. Their dignity had to be restored and strengthened as long as any change reinforced a hierarchy in which the emperor constituted its apex and retained the ultimate authority.[67]

The Senate was refashioned in Augustus's image. He purged its membership from 1,000 to a fixed number of 600. The status was also made hereditary, and it was assumed that the senators' male heirs would follow the path of their fathers—a career in the military and eventual role in the state's civic administration, that is, "a career of service to the state." Augustus also established the standard that aristocrats should possess a certain amount of wealth to retain qualification for the Senate, although he was willing to use his own money to make sure that certain families would not be deprived. He made clear that the next social rank, the equestrian, should be understood as a "reservoir" and "training school" for new members of the Senate for a return to the ancient ways, wherein they were the leaders, together with the aristocrats, of the Roman army. What August wanted was a ruling class combining wealth with "merit, moral rectitude, and industry." This did not mean that the emperor cared only for the wealthier people. Augustus's view included the protection of humbler citizens, whose rights had to be defended against any threat, whether private or public.[68]

The Senate kept some of the old administrative functions. Membership to the body was, for instance, a prerequisite for a proconsul (provincial governor) appointment. But Augustus retained control over all matters relating to the armed forces, financial affairs, and foreign policy. The key, as mentioned earlier, was control over the provinces—meaning their resources and the legions stationed there. The normal administrative practice had been to divide the conquered territories into provinces *(provinciae)*, the control of which remained in the hands of governors appointed by the Senate. In 27 B.C. Augustus was appointed proconsul of a sprawling province that included Spain, Gallia, Egypt, and Syria. The area was extended over time, and Augustus's authority was renewed. Most of the legions were stationed there, and so this is where most of the revenues were generated; this strengthened his military and economic power. The rest of the territories (i.e., the senatorial provinces) remained under the control of the Senate, but in practice Augustus could enforce his will there as well, and in any event the senatorial provinces did not constitute a political threat to his supremacy (see Figure 5.1).

Augustus thus concentrated into his hands all the tools to control the army. He was supreme commander; he retained direct control over the legions, even if he delegated authority to trustful associates (any challenge to his rule was quickly smashed); and he was the paymaster, either using his own finances to pay them or organizing the method of disbursement. This allowed him to separate soldiers from close associations with other commanders; he made them dependent on him alone for their economic well-being.[69]

Paying legions in active service remained the burden of the imperial treasury, but all other military expenses needed a different system. Augustus established a military treasury *(aerarium militare)* to which he annually pledged a personal gift and, later, the revenues of a 5 percent inheritance tax and a 1 percent sales tax, thereby ensuring a constant flow of money to the fund.[70] The salary of the legionnaire was fixed at 275 silver *denarii* per year, which was raised to 300 under Domitian (81–96), probably 600 under Septimius Severus (193–211), and 900 from Caracalla to Diocletian (211–284). These increases, however, must have benefited the soldiers' lifestyle only modestly because of serious inflation beginning with Marcus Aurelius's reign (161–180). In A.D. 13 Augustus also established a fixed severance gift

FIGURE 5.1   Roman Empire, A.D. 14

(praemium militiae) of 3,000 *denarii*, the equivalent of almost fourteen years' pay, which was raised to 8,250 *denarii* in 212. The salary and severance gift of the permanent garrison in Italy were much higher, especially for the praetorians, who received 750 silver *denarii* per year under Augustus then 1,000, 1,500, and 2,250. Their severance was 5,000 *denarii* to start.[71]

Granting lands to veterans had been an established policy under Augustus, who in his political will claims that in 31 B.C. he settled 120,000 veterans in colonies in Italy, 100,000 more in 14 B.C. in Spain and Gallia Narbonensis, and 96,000 in A.D. 2. We also know that he spent 150 million *denarii* (or 600 million *sesterces*) for the veterans' settlement in the peninsula and 50 million (200 million *sesterces*) elsewhere for a total of 200 million *denarii*. More land grants were given in other periods—7, 6, 4, and 3 B.C.[72]—but as time went by the policy of giving land to the legionnaires at the end of their careers would prove unsatisfactory to both the emperor and his soldiers. Under Augustus, starting in A.D. 13, cash payments were usually substituted for land grants except in certain cases. The Romanization of the empire and the decrease in conquest meant that fewer and fewer territories were available, unless expropriation would be used, a very unpopular and illegal measure, or unless the soldiers would be rewarded with lands located in abandoned and infertile regions. Hadrian (117–138) finally abandoned the policy altogether.[73]

Forni suggests that the financial rewards were not as attractive as they might appear.[74] Army life made soldiers affluent only occasionally; yet there is no reason to doubt that it was an alluring occupation given the paltry opportunities available to the lower classes and the impoverished. Most certainly, civilians at this time stereotyped the soldier as rich and military service as highly remunerative.[75]

In addition to the usual salary and severance, soldiers received special gifts—the *donativa* and *liberalitates*—upon the instauration of a new emperor or as legacy in his will, although the beneficiaries were regularly the praetorians located in Rome, less so the legionnaires at the frontiers.[76] Some benefits also accrued from the agricultural lands near where the legions were stationed. But even more important were the legal rights to which the soldier was entitled. Normally he received Roman citizenship upon enrollment, something he could pass on to his children, together with other legal privileges like the ability to draw a will, the right to buy and sell, and the right to be judged by a court drawn from his legion if he committed a crime. In the end, at least starting with Claudius, the prohibition on marriage was relaxed, the presence of an "informal bride" tolerated, and offspring recognized.[77]

Augustus reinstituted the strictest discipline, one of the features that had made the Roman army so strong in the past. Gone were the days when soldiers married or took their women along, a privilege no longer enjoyed even by generals.[78] Serving the state was an obligation that no one, if called to serve, could shy away from. When one Roman from the equestrian order tried to avoid military service for his sons by cutting off their thumbs, Augustus put the father and his property on sale at a public auction, although at the last moment he commuted the penalty by reducing the culprit's status from equestrian to freedman to prevent him from falling to a commoner as a slave. Doing so would have created scandal and damaged the rigid social structure that Augustus thought essential for the internal peace of the state.[79]

He was spare in awarding the highest symbols of honor on the battlefield, like the crown, but he was generous with material rewards, like silver and gold collars, to those who distinguished themselves.[80] But he had no pity for cowards and those who shied away from their duties. He executed one man in every ten in any cohort that had given way to the enemy (a punishment known as decimation); the rest were punished by being placed on barley rations—a humiliating condition. Death was also the punishment for any centurion who left his post; degradation was the punishment for many a fault; soldiers might be forced, for a whole day in front of their general's tent, to hold a ten-foot pole or a clod of earth while in their tunics and without their sword belt, the symbol of the legionnaire. When the tenth legion demanded its discharge with insolence, Augustus disbanded it without granting the rewards due for service.[81]

Finally, Augustus reestablished a more proper distance between himself and the soldiers. He discontinued Caesar's term of referring to them as *commilitones* (comrades), reviving the more distant term *milites* (soldiers), used before the civil wars. He even forbade members of his own family from using the term *commilitones*, for it was "too flattering for the requirements of discipline, the peaceful state of the times, and his own dignity and that of his household."[82]

The New Army

Augustus claimed that his military changes were not revolutionary but rather the natural evolution of the Roman state, perhaps even the restoration of ancient and revered customs. Such was not the case, however, for his changes were profound and unprecedented. The imperial army had only one immediate ancestor, his great-uncle Iulius Caesar, and a very distant and feeble one in Marius (another relative through his mother).

Marius was the first to abolish the property qualification and establish an army of volunteers, which abandoned the old republican system based on the principle that only men of means were responsible enough to be soldiers. Marius's reforms, however, created strange armies whose loyalty was not to the state and, sometimes, not even to the general if he was hesitant or unsuccessful in enriching his men. The aim of the civil war armies was simply to loot and despoil any political opponent. Discipline, one of those cherished *mores maiorum* (customs of our ancestors) longed for by many Romans, was also abandoned. Caesar began to reverse this trend. He doubled the soldiers' pay, making them less prone to undisciplined looting; converted them into unbeatable machines that could defeat not only non-Roman armies but also hosts of fellow Roman citizens; and instilled a new sense of civic duty so the troops saw themselves not as vultures at the margin of society but as responsible citizens defending the state. In turn, the common soldiers felt they had achieved a position of importance in society and received rewards for their labor if not the chance to play a political role.[83]

Caesar began this process, but it was Augustus who brought it to completion. Augustus surely owed a huge debt to his great-uncle, but the changes he brought were extraordinary on their own. He reduced the number of legions from sixty to twenty-eight and then to twenty-five, cutting costs while increasing efficiency; made them into a permanent army; deployed them at the borders or in recently annexed lands, like northwestern Iberia, which were potential hotspots; clarified and strengthened the career path and the rewards; strengthened the already dominant position of Rome in the Mediterranean; transformed Rome into a garrison by creating new forces that were stationed in the city or nearby, a radical departure from custom; and reconstituted the auxiliaries into a permanent part of the Roman army. True, one can recognize Caesar's imprint in most of these developments, yet some were far-reaching. Not only did the old world of the republic disappear; Caesar himself would have had difficulty recognizing it.

For his part, Caesar considered war something like a continuously moving target to which his soldiers would react and destroy; for Augustus supremacy would be defined as establishing a permanent army in fixed locations. The process of integrating non-Romans had far to go, but by making the auxiliaries a permanent part of the Roman armies Augustus opened a new process that would eventually Romanize the whole empire. In part the development would be fruitful, as it maintained Roman supremacy, yet in a way it strengthened the tendency of Roman citizens to rely on noncitizens to fight Rome's wars. For the moment, all this would be a positive development, the harbinger of a cosmopolitan and seemingly eternal civilization. In the fourth and fifth centuries, however, it would lead to the fall of the empire. Once Italy lost its primacy by becoming just another province within the Roman Empire, Rome itself would decline until Italy was overshadowed by the eastern empire, Rome by the emergence of Constantinople. For the newcomers from across the Alps, a path to conquest would be opened.

Although Augustus's military reforms were varied and far-reaching, we can look at three in particular in an attempt to evaluate their importance. For the first time in its history Rome became an armed city, wherein the commander in chief of all the forces was the emperor himself. Thus a city that had relied on custom and tradition for defense (i.e., social harmony was absolutely necessary for peace and safety) was now a capital, wherein one man could implement his will by force. Marius, Sulla, and Caesar briefly did so; but now the power of one man—the emperor—could in theory be eternal and passed on to an individual whom he personally designated. The emperor was the commander in chief, the provider, the benefactor—even a god. But another crucial change, one that first appeared under Caesar, was associated with the imperial soldiers. The rapacious vultures of the civil wars became men of destiny. They were the messengers of Rome's mission—a myth that has lasted for millennia and may never disappear. Indeed, this myth has been hijacked by other people in different guises, whether barbarian kingdoms or the Catholic Church.

From the very beginning, Roman citizens were of a different makeup than any other ancient society. This may help explain their success in erecting an empire that lasted centuries in the west and almost two millennia in the east.[84] The devotion to the state was an obsession permeating civil society and the citizens' subconsciousness. It implied that the citizen was a soldier who blindly believed in the destiny of the republic—to rule the world. That belief sustained the state during its bleakest years, as when the Samnites forced the republic to accept humiliating surrender at Forche Caudine in 321 B.C.; when the Celts sacked Rome circa 387 B.C.; when Hannibal destroyed a generation of young men at Trebia, Trasimene, and Cannae (218–216 B.C.) and threatened to break through Rome's gates at any moment; when consul Atilius Regulus, the prisoner of Carthage sent to Rome to ask for peace in 256 B.C., urged the Senate to continue the war knowing the horrible punishment that awaited him upon his return to Carthage; when after the early stages of the Cimbric and Teutonic War (105–101 B.C.) thousands of Roman citizens stained the earth with their blood; when the republic was torn apart by civil wars in the years after the reform of 107 B.C.; and especially when the later emperors became an example of debauchery and vice, not symbols of probity and strength and civic virtue.

This conviction never really disappeared, although it was no longer in practice, and many warring societies would learn to apply to it in their own environments. And Rome never demobilized, even after it conquered the world.[85] As Virgil would write, "Remember thou, O Roman, to rule the nations with thy sway; these shall be thine arts—to impose the law of peace, to spare the humbled, and to tame in war the proud."[86] It is no surprise, then, that for centuries western Europeans and their descendants saw themselves as heirs of the Roman tradition. The Roman eagle would triumph, but in a different guise and for different purposes, among Americans, Germans, and Russians. Rome remained the ideal state despite its brutality even during the best years, despite the legacy of conquest, poverty, and dispossession throughout the empire.

The Reluctant God

Augustus was not the first or last personality whose arrival carried messianic implications. Indeed it was not unusual for his contemporaries to share such hopes following decades of civil turmoil, the murder of a great man in the holy Senate, the disappearance of distinguished families, and the transformation of the state into a pawn of power-hungry generals and greedy soldiers.[87] Many centuries later, French King Charles VIII would be hailed in the Italian states as the deliverer from political misery and social injustice.[88]

Augustus's conception and birth were clouded in mystery. It is alleged that ten months before his birth, his mother, Atia, went to the temple of Apollo to perform a ritual, but she fell asleep on the temple floor. A snake, people said, appeared and laid with her before disappearing again. When she woke up, she performed the rituals customary after intercourse with her husband. Since that night at the temple a mark similar to a snake had appeared on Atia's body; ten months later Augustus was born. Thus Augustus was hailed as the son of Apollo.[89] Also, the year that he was born the Senate was warned that a neonate would become king of the Romans, news that at first terrified the senators. As King Herod of Judaea would a few years later, they decided to kill all the children born that year; then, hopeful that the king would come from one of their own families, they refused to carry out the deed.[90] Good omens continued. When Augustus arrived in Rome after Caesar's death, a rainbow appeared in the clear and cloudless sky, and lightning struck the tomb of Caesar's daughter, Iulia. When Augustus took the auspices of his first consulship, twelve vultures flew overhead, as they had during the founding of Rome by Romulus.[91]

Such signs were interpreted as the visual projection of divine favors. They tied Augustus to the king of the gods—Jupiter the Thunderer—and to Apollo; they showed that like Romulus he would be the founder of a new era; they stated that he would become a king. But Augustus's presumption to divine status was not an immediate and forceful process: It was "a typically Augustan exercise in carefully nuanced suggestiveness."[92] It continued in this manner throughout his life, a decision over which he had no control; it would be a process desired by the gods, by the Senate, and by the Roman people.

Karl Galinsky identifies several steps in Augustus's march to divinity.[93] Two had existed even before he gained political power. The first was the messianic idea; the second, much more important, was his familial relationship with a person who had been proclaimed a god—Iulius Caesar. This was the tie that Augustus would emphasize throughout his life: He was the son of a god who had adopted him. Every action that tended to strengthen Caesar's divinity also strengthened Augustus. Other steps in the process of his divinity were the result of military successes and his establishment of peace and order in a society ravaged by civil wars. In 36 B.C. Augustus was granted the sacred status *(sacrosanctitas)* of tribune for life, his vote cast in the name of the goddess Minerva, following his victory in Spain against another leader of the Pompeian faction; and when he began building a temple to Apollo on the Palatine, the cities of Italy followed suit by honoring him in their temples.[94] His victory over Marcus Antonius and Cleopatra at Actium in 31 B.C. left him master over the Hellenistic monarchies, where the ruler cult had a long tradition. It is no surprise, then, that Augustus would soon be portrayed in the image of a god, whether as a statue modeled on Apollo or on the Roman coins minted during this period. The Senate was also influential in shaping the process. A festival was established to honor his birthday; priests and priestesses added his name in the customary prayers for the Roman commonwealth; the Salian hymn (a martial ritual) placed him next to the name of the gods, combining divinity with warlike memories.[95] Then, in 27 B.C., he took the title *augustus*—synonymous with the holder of imperial power and a sacred term used in ritual.[96]

Augustus's assumption of the divine was not uniform throughout the empire. While alive he was never considered a god in Rome, although he received honors associated with the divine. Yet he was unlike any other human. Combining native Italian tradition with Hellenistic influence, he played an intermediary role between gods and humans.[97] When he reordered the wards of Rome, the ward leaders included his *genius* (the double of Augustus's living self) and his *Lares* (the guardians of his family) among the entities to be worshiped; they made a family cult into a public cult. Writers like Horace and Virgil accepted the Stoic canon that men who benefited humankind and the commonwealth acquired an aura of divinity and that eventually they would be deified after death. Augustus's funeral would have all the characteristics of an apotheosis—a human had joined the gods.[98]

Acceptance of the Augustus cult was more evident outside the gates of Rome—in Italian cities, in the east, and in the west. In Italy, Augustus had already acquired the honors of a divinity soon after destroying the last Pompeian threat in 36 B.C. in Spain. In the east the deification of the emperor while alive was accepted and easy to promote. Temples were erected in his honor—an impulse restrained at times by Augustus himself. The promotion of the easterners' ruler cult was motivated not only by tradition but as a visual construction of the reality of power. The easterners were eager to express their gratitude to a man who had put an end to the civil wars; they also felt compelled to visually and symbolically display their loyalty because most of their regions had sided with Marcus Antonius against Octavian.[99]

The west—that is, the territories of western Europe—had no sacred tradition of this kind. But the western empire soon followed the example while Augustus was alive. And an interesting aspect of this is the direct role of the Roman government and the army. Here different values were paramount—the loyalty of the soldiers to their commanders, the worship of the successful military leader.[100] Images and statues of Augustus became part of the standards in the soldiers' camps, and important events of his life marked many special holidays. As Galinsky explains, "The soldiers regarded his cult as a means to promote loyalty to him and Rome in the newly conquered regions."[101] During Augustus's lifetime there were four expressions of the cult at the provincial level and at least thirty-seven at the municipal level.[102] It was a trend that Augustus and the imperial family fostered in a variety of ways, beginning as early as 40 B.C. The propaganda included coins, monuments, sculptures, and inscriptions ending, ultimately, in Augustus's worship.[103]

This development suited later leaders of the empire who, except for Gaius, Caligula, and Commodus, generally followed the pattern set by Augustus: divine honors in Rome—he was the intermediary between the city and the gods—and, elsewhere, actual worship. It strengthened the emperor's rule, made challenges to his power religious and social offenses, and bolstered the sense of hierarchy and thus political obedience within the empire. It is no surprise that the cult received the allegiance of the highest social groups in the east and that it became a prop for the hegemony of Roman arms in the west.[104]

A Physician for a Disease-Ridden Body

At Augustus's funeral in A.D. 14 his successor, Tiberius, said that his stepfather had wealth, weapons, and power to become the "sole lord of all" but that he had refused to do so: "Like a good physician who takes in hand a disease-ridden body and heals it, he first restored to health and then gave back to you [the Roman people] the whole body politic."[105] It was the kind of public image that Augustus had carefully fashioned all his life. The process had begun before he had disposed of the other pretenders who threatened his hegemony, in the "autobiography" that he began early in his career but never completed. At that time his concerns were mainly defensive—to affirm that his paternal ancestry was not ignoble, as his enemies claimed; to boast that even as a child he had shown great virtues; to state that he was not a treacherous, ruthless, cruel individual; and to deny the label of coward that his adversaries had thrown at him after his performance on the battlefield.[106] And he had strong reasons to clean up his public image, for the young Augustus was indeed ruthless, cruel, and untrustworthy. Cicero, who eventually came to admire him, was aware that he was a dangerous man. "That young man," he said, "should be lauded, glorified, and eliminated."[107] But beginning in 22 B.C., after his successful campaign against the Cantabrians, an Iberian people northeast of the Astures, Augustus realized that he did not need to defend his conduct anymore. From then on until 2 B.C. he spent his time drafting and redrafting his political will. His tone would be different there, not "the language of an usurper, but that of a savior."[108] He assumed the persona of the physician restoring the Roman commonwealth to health and glory through a masterful display of reforms and a literary and artistic campaign of public images. He became the *vir gravis et sanctus* (the civic-minded holy man), the *pater patriae* (the father of his country), *augustus* (divine), and *imperator* (commander) of his forces. How he achieved these goals is a textbook example of the manipulation of power.

Augustus's legal powers were less all-encompassing compared to those of the later emperors. Still, he exerted greater influence than any other before or after because of the consensus and the resultant authority that he enjoyed after bringing peace at home and supremacy in the conquered lands. He was the symbol of the state to whom allegiance was due, not only because his actions were based on the concept that he pursued the interest of all but also because the citizens obeyed the higher interests of the empire by accepting Augustus's dominance.[109] According to Galinsky, the components of Augustus's prestige and influence included his enormous wealth, his unmatched generosity for public purposes, his constantly repeated connection to Caesar, his role as the army's commander in chief, and his careful campaign to imprint in the collective mind of the Roman commonwealth all the great attributes that he represented.

Buildings, statues, coins, literary works—all portrayed what he had done and what the Roman people should be grateful for. In the past, constructing buildings had been a traditional means of self-representation by the Roman nobility. Augustus monopolized this activity, making it the privilege of his family, thus leaving the senators—many of whom were from provincial cities by this time—to grandiose constructions outside of Rome and, even there, often to honor Augustus and his house. Augustus never conveyed the impression that his Rome—as in the new Augustan Forum, for instance—was for his own glorification and the symbol of a new period of history; rather it was a restatement of the old values of Republican Rome. He was the restorer, not a man interested in *novae res*, that is, the innovation of new destructive values. Between the old Roman Forum and the new Augustan Forum, there was a mutually embracing relationship of Rome's greatness with the emperor's prestige. Statues in his image and inscriptions with his name were everywhere. Today, only 3,000 inscriptions survive from five centuries of republican rule; the five centuries of the Roman Empire would leave 300,000. Traveling along the old Roman roads, one would find the name of the emperor on every milestone.

Buildings, statues, and milestones helped to make the emperor ever-present, but the most important contributors to Augustus's prestige were his deeds.[110] Of these, the most important was his ability to create consensus in all sectors of the population, in addition to his caring but strict control over the army. Choosing an emperor was a delicate matter that included the man's birth (or adoption) as well as the support of the Senate, the equestrian order, and the commoners together with the praetorians in Rome and the governors and soldiers stationed throughout the empire. His safety rested on controlling two potential threats: conspiracies from those near his person, and rebellions from the armed forces. Augustus solved this problem by establishing the praetorians and by making the generals dependent upon him for appointments, favors, and rewards.[111] He cherished the power that the soldiers gave him but also made sure that a certain distance existed between the commander in chief and his armed forces. It was a system that worked well for his immediate successor, Tiberius, but it would require careful adjustments by his successors (e.g., Claudius and Nero). It would break down about two centuries later with the emergence of Septimius Severus.

In many ways, for Augustus the state was a giant household with the emperor acting as father, holding all the traditional powers of the *paterfamilias*. He possessed undisputed control and the ultimate decisions over life and death, although he had to act always in the household's best interests as would any good father. He had to present an image of restraint, moderation, and caution. He even became tolerant as the years advanced, although he would remain suspicious of the motivations of friends and enemies alike. He wanted to be and became, despite venomous portrayals by writers like Tacitus, the personification of the best interests of the commonwealth.

This was the way Augustus ran the state once his competition had been eliminated. The last serious threats were Antonius and Cleopatra, both of whom died a few months after their defeat at Actium in 31 B.C. And among all his interests, the most important was to refashion the army into a tool that would enhance the emperor's hegemony and the security of the dominion. Uppermost in Augustus's mind would be achieving victory on the battlefield against all enemies as well as establishing safe frontiers.

Only thus could Roman supremacy endure for centuries.

Notes

1. Svetonius, *Divus Augustus* 46.1.
2. Ibid., 1–4.
3. Ibid., 79–80.
4. Plutarch, *Caesar* 66.4.
5. Res Gestae Divi Augusti 15, 30, 26.
6. Svetonius, *Divus Augustus* 24.1.
7. A. Ferrill, *Roman Imperial Grand Strategy* (Lanham, MD, 1991), p. 1.
8. Cf. E. Luttwak, *The Grand Strategy of the Roman Empire from the First Century A.D. to the Third* (Baltimore, 1976), p. 17, and Ferrill, *Roman Imperial Grand Strategy*, p. 2.
9. Ferrill, *Roman Imperial Grand Strategy*, p. 3.
10. Kurt A. Raaflaub, "The Political Significance of Augustus' Military Reforms," in *Roman Frontier Studies 1979*, edited by W. S. Hanson and L.J.F. Keppie (Oxford, 1980), p. 1005.
11. Lawrence Keppie, *The Making of the Roman Army from Republic to Empire* (Norman, OK, 1998), pp. 134–136.
12. Brian Dobson, "The Empire," in *Warfare in the Ancient World*, edited by John Hackett (New York, 1989), pp. 192–195.
13. Vegetius i.6.
14. G. R. Watson, *The Roman Soldier* (Ithaca, 1969), pp. 39–40.
15. Brian Campbell, *The Roman Army, 31 B.C.–A.D. 337: A Sourcebook* (London, 1994), p. 11.
16. See Y. Le Bohec, *L'esercito romano: Le armi imperiali da Augusto a Caracalla* (Roma, 1992), p. 98; see also Watson, *The Roman Soldier*, pp. 37–42.
17. Josephus, *Jewish War* iii.72–76.
18. An African inscription of A.D. 128 by Emperor Hadrian shows this. For the text of the inscription, see Campbell, *The Roman Army*, pp. 18–20.
19. Svetonius, *Divus Augustus* 49.2.

20. Dio liv.25.5–6.

21. Ibid., lv.23.1.

22. Campbell, *The Roman Army*, p. 20.

23. Patrick Le Roux, *L'armée romaine et l'organisation des provinces ibériques d'Auguste à l'invasione de 409* (Paris, 1982), p. 263.

24. Keppie, *The Making of the Roman Army*, p. 154.

25. See A. Passerini, *Le coorti pretorie* (Roma, 1939); M. Durry, *Les cohortes prétoriennes* (Paris, 1939); and the short but lucid summaries in Le Bohec, *L'esercito romano*, pp. 28–29; Watson, *The Roman Soldier*, pp. 16–18.

26. Dio liv.25.6; lv.23.1.

27. Le Bohec, *L'esercito romano*, pp. 28–30.

28. Ibid., p. 29.

29. Campbell, *The Roman Army*, pp. 38, 40.

30. Le Bohec, *L'esercito romano*, pp. 31–32.

31. Ibid., p. 30; Campbell, *The Roman Army*, p. 38; Keppie, *The Making of the Roman Army*, p. 154.

32. Le Bohec, *L'esercito romano*, p. 31.

33. See G. L. Cheesman, *The Auxilia of the Roman Imperial Army* (Oxford, 1914); Y. Le Bohec, *Les unités auxiliaires de l'armée romaine en Afrique Procunsolaire et Numidie sous le Haut Empire* (Paris, 1989); P. A. Holder, *Studies in the Auxilia of the Roman Army from Augustus to Trajan* (Oxford, 1980); D. B. Saddington, *The Development of the Roman Auxiliary Forces from Caesar to Vespasian, 49 B.C.–A.D. 79* (Harare, 1982); Adrian Goldsworthy, *The Roman Army at War, 100 B.C.–A.D. 200* (Oxford, 1996), pp. 15–31, 35–37.

34. Le Bohec, *L'esercito romano*, pp. 34–38; Campbell, *The Roman Army*, pp. 33–38.

35. Le Bohec, *L'esercito romano*, p. 38.

36. Campbell, *The Roman Army*, pp. 33–34.

37. Le Bohec, *L'esercito romano*, pp. 44–46.

38. Goldsworthy, *The Roman Army at War*, p. 38.

39. Giovanni Forni, "Estrazione etnica e sociale dei soldati delle legioni," *Aufstieg und Niedergang der Römischen Welt (ANRW)* 2(1) (1974): 355.

40. Campbell, *The Roman Army*, pp. 61–62.

41. Le Bohec, *L'esercito romano*, pp. 51–53, 84.

42. F. E. Adcock, *The Roman Art of War under the Republic* (New York, 1981, reprint of 1940 ed.), pp. 99–124.

43. Campbell, *The Roman Army*, pp. 46–47, 50.

44. Ibid., p. 47.

45. Caesar, *De bello gallico* vii.51.

46. Forni, "Estrazione etnica e sociale," p. 354.

47. Le Bohec, *L'esercito romano*, p. 95.

48. Le Roux, *L'armée romaine et l'organisation*, p. 263.

49. Forni, "Estrazione etnica e sociale," pp. 382, 383.

50. Le Bohec, *L'esercito romano*, pp. 108–111 based on calculations in Giovanni Forni, *Il reclutamento delle legioni da Augusto a Diocleziano* (Roma, 1953), pp. 339–391.

51. Jacques Harmand, "Les origines de l'armée impériale: Un témoignage sur la réalité du pseudo-principat et sur l'evolution militaire de l'Occident." *ANRW* 2(1) (1974): 290.

52. Forni, "Estrazione etnica e sociale," p. 344.

53. Le Bohec, *L'esercito romano*, p. 127.

54. Forni, "Estrazione etnica e sociale," p. 384.

55. Tacitus, *Histories* ii.17.1; Forni, "Estrazione etnica e sociale"; Forni, *Il reclutamento delle legioni*, p. 384.

56. Forni, "Estrazione etnica e sociale," p. 384.

57. Ibid., p. 386. Michael Speidel suggests a slightly different demarcation line; see "Legionaries from Asia Minor," *ANRW* 2(2): 742–743.

58. Speidel, "Legionaries from Asia Minor," p. 744. For Egypt, see Hubert Devijver, "The Roman Army in Egypt (with Special Reference to the Militiae Equestres)," *ANRW* 2(1) (1974): 452–492.

59. Forni, "Estrazione etnica e sociale," p. 385.

60. Ibid., p. 385.

61. Ibid., pp. 386–390.

62. Le Bohec, *L'esercito romano*, pp. 98–103.

63. Zeineb Ben Adallah and Yann le Bohec, "Nouvelles Inscriptions concernant l'armée romaine," *Mélanges de l'École Française de Rome* 109 (1997): 79–80.

64. Forni, "Estrazione etnica e sociale," p. 390.

65. Ibid., pp. 390–391; Le Bohec, *L'esercito romano*, pp. 113–120.

66. J. Béranger, "Fortune privée imperial et état," *Mélanges Georges Bonnard* (Geneve, 1966), p. 151.

67. See also Kurt Raaflaub, "The Political Significance of Augustus' Military Reforms," in *Roman Frontier Studies 1979*, edited by W. S. Hanson and L.J.F. Keppie (Oxford, 1980), pp. 1005–1021.

68. C. Nicolet, "Augustus, Government, and the Propertied Classes," in *Caesar Augustus: Seven Aspects*, edited by F. Millar and E. Segal (Oxford, 1984), pp. 89–128.

69. Keppie, *The Making of the Roman Army*, p. 149.

70. Dio lv. 24.9–25.1–5; Svetonius, *Divus Augustus* 49.2; Keppie, *Roman History*, p. 148.

71. Le Bohec, *L'esercito romano*, pp. 280–285; Dio lv.23.1.

72. Le Bohec, *L'esercito romano*, pp. 298–299.

73. Forni, "Estrazione etnica e sociale," pp. 357–358.

74. Ibid., pp. 354–355, 357.

75. Le Bohec, *L'esercito romano*, p. 280, on the basis of Tacitus, *Annales* i.17.6; Dio lix.5; Talmud, *Sheqalim* v.1.

76. See the interesting tables of *donativa* and *liberalitates* in Le Bohec, *L'esercito romano*, pp. 287–290.

77. Ibid., pp. 280–305.

78. Svetonius, *Divus Augustus* 24.1.

79. Ibid., 24.1.

80. Ibid., 25.3.

81. Ibid., 24.2.

82. Ibid., 25.1.

83. See Harmand, "Les origines de l'armée impériale," pp. 271–272; also Raaflaub, "The Political Significance of Augustus' Military Reforms," p. 1008.

84. The key to the Romans' success is eloquently presented in a few pages of C. Nicolet's work on the citizen in Republican Rome. Nicolet, "Augustus, Government, and the Propertied Classes," pp. 89–93.

85. Ibid., pp. 89–90.

86. Virgil, *Aeneid* 6.851–853.

87. A. Passerini, *Linee di storia romana in età imperiale* (Milano, 1972), pp. 68–70.

88. Anne Denis, *Charles VIII et les Italiens: Histoire et mythe* (Genève, 1979).

89. Svetonius, *Divus Augustus* ii.94.4.

90. Ibid., 94.3.

91. Ibid., 95.

92. K. Galinsky, *Augustan Culture: An Interpretive Introduction* (Princeton, 1996), p. 312.

93. Ibid., pp. 312–322.

94. Appian v.546; Dio li.19.6.

95. Dio li.19.6–7; 19.1.

96. Res Gestae Divi Augusti 6.34.

97. Passerini, *Linee di storia romana in età imperiale*, pp. 70–71.

98. Galinsky, *Augustan Culture*, pp. 301–306, 206–207.

99. Ibid., pp. 323–326.

100. Ibid., pp. 326–331.

101. Ibid., p. 328.

102. Ibid., p. 323.

103. E. S. Ramage, "Augustus' Propaganda in Gaul," *Klio* 79 (1997): 117–160.

104. Galinsky, *Augustan Culture*, pp. 324–325, 328.

105. Dio lvi.39.1–2.

106. Zvi Yavetz, "The Res Gestae and Augustus' Public Image," in *Caesar Augustus: Seven Aspects*, edited by Fergus Millar and Erich Segal (Oxford, 1984), pp. 1–4.

107. Cicero, *Fam.* 11.20.1, as translated by Z. Yavetz, "The Personality of Augustus: Reflections on Syme's Roman Revolution," in *Between Republic and Empire: Interpretations of Augustus and His Principate*, edited by Kurt A. Raaflaub and Mark Toher (Berkeley, 1990), p. 32.

108. Yavetz, "The Res Gestae and Augustus' Public Image," pp. 4, 8.

109. M. Pani, *Potere e valori a Roma fra Augusto e Traiano* (Bari, 1993), p. 309.

110. Galinsky, *Augustan Culture*, pp. 376–389. Also T. Höscher, *Pax Romana* (Mainz, 1967); E. Simon, *Ara Pacis Augustae* (Tübingen, 1967); and especially P. Zanker, *The Power of Images in the Age of Augustus* (Ann Arbor, 1988).

111. R. P. Saller, *Personal Patronage under the Early Empire* (Cambridge, 1982), p. 74.

6

How to Manage an Empire: Strengths and Pitfalls

That the Roman people should be subject to other people is contrary to divine law; the immortal gods have willed it to rule all nations.

Cicero, *Philippic* 6.19

Augustus died in A.D. 14 after a lingering illness. The day of the funeral Tiberius ordered his son, Drusus, to read the instructions and injunctions that Augustus had left in four documents. One of them instructed the new emperor and the Roman people to keep the empire within its existing frontiers.[1] According to Cassius Dio, Augustus advised Tiberius and the Roman people "to be satisfied with their present possessions and under no conditions to increase the empire to any greater dimensions." Cassius continues: "It would be hard to guard . . . and this would lead to danger of their losing what was already theirs. This principle he had really always followed himself not only in speech but also in action." While still alive Augustus "might have made great acquisitions from the barbarian worlds, but he had not wished to do so."[2]

This advice is at the root of a conviction among ancient and modern historians that after Augustus's death the empire lived under the constant threat of disintegration and that later emperors were compelled to defend what Rome had acquired during the late republic and under Augustus. At first glance such an evaluation would be accurate: Not many new lands were conquered after A.D. 14 (Britain in 43, Dacia in 105–106, and Mesopotamia after the wars of 162–166 and 194–198). The conquests of another warlike emperor, Trajan, were ephemeral. Roman power in Armenia, Mesopotamia, and the Parthian lands of the Persian Gulf was already crumbling even before Trajan's death and the ascension of his successor, Hadrian.

The Limits of Roman Imperialism

The practical nature of Romans and the characteristics of Roman deities cause many to downplay their commitment to religion. Yet religion played a fundamental role and was subtly intertwined with ritual and the application of military conquest (e.g., the gods were the guarantors of all treaties, and only "just" wars could be waged). "The gods were the guardians of city and empire,"[3] the Romans claimed, because their state enjoyed the wisest, most balanced constitution and their rule was just and pious and thus willed by the divine. This belief found expression among the most influential intellectuals of the Principate (the period from Augustus to the end of the third century) and became a leitmotiv in the work of almost all later writers. Rome's mission had in fact been announced more than a century earlier by the Greek historian Polybius, who claimed that Rome's hegemony embraced the known world (i.e., the nations, according to Polybius, that mattered politically). In 7 B.C. another Greek, Dionysius of Halicarnassus, thought that Rome's supremacy knew only two limits: the ocean, understood as the great sea-river marking the confines of the earth; and those places troops could not access because of unsurpassable physical barriers. Cicero, concerned about waging just wars but also glory and empire (which were just motives in his eyes), was proud of Rome's imperial accomplishments: No people could threaten Rome because it ruled the world. Its power extended over alien territories physically as well as politically, because Rome was the "master of kings" *(dominus regum)*. In his classic work *Aeneid*, Virgil makes the king of the gods, Jupiter, foretell that Rome's conquest of the world will bring peace to humankind. Similar views are also found in Horace and Ovid and in later writers like the geographer Strabo and the biographer Svetonius.[4] Even when no efforts were made to annex new people and lands, the ideal of continuous conquest and hegemony continued,[5] another example of how ideals persist even after the disappearance of the structural apparatus that had justified them in the first place.

Despite the ideal of interminable conquest and sacred imperialism, Romans did stop at certain boundaries, which later historians identified as the limits of their empire: Hadrian's Wall in Britain, the Rhine and the Danube in Europe, the Euphrates in the Near East, and the desert in most of North Africa. Why did the Romans stop their expansion? Did they adopt a defensive policy? The view that the Romans endorsed a grand strategy based on a tenacious defense of the borders as established in the first century A.D. found influential and controversial expression in *The Grand Strategy of the Roman Empire* (1976), by military analyst Edward N. Luttwak. According to Luttwak, Roman imperial strategy went through three stages. First the Romans harshly suppressed internal disorder while cordoning their borders with client states. In turn the buffer states used their influence to control the satellite peoples immediately outside their frontiers. This meant that any serious threat had to go through two obstacles before reaching the territories directly controlled by Rome: first the satellites, then the client states.

The Romans followed this policy until the A.D. 60s, when they began to systematically incorporate clients and satellite states into the empire. Thus in the second stage they took direct control over border defense, making the empire in effect a sprawling fort, one that was protected by linear fortifications (actual walls and palisades) and deterrents like rivers, chains of forts, towers, fortified farms, and the rugged and forbidding nature of the terrain itself. As Arther Ferrill argues, however (supporting Luttwak's thesis), the Romans used an effective system of forward defense by attacking and defusing any potential threat by moving against it before it reached the border.[6]

The last stage of the imperial grand strategy was installed after the traumatic invasions of the third century A.D. when the Romans switched to a defense-in-depth—that is, loose vigilance at the borders but increasing opposition as enemies penetrated the empire—with the creation of fixed fortified camps, fortresses, and towers. This approach failed in the end.

In other words, Luttwak's argument and its revision as exemplified by Ferrill and in others like E. L. Wheeler[7] are based on the assumption that the Romans applied a coherent, logical, consistent imperial grand strategy. It blended diplomacy, coercion, and continuous vigilance, rapid movement of the legions, effective logistical support, an impressive road and river communications network, and intelligence operations. The core of the strategy was defensive. Its premises evolved from relying on client states and their satellites to stop any invader to forward defense. In other words, it evolved into attacking the enemies before they arrived at the borders, where impressive manmade or natural obstacles were used. But by adopting the strategy of defense in depth—that is, allowing enemies to penetrate the frontiers and slowing them with obstacles before challenging them to a pitched encounter—the Romans committed a grave error.

The Romans gave the impression that they encircled the empire with a defensive structure; the existence of impressive artificial barriers supports this argument. They included major fortifications like two walls in Britain, a *fossatum* (essentially a defensive ditch to keep invaders at bay) in Africa, and a defensive system in southwest Germany. The Antonine Wall, built in Britain between 139 and 142 by Antoninus Pius, ran for 59 kilometers from Bridgeness on the Forth to the Old Kirkpatrick on the Clyde. It included a ditch, about 7 meters in front of the wall, some 12 meters wide and 3.6 meters deep. At least sixteen small forts were constructed along its perimeter. The occupation of the line did not last long. The structure was evacuated first around 154–158, reoccupied soon thereafter, then abandoned around 164.[8] Hadrian's Wall ran south of the Antonine Wall for 118 kilometers from Wallsend-on-Tyne to Bowness-on-Solway. Fortified gateways were erected roughly every 1,500 meters with surveillance turrets every half a kilometer. A ditch protected the wall, excavated about 6 meters in front of the wall, 8 meters wide and 3 meters deep. Begun around 122, Hadrian's Wall, except for brief periods, was probably occupied until the later stages of the empire.[9]

The linear constructions in Africa (the *fossatum* and *clausurae*) were much less impressive than the two British walls. They were intermittent, constructed along the fertile areas from Tripolitania to southern Algeria. The area was also strengthened with fortified buildings and soldiers posted in oases, probably to control the caravan routes. The linear fortifications in southwestern Germany were built over a long period. They began under Domitian in 83 in the form of wooden towers and stone forts; Hadrian (emperor, 117–138) erected a wooden palisade; by the beginning of the third century the frontier was moved about 30 kilometers forward with a stone wall marking its limits.[10]

These fortifications were the most prominent, leaving extensive evidence for us to analyze today. Most likely other fortifications will be discovered. Recently, an impressive defensive line was found at Porolissum in the northwestern corner of Dacia (Transylvania), consisting of timber and stone fortlets, three watchtowers, an entrance gate, and a continuous defensive wall about 3.5 kilometers long. The defensive line, which blocked access to the two valleys leading to the Roman military site in the area, is located at about 6–7 kilometers away from another linear defense formed by banks and ditches.[11]

In addition, the Roman frontier appears to have been studded with all types of military strongholds. By the fourth century an anonymous writer advised that "an unbroken chain of forts will best assure the protection of these frontiers, on the plan that they should be built at intervals of one mile, with a solid wall and very strong towers."[12] Of course at this time the empire was under enormous stress; yet it seems to have been common practice to construct all types of fortifications near or at the frontier (or sometimes behind the frontier, as during the first two centuries of the empire). Such constructions, often protected by ditches, could be large (e.g., garrison forts) or increasingly smaller, including detachment forts, watchtowers, and fortified landing places along major rivers. They fulfilled several functions: control over the countryside, surveillance, defense, and jumping off for offensive operations in enemy territory. The chain of forts on the middle Danube began under Augustus and his successor, Tiberius, and it was renewed after the brief civil war of A.D. 69. In Scotland and elsewhere the forts seemed to have been an innovation of the later Flavian period.[13] They became a typical feature of the Roman landscape in the Near East as well.

The Roman penchant for defense is also confirmed by the location of the borders, which coincided with the three great rivers—the Rhine and Danube in Europe and the Euphrates in the Near East. This does not imply that the frontier was static, because at times the Romans occupied territories across the rivers, and they were always ready to strike into enemy territory and extend territorial control. Generally, however, Rome stopped at river's edge, that is, the obvious obstacle. Beginning with Augustus, the location of the legions suggests that the Romans adopted a defensive stance. The majority of troops were stationed at the farthest borders.[14]

Peoples in continental Europe west of the Alps offered few challenges to Roman supremacy. Revolts in the Gallic territories were rare, and the few troops deployed there were to protect the Lyons mint or to bring relief to a notorious trouble spot—the Rhine frontier. The Iberian peninsula, especially the northern part, was a different matter. Despite what seemed to be its final subjugation with the victorious campaign of Agrippa (29–19 B.C.), the region remained a source of great concern during Augustus's time. Five legions were stationed there, but the situation must have improved with the passing of time. There were three legions during Tiberius's tenure, two under Claudius, and only one afterward. Britain offered a different situation. The northernmost limit of Roman conquest was the River Tay, at the foot of the Scottish Highlands, but after a series of reverses, attacks, and counterattacks the Romans had to withdraw at the line between the Tyne and the Solway.

Augustus and his successors were aware of the vulnerability of the Italian plains to attacks originating northeast of the Alps. Besides the troops available in Rome and the sailors of the two Italian naval bases, which could have functioned as foot troops in an emergency, Augustus deployed three legions in the Illyricum and probably two in Macedonia. Tiberius reduced them to two (both in the Illyricum), Claudius to one. But the greatest European threat was along the Rhine and the Danube. On the Rhine Augustus stationed a minimum of five legions, Tiberius (14–37) eight, and Claudius (41–54) and his successors until Vespasian (69–79) seven. Then from Trajan (98–117) onward until Aurelian (270–275) there were only four. While the number of soldiers on the Rhine declined somewhat, those on the Danube increased. From the four legions under Augustus to the three under Tiberius we see a dramatic increase to eight (Claudius), six (Vespasian), twelve (Trajan), ten (Antoninus), thirteen (Caracalla), and twelve (Aurelian). In the first two centuries of the empire, securing the Danube—with Germans, Celts, and Asiatic people like the Sarmatians, a nation of Iranian descent, across the river—was the Romans' great concern. The Near East frontier required similar measures: The legions stationed there, only three and then four under Augustus and Tiberius until Claudius, increased to six and up to eight until Antoninus (138–161) and then to ten and twelve under Caracalla (211–217) and Aurelian. Africa seems to have posed little threat: There were three legions, soon reduced to two and then to one in Egypt, and two more soon reduced to one for the rest of Africa from the western border of Egypt to the Atlantic.[15]

Assuming that each legion roughly equaled 5,000 men, we can count 25,000 legionnaires on the Rhine and 20,000 on the Danube under Augustus. This rises to 35,000 and 40,000 under Claudius, and finally to 20,000 and 60,000 under Aurelian. In the Near East we can count 15,000 legionnaires under Augustus, 20,000 under Claudius, and 60,000 under Aurelian. These figures can be doubled if we assume that the auxiliaries matched the number of legionnaires.

Thus we can point to several things that support the thesis that Rome adopted a defensive posture for securing the imperial borders: Augustus's last instructions, the unchanging nature of the borders, the lack of a continuous expansion policy, the choice of natural barriers and obstacles to mark the farthest limits, and the location and positioning of the legions. Yet many historians challenge this idea on two grounds: The Romans, although they had strategic notions, were incapable of forging the complicated interrelationships of grand strategy; moreover, it was in the nature and makeup of the Roman worldview to conquer and dominate—thus they could never adopt a defensive strategy.

The Romans had a rudimentary understanding of geography. When they translated geographic knowledge into practical knowledge, they did so in terms of directions. For instance, to carry, say, wine from the Mediterranean to Britain, the faster and much cheaper route would have been by sea, because transportation costs followed the ratio of 1:5:34 (i.e., sea:river:land). Yet the most common route was overland, for Romans understood itineraries on the basis of land spots.[16] Moreover, the people who fashioned foreign policy—that is, the emperors—had neither the practical nor the intellectual understanding of the intricacies of grand strategy. As C. R. Whittaker says, "Rational decisions [of the emperors] were fatally flawed owing to the absence of any sophisticated concept of strategy and to a chronic lack of information."[17] He agrees that the Romans had "some, rather limited evidence of strategic planning, and perhaps in the later empire of something more sophisticated," yet there was "nothing which really qualifies for the description of a Grand Strategy."[18] As Benjamin Isaac emphasizes, Romans tended to expand ethnically, not geographically: They "conquered peoples, not land."[19] Certainly without adequate maps and a keen understanding of the physical environment, it would have been impossible to fashion a complex strategic plan. Caesar's invasion of England is an example of how limited the Romans' knowledge was of an enemy prior to an invasion.

Yet there is no doubt that a certain strategic pattern can be discerned in imperial foreign policy. Generally emperors were convinced that they could acquire new territories only by making sure that the launching bases for the attack were well protected. In other words, cautious defense of Roman-controlled territory was combined with a tendency to move the frontiers forward or at least to control the terrain beyond where the Romans decided to stop for the time being. The problem with Luttwak's thesis is that he makes things too clear and logical, whereas in reality the Romans must have planned goals in a fog, sometimes thick, sometimes light, never in crystal-clear conditions.

The argument that Roman imperialism went into a defensive shell is weakest at least until the early third century A.D. Whittaker, who has synthesized the recent works on Roman frontier studies, argues that the Romans' main concern was to expand, not to defend.[20] The border with the Parthians, the successors of the Persians in the Near East, remained a concern for the Romans—which in itself leads many to believe that the Romans were normally poised in a defensive stance. But Isaac argues instead that "the frontier policy of Rome in the East intermittently but persistently aimed at expansion" from the beginning of the empire until at least the reign of emperor Diocletian (285–305). If one counts the attacks engineered by Parthians and Romans against one another in the first 300 years of our era (i.e., A.D.), the Romans were responsible for twice the number of strikes, and in all cases the Romans were the initiator of the hostilities.[21] Even though the efforts to expand in Britain, in Germany, and on the Danube became increasingly less frequent after Trajan, such was not the case in the east. Rome never gave up the idea of subduing Parthia and to control Mesopotamia. And whereas the wars against the Parthians were almost always begun by Rome, on the European borders Rome seemed increasingly reactive to what happened across the rivers.[22]

The Romans did not consider borders to be the limits of their sovereignty, for anyone who had somehow recognized and shown homage to Rome was considered to be a subject of Rome. The most obvious example was of course the annexation of a territory into a province; the power to tax the inhabitants followed. Vassal states were also interpreted as being part of the empire. Sovereignty was also exercised if they appointed the king as it would in the case for Armenia; if foreign people, like the Indians during the time of Augustus, sent their representatives to the emperor; and if any civilizations sought Rome's friendship like some German tribes.[23] But the presumption went even further: Any territory that the Romans could easily threaten would be considered subject to Rome's supremacy. This included any people, even if they were hostile to Rome, that had settled within a certain distance from the legions' most advanced positions.

Although rivers and linear constructions obviously fortified the defensive position of any region, modern scholars argue that they functioned mainly as communications arteries.[24] The Roman *limes* (a border of the empire) was never a boundary in the modern sense (see Figure 6.1). Rather it was a wide strip that included territories under direct Roman control as well as nearby territories belonging to both hostile and friendly people whose existence rested on recognizing Rome's arbitration over their affairs. Thus it was an area within which Roman troops exercised not just military control but also social and economic functions crucial to the safety and efficiency of the *limes* and adjacent territories. The *limes* from Asia Minor to the Red Sea, for instance, was "in essence a line of communication," a base from which "the Romans extended their control without any sense of boundaries." Rivers "were not natural frontiers but lines of communication and supply." The borders of other people were never sacred boundaries: The emperor was always ready to cross them if it was in his interest to do so. In A.D. 100 Pliny the Younger de-

FIGURE 6.1   Roman Empire, A.D. 116

scribes Trajan commanding the banks of the Danube ready to attack any barbarian: "Nothing will protect from our very territory taking him over."[25]

Yet the Romans did stop in places where they implied they would not.
They tried to push their line of advance to the Scottish Highlands by erecting the Antonine Wall but then withdrew quickly to Hadrian's Wall. At least
under Augustus they marched to the Elbe River in a complex operation
combining land advance with naval support in the North Sea, yet there, too,
they abandoned their goal, withdrawing to the left side of the Rhine. In the
Near East the Euphrates always seemed to be a fluid barrier that many emperors—Trajan, for instance—would have liked to extend over the whole of
Mesopotamia and beyond. The truth is that the Romans' fabled machinery
of war also had its weaknesses and had to recognize its limits. Some limits
were perfectly logical, given their poor understanding of geography and
natural resources that may exist. The geographer Strabo explains why it was
useless to conquer territories with poor resources: Keeping them would out-
strip economic and strategic benefits. Despite the importance of glory in
war, Romans always considered the necessity of making the enterprise
worthwhile economically.

Another limit was the great length of the frontiers and the limited man-power available to patrol them. More men could have been recruited, but this would have handicapped Rome, a society of limited technological knowledge. In other words, many adults had to work the land in order to feed the rest of the population. Hiring more men for the legions would have required larger expenses and more taxation, and the expenses could not be recouped (except perhaps for a place like Parthia). And in the long run the traditional recruiting pools tended to dry up as populations decreased and as more attractive lifestyles lured away potential recruits. Other things curtailed the possibility for unending aggression. Despite paying lip service to martial ideals, some emperors were not interested in leaving the comforts of Rome to wage war in the hinterland. Thus we see Roman aggressiveness under Trajan, relative peace under Hadrian, aggressiveness again under Marcus Aurelius, and outright reluctance by Antoninus Pius.

Sometimes the Romans were unable to solve the problem of enduring conquest. In such cases (e.g., Parthia and German lands not under Roman control) there were tactical problems, but terrain and sometimes the enemy's social structure prevented a permanent victory. Success alternated with defeat, and defeat brought the realization that defensible borders were enough, especially if they could accommodate future expeditions.

On the Rhine frontier, for example, the question remains why the Romans conquered the Gallic Celts so easily but failed against the Germans. The terrain made the legions efficient in Gallia, but the lands populated by the Germans presented an obstacle. And the Germans were fierce warriors (although the Celts showed great bravery in battle time and again). A more interesting explanation has been offered recently by the German scholar Jürgen Kunow.[26] Adapting the theoretical model offered by J. Galtung for modern imperialism, Kunow argues that Rome's failure in Germany was its inability to establish a bridgehead between German and Roman society. The key to the bridgehead, he says, was control over the key holders of power in both societies. This had been relatively easy in a stratified civilization like Gaul: The aristocracy monopolized power, and the main strength was located in cities and *oppida* (fortified towns). Thus Caesar's policy was to destroy the fixed power bases of the *oppida*, to eliminate the chieftains who opposed him (e.g., Vercingetorix), and to "corrupt" the rest. In this case, corruption meant to make the interests of the ruling class coincide with the interests of the imperial power.[27]

This was impossible in the lands inhabited by the Germans. The promise of booty was paltry compared to Gaul; German society was relatively primitive; fixed targets like the Gallic *oppida* were nonexistent; and the social centers of power were not clearly fixed, except in the case of a few tribes. In other words, it was impossible to build a bridgehead between Roman and German society. Defeating one tribe did not mean the subjugation of the rest. Indeed in most cases the appearance of new tribal leaders meant that even the initial conquest was ephemeral. Like the phoenix, the destroyed German tribes would rise again and again, making foreign domination impossible.[28] Containment thus became the key strategy, but this did not mean that the Rhine was used in the manner of a modern border. The wide strip of terrain represented by the *limes* was applied against the Germans, and Roman control extended for some distance beyond the right bank.

Generally, then, the Romans made sure that a wide strip of the Rhine's right bank was kept free of German settlements at least until Vespasian (69–79). Kunow describes a more fluid situation south of the Lippe River, which flows into the Rhine at a right angle north of Bonn. Archaeological evidence, says Kunow, shows the presence of both Romans and Germans on the right bank. In the case of the Romans it is clear that as elsewhere they used the area not for settlement or for military camps but to exploit natural resources. After a period of depopulation following Varus's defeat in A.D. 9, the Germans were apparently allowed to resettle the region toward the end of the first and continuing until the early third century, at least in numbers that the Romans did not consider threatening. The peace reigned for about 150 years here until the Frankish invasion of the third century. In the aftermath of the Frankish invasion the Romans made certain that the *limes* on the right bank of the Rhine would be depopulated again. This was the situation south of the Lippe River, where the Romans faced the greatest hostility; the region north of the Lippe was easily controlled due to the nature of the terrain (swamps) and the subordinate attitude of local allied tribes (e.g., the Batavians).[29]

In conclusion, the strategy of the Roman Empire changed in its efficiency and application according to obstacles like terrain, a lack of economic gain, and even an unwillingness to be aggressive. The Romans considered their borders to be temporary launching pads for conquest and glory, at least until the third century. Yet Rome's offensive strategy was more complex, and it assumed that a good offense was based on a strong defense. And in the long run the dangers inherent to some territories and the inability to make permanent and fruitful advances must have convinced the emperors to give priority to defensible borders. But it was not until the third century that defense prevailed over offense along the Rhine and Danube. However, the Roman policy remained offensive in the Near East.

The Emperor as Manager of War

The motivation behind Roman imperialism was complex, as William V. Harris has brilliantly shown for the republican period.[30] The imperial age would retain some of the characteristics of the past, like the desire for glory, security, and material acquisition. Conquest for political gain remained the privilege only of the emperor and his family, for Augustus and his successors would make sure that victory on the battlefield was a personal monopoly— and jealously guarded. There was no limit in the motive for expansion: The territories controlled by Rome, as Cicero said of Macedonia, were wherever the swords and spears of her soldiers were.[31] The Roman frontier was an eternally shifting boundary.[32]

As we pass to the imperial period, another motivation becomes increasingly dominant: the superiority of Roman culture. It was proper for Romans to conquer barbarians because Romans were culturally superior. Non-Romans and non-Greeks were inferior not because of their blood but because they did not yet share the value system, the language, and the sophistication of the Romans. Thus Roman imperialism was not racially motivated, although the Romans did use the stereotypes of imperialism. Those beyond their frontiers deserved to be conquered because they were not quite human (at least according to the Greco-Roman definition of humanity). Such dehumanization implied moral and legal authority to act cruelly; their very inhumanity was the justification.[33] Only the oceans defined the limits of the Roman world.[34] These were the ideas prevailing at the center of imperial power.

Ancient Rome had no foreign ministry, no department as such to direct foreign policy and wage war, although some individuals must have exerted great influence. Marcus Vipsanius Agrippa (ca. 64 B.C.–A.D. 12), for instance, boasted familial, emotional, and friendly ties to Augustus. Civilians, especially those residing outside Rome, had little or no influence: "The decision to engage in a war of conquest was determined by the imperial will and not by pressures from definable groups with interests at stake."[35] And the harsh reality was that it was beneficial for emperors to be warlike. Wars strengthened their power base and fulfilled the main value of being an upper-class Roman. By being warlike the emperor fulfilled the desires of his people.

Peace did not suit the military rank and file. The standard term of service were close to two decades, sometimes more, and a comfortable life afterward depended on how much money one accumulated during service and received upon discharge. Peace brought physical security, a condition to be treasured no doubt—but at what cost? Violence must have permeated everyday life: Suicide was a solution to problems, games pitted humans against humans, and people were offered as prey to wild animals. As Harris argues in regard to republican Rome,[36] *bia* (violence) was part and parcel of the Roman ethos. Thus after Augustus, Roman soldiers did not transform into mild-mannered individuals concerned about the bloodletting. More likely they stood ready to put their lives in danger in a legal occupation that was supported and glorified by society, a job that could bring them considerable material gain.

Victory brought eternal glory to most upper-class Romans, promotion to some, and booty to all. After the conquest of Jerusalem, so much gold was distributed to the soldiers that its value fell in Syria. Glory and spoil were the promises of commanders before a campaign or battle began. And the fringe benefits for people accustomed to violence included, besides the massacre of all adult men, the enslavement of the rest of the civilian population and a share in the material plunder.[37]

Keeping soldiers happy and satisfied was an absolute necessity for all emperors, for their rule was secure only as long as the army remained loyal. And the standing army established by Augustus could create more problems than the armies of the early republic. Back then the soldiers were sent home at the end of a campaign, whereas after Augustus they remained under arms until the end of many years of service. It is no surprise that the triumph—the most visible expression of a victorious general—would increasingly be the private reserve of the emperor or members of the imperial house, that the tenure of military commanders became increasingly shorter to prevent them from building a power basis, and that in most cases the emperor or his family members led the armies in person.

Yet military glory (or at least the appearance of it) was a necessity even for rulers who preferred peace. Glory defined him as a great Roman. Success on the battlefield was the direct avenue to esteem and respect. Thus all rulers were potentially warlike in thought if not in deed, even when the emperor-as-great-soldier became less common. Even Augustus himself, often considered the prototype, can be viewed in this different light if we take his final instructions to Tiberius at face value. He must have been sincere when he spelled out the defensive policy. Yet his instructions were written at a time of mental and physical deterioration; he was in great distress after Varus's defeat in Germany in A.D. 9.

Still, Augustus not only consolidated what the Romans already had but also gained new lands for the empire. Thus it is conceivable that his advice was intended only for the situation as it then existed. The frontiers, which he ordered Tiberius to defend, were different from his previous policy—including proceeding past the Rhine to the Elbe—which would have required expansion north of the Danube. He also never gave up his interest in advancing the Roman border beyond the Euphrates.[38] Thus Augustus's tenure assumed secure but stronger borders—and thus aggression. He extended Roman control over all corners of Spain, a task that had been left unfinished for about 200 years; he subjugated Alpine tribes who had thus far maintained independence and remained a potential threat to Italy and Rome; and he sent expeditions to Arabia and Ethiopia in hopes of conquering new land and riches. Roman imperial policy thus followed these guidelines: to expand the empire, but cautiously and in stages; to make the waging of war the monopoly of the emperor and his family; and to concentrate on the European frontiers.[39]

The Verdict of the Battlefield

The Romans were successful not only because of superior strategy but also superior tactics. Although standardized for most units, the armor worn by the legionnaires varied. Officers seemingly preferred the muscled cuirass typical of Hellenistic civilization, sometimes with a band wrapped around the waist to indicate status. Their cuirass was cut shorter with the passage of time, probably to distinguish officers from the rank and file, who at times adopted similar armor. The rank and file wore a mail shirt in the early decades of the first century; later other armor types became more common—the scale *(lorica segmentata)* and the muscled cuirass. The first one, the *lorica segmentata*, was the dominant type. Metal plates were held together with hooks, rivets, and hinges giving the legionnaire more flexibility, providing a lighter weight (9 kilograms versus the 12–15 kilograms of the mail shirt), and spreading it evenly over the body.[40]

The shield *(scutum)* underwent a design change. The legionnaires used the oval shield typical of the republican period until the early years of the Principate. Then the oval top and bottom were cut in such a way that the shield became rectangular. At times it kept its convex form, and at times (probably among the auxiliaries) it was flat. A sample from Dura Europos in Syria shows that it was made of laminated strips of wood covered with leather that could be heavily decorated. The plywood was thicker at the center, where a round boss stood (oval in the past). The shield edge was reinforced either with rawhide or more commonly bronze. The *scutum* remained large and heavy—about 5.5 kilograms, 7.5 kilograms if the center was thickened.[41]

Whereas the auxiliary used primarily a spear *(hasta)* and a long sword *(spatha)*, the legionnaire's offensive weapons were much more varied. They could include javelin *(pilum)* or spear, short sword *(gladius)*, and dagger. But the two weapons that reflected best the legionary's offensive characteristics of the first two centuries were the *pilum* and *gladius*.[42] But the *pilum* might have been used increasingly less often during this period, and the Roman soldier may have been primarily a swordsman.[43] Although the *gladius* was the legionnaire's primary weapon, it is likely that the *pilum* remained an important weapon until substituted by the spear during the late empire.

The *gladius* blade, fairly wide and initially tapered but eventually with straight sides, measured between 50–56 centimeters if tapered and 44–55 centimeters if straight.[44] It was the ideal weapon for thrusting, seemingly the preferred tactic of the Roman soldier. Agricola, for instance, urged his German auxiliaries, when they faced the Britons, to take advantage of the awkwardness of their opponents' long swords by coming quickly to hand-to-hand fighting, then to hit them first with the shield bosses and finally to stab their faces with the swords.[45] At Mons Graupius, also in Britain, Agricola again urged his soldiers to come to close quarters and to use both shield and sword.[46] And Vegetius, writing between the end of the fourth century and the first half of the fifth century but reflecting the military usages of the past, advises thrusting, which can be more deadly.[47] Peter Connolly, an expert on Roman weapons, also maintains that until the middle of the first century A.D. the smaller Roman soldier must have fought from a crouching position to strike at his opponent's stomach, at least against the taller Celts. Connolly concludes this on the basis of the changes in the helmets used by the Roman soldier. During the end of the first century B.C. the Montefortino helmet was abandoned for the Coolus helmet, which raised the neck peak to eye level and set a sturdy frontal peak to the brow of the helmet—all changes that facilitated a crouching posture for the attacker.[48] Adrian Goldsworthy disagrees. Crouching, he says, would have been an impractical and awkward posture that would have made the legionnaire an easy target for the Celts' slashing long swords.[49] Yet at some point crouching, at least briefly, must have been a good option for a shorter man wielding a much shorter weapon. Goldsworthy also seems unconvinced on the priority of thrusting over slashing. There are numerous visual instances, he writes, of delivering other forms of sword blows, especially cutting.[50] Such evidence does exist on Trajan's famous column, for instance; yet one must wonder whether this was an unrealistic depiction, an artistic homage to the classical Greek representation of close-quarter fighting.[51]

Le Bohec argues that the combination of long sword and spear is typical of the auxiliary infantry. It is also likely that during the first century auxiliary defensive armor (a leather cuirass) was of poorer quality than legionary armor. However, horsemen (about 120 to a legion), normally all composed of auxiliaries, are shown wearing mailcoats over leather and oval or rectangular shields on Trajan's column.[52]

Any marching order for the Roman army was of great concern to the commander, because an army strung out in a long column—the norm being six men abreast—must have been an enticing target. The order must have varied depending on the circumstances and the terrain, although certain principles prevailed. The baggage containing the supplies and the personal assets of the legionnaires was placed in the most secure position, normally the center of the long column, nearest the legionnaires. The cavalry led the column; other units of horsemen, and sometimes infantry, moved ahead as lookouts, surveying the terrain and ascertaining that no enemy was deployed for battle or waiting in ambush. The march was closed by light and heavy auxiliary infantry together with a sizable part of the cavalry.[53]

A marching army set a fortified camp every night. The camps' layout was standardized in the sense that the command, the units, and so on were always placed in similar locations, making it easier to organize a defense or an attack. Defensive works—ditches, walls, palisades, ramparts, sharp stakes embedded in the terrain—meant any attacker had to overcome a series of obstacles before reaching the soldiers. Ditches and other obstacles were sometimes built to protect the Roman line during the early stage of battle.

Roman battles did not always follow the same canon, as the Greek hoplites did. The Romans retained considerable flexibility in their tactical approach, adapting it to the characteristics of the terrain and those of the enemy. They were mostly successful in this, although at times (e.g., against the German tribes and the Parthians) they were unable to solve the problem of how to subdue those threats even though their failure was dictated not by their battlefield performance but by complex logistical difficulties or the social structure of the enemy.

Roman battle tactics were characterized by cavalry deployment as flank protection and to guard against encirclement, careful arrangement of the lines, with soldiers ready to provide mass or mobility as required, the use of reserves to exploit a break in the enemy line or to strengthen a vulnerable position in their own, and skill to counter enemy maneuvers.[54] One must also add aggressiveness, flexibility of maneuver, superiority in hand-to-hand encounters, good training and discipline, competent leadership, competent and brave noncommissioned officers like the centurions, and a belief in the ability to recover from any setback. It was not a perfect army, but it was superior to any other up to that time in the Mediterranean and Near East. It almost always won on the battlefield.[55]

The introduction of the cohorts—480 men each, ten per legion—and of identically armed legionnaires helped along the introduction of different line deployments.[56] There is no mention of the checkerboard formation that was used during some stages of the republican period. Roman armies from the late republic (e.g., under Caesar) through the first two centuries of the imperial age could deploy in single, two, three, or even four lines. A typical deployment per legion in three lines could have seen four cohorts in the first and three each in the second and third.[57] In reality the Romans tended to adopt the deployment that best suited the terrain or the type and number of adversaries. We find Caesar using four lines on the right of his battle line against Pompeius at the Battle of Pharsalus to counter an expected cavalry assault. Pompeius himself had deployed his men in three rows.[58] Caesar also deployed three lines against the Germans under Ariovistus in 58 B.C.,[59] but more often two,[60] which seems to have been the Romans' favored deployment. At times, however, Roman generals (Caesar again) also lined their men in a single formation if a numerically superior enemy threatened their flanks.[61]

The basic fighting unit of the legion, the cohort of 480 men at full strength or double the strength for the first cohort starting in the second half of the first century A.D., was large yet small enough to provide flexibility. As Hans Delbrück brilliantly argued long ago, the Romans first made their legion into a phalanx with "joints"—that is, flexible and thus unlike the Greeks' rigid phalanx; deployed it in different lines that could support each other or perform different functions; and finally joined the smaller units (the centuries) into larger, compact formations (cohorts), which could provide flexibility and power at the same time. "The cohort tactics marked the apogee of the development which the fighting skill of ancient infantry could reach."[62]

Repeated drilling and discipline were among the secrets of Roman success; discipline is a continuous refrain among ancient authors in comparing legionnaires to barbarian enemies. The Britons, says Tacitus, "fight individually and are collectively conquered."[63] And while the Pannonians formed for battle at daybreak, Tiberius held back his men, leaving the opponents standing in full battle array amid fog and driving rain; he signaled to attack only when he felt that the Pannonians were faint from exhaustion and exposure.[64] The Jewish writer Josephus marvels at the discipline and training of the Roman soldiers.[65] Seemingly born with weapons in their hands, "they never have a truce in training, never wait for emergencies to arise." They are at perfect ease in the shock of battle: "No confusion breaks their customary formation, no panic paralyzes, no fatigue exhausts them."[66] Even the strongest barbarians would attack in scattered parties (later they learned to imitate the Romans).[67]

The mechanics of face-to-face confrontation in the first two centuries of the imperial period must have been similar to the encounters following the Second Punic War. Deployed in lines eight to three men deep (three or four against infantry, six to eight against cavalry), they disrupted the enemy with the *pila* then moved in for the kill with shield and *gladius*, hitting first the enemy buckler and then trusting the weapon into an opening in the defenses.[68] As the cohorts' deployment indicates, there must have been a tendency to attack in waves—to pull back the frontmost line while pushing forward with the next.[69] This did not make the Romans invincible—at times they suffered terrible reverses—but they were always ready to fight another day and believed that defeat in one battle did not mean defeat in war. Even typical examples of Roman successes illustrate their overwhelming power: the crushed rebellion under Boudicca (see next section), defeat of the German tribes, masterful engineering in Gaul and Judaea.

Boudicca's Rebellion

When Boudicca's Rebellion broke out, the Roman legate Gaius Suetonius Paulinus was away on a punitive expedition against the Druid stronghold of the island of Mona (Anglesey) in the Irish Sea (see Figure 6.2). The Romans accused the Druids of savagery: They offered their prisoners' blood on the altars of their deities and used human entrails to consult their gods. In reality, what troubled the Romans about the Celtic priests was their association with fomenters of rebellion against Roman rule.

The campaign in Anglesey was successful, although fear struck Paulinus's soldiers during the first encounter with the Druids. Anglesey's beach was lined with a crowd of men and women. The women, attired in black, with wild hair streaming over their faces and shoulders, held torches as a circle of Druids lifted their hands to the sky asking the gods to punish the invaders.

FIGURE 6.2   Roman Britain

Paulinus's men stood in dismay, then charged and cut the priests and their followers to pieces.[70]

Queen Boudicca's tribe—the Iceni—occupied a territory across the Irish Sea on the British mainland that included parts of modern Norfolk and Sussex, north of Cambridge and Colchester. Upon his death, Boudicca's husband had named his two daughters and the Roman emperor co-heirs to his throne, probably in the hope that the Romans would not destroy his family's rule as he had recognized the emperor. His decision would have made sense under normal circumstances: "A long and established principle of Roman policy," says Tacitus, "[was to employ] kings as the instruments of their servitude."[71] In this case, however, the Roman soldiers stationed in

England—displaying callous indifference, cruelty, and greed—undertook a campaign of exploitation: Centurions pillaged the kingdom, Boudicca was subjected to the lash, her daughters were violated, and the Iceni elite was robbed of its estates.[72] Moreover, a prior gift of cash and a money loan forced upon the Iceni were recalled.[73]

Dramatic omens—harbingers that seemed to favor the Britons—fostered the queen's thirst for revenge. The statue of Victory, a symbol of Roman rule in the colony of Camulodunum (Colchester), fell to the ground for no apparent reason, her back turned as in flight. In Rome, women started to shriek that destruction was near, and people reported that alien cries had been heard in the Senate; a vision of the ruined British colony had appeared. The sea around England had become red, and human corpses washed upon the beaches.[74] The time to act had arrived, especially because the commander in chief, Paulinus, was at Anglesey in the Irish Sea, and the Romans had failed to prepare for any threat.

Boudicca cut an impressive physical appearance. Very tall, with fierce eyes, a commanding voice, and tawny hair reaching her waist, she would wear a golden necklace and a dress of many colors over which a brooch fastened her thick mantle.[75] She gathered the support of another tribe, the Trinovantes, who had settled in Essex, probably relocating from what is now Belgium. The rebels easily overpowered the Roman posts. They captured Camulodunum and defeated the soldiers that tried to stop their operations. Even Paulinus, by now returned from Anglesey, did not dare face Boudicca's men immediately. He withdrew, leaving two other cities, Londinium (London) and Verulamium (a town adjacent to St. Albans), to fall to the rebels despite the laments of their inhabitants. By now the rebel army had grown from 120,000 to 230,000;[76] they had slaughtered close to 70,000 Roman citizens and allies, some of them after horrible torture, and they took no prisoners.[77] Dio Cassius reports that they subjected even the noblest women to great brutality.[78]

Enemy acts of cruelty described in the ancient Roman sources should be viewed with caution, yet the Britons would have been justified to react with great anger and violence. And there is little doubt that the Romans were heavily outnumbered; Paulinus's forces totaled some 10,000.[79] He had no choice but to stand and fight: The Britons were pressing him relentlessly, and his food supplies were dwindling.[80]

Characteristically Roman, Paulinus moved over to the offensive. Since the enemy could have outflanked him in any pitched battle, he faced three problems: how to choose terrain that gave some protection to the flanks; how to retain the initiative and exploit the element of surprise; and how to maximize the legions' strength against the Britons' style of warfare. He withdrew near St. Albans in a position where his rear was protected by woods and his flanks by a defile. He deployed the armies in the usual three wings but added several refinements. The legionnaires held the center in close order; the auxiliaries flanked them; and the cavalry covered the extreme wings.[81] However, the Roman phalanx would assume the attack, for when the moment came the legionnaires at the center and the auxiliaries on the right and left wings engaged the enemy in wedge formations, a deployment typical of a host that intends to smash the enemy's line and cohesion.[82]

The Britons may have been certain of victory, for they moved without the tight discipline and order of the Romans, the women following to take part in the slaughter.[83] As they rushed carelessly through the defile, they threw their javelins at the Romans, who had been instructed to stand motionless for the moment. Once the enemies had exhausted their missiles, the Romans, as Paulinus had instructed, rushed forward in a wedge formation in close order. In face-to-face battle, the Romans would surely win. The close quarters gave advantage to the Romans, who used their heavy shields to strike their opponents before dispatching them with their short swords. The Britons' long swords must have hampered them, and the small, round shields they favored offered little protection against the Romans' *gladius* and *scutum*.[84]

Eventually the Briton line withdrew in disorder from the battlefield, encumbered by their chariots and the presence of many noncombatants. In their customary manner the Romans spared no one that could be reached—men, women, even the baggage animals. The Romans suffered only 400 casualties, the Britons a little less than 80,000. Boudicca escaped and probably chose suicide by poison soon thereafter.[85] Paulinus's punishment did not stop there. He was so harsh in his reprisal that Rome replaced him with another commander.[86] It made better sense to be lenient, for the Britons promptly paid their tribute, as long as the conquerors were not engaged in harsh wrongdoing.[87]

The Germans

Two events were instrumental in curtailing Rome's supremacy over the Germans east of the Rhine and north of the Danube: Varus's defeat and Tiberius's expedition. Yet this does not mean that all Germans escaped Rome's hegemony everywhere and at all times. Rome controlled the right

FIGURE 6.3   *German Lands and Tribal Groups Around the First Century A.D.*

banks of both rivers at least up to a certain distance from the waters (see
Figure 6.3). Moreover, they founded and settled German towns like Cologne
(Colonia Agrippinensis, an important imperial city) and Bonn (Bonna),
where a fortress was manned by auxiliaries until the third century.

The Romans remembered defeats as well as victories with equal intensity,
whether they be the sack of Rome by the Gauls (ca. 387 B.C.), Hannibal's
victory at Cannae (216 B.C.), or Crassus's defeat to the Parthians at Carrhae
(53 B.C.). And Varus's defeat to the German Cheruscan leader Arminius in
the Teutoburg Forest in A.D. 9 was burned in their collective memory. It certainly impacted Augustus's expansion policy toward the end of his life. From
then on, emperors looked at new conquests with great caution.

In A.D. 6, three years before Varus's defeat, Augustus had instructed his appointed heir, Tiberius, to solve the German problem. Tiberius had experience with Germans. In A.D. 4 he penetrated lands beyond the Weser River; one year later he reached the Elbe. As a fleet on his left flank carried supplies, he moved forward with his army, conducting an exploration survey up to the Jutland.[88] These two campaigns probably convinced Tiberius of the importance of subduing the Germans: As long as Rome did not control the highlands of the Germans' southern territories (roughly modern-day Bohemia), any submission by the Germans would be fleeting; they would probably renege as soon as the Roman troops moved back to Gaul.[89]

In Bohemia the Germans had established a strong kingdom under Maroboduus, the king of the Marcomanni; around 9 B.C. the Romans had expelled them from the upper and middle Main, where the Marcomanni had settled almost a century earlier from ancestral lands in Saxony and Thuringia. Maroboduus—tall, strong, courageous, and intelligent—skillfully extended his power over neighboring German and Celtic tribes, trained his men in the Roman manner of discipline, and gained great influence over the German tribes in the north (in fact, Arminius sent him Varus's head in homage after his Teutoburg victory).[90] The Romans feared Maroboduus, for he was a serious threat even to Italy; his kingdom bordered on the west and north with other German tribes, on the southeast with Pannonia (the lands south and west of the Danube), and on the south with Noricum (roughly modern-day Austria), offering a route to the Italian plains through mountain passes.[91]

Tiberius prepared his campaign with care. The attack against Maroboduus had to be carried out from two directions—five legions from the west, coming from across the Rhine, and twelve more from the east, from across the Danube. It is likely that this mass of forces was intended not just to destroy Maroboduus's power but to use his territory as the launching pad for extending Rome's control from the Danube to the North Sea, thereby moving the frontier from the Rhine to the Elbe. The campaign failed to materialize, for, as Tiberius began, great troubles emerged on his rear. They started among the Illyrians of Dalmatia and then spread to the other Balkan regions (modern-day Croatia, Slovenia, and Serbia). Almost three years passed before the insurgents were brought to bay—on the eve of news of Varus's disaster. One might even argue that it was Bato (the Illyrian leader), and not Arminius, who prevented Rome from dominating the entire continent.[92]

The battle in the Teutoburg Forest in A.D. 9 is a low mark in Roman military history (see Figure 6.4). The legate in charge was Publius Quinctilius

FIGURE 6.4   *Area of the Teutoburg Battle*

Varus. Varus's father, a follower of Caesar's murderers, had covered his body
with the insignia of his office and asked his freedman to end his life when
his faction was defeated at Philippi (42 B.C.).[93] Slow of mind and weak of
body, Varus was an administrator more than a soldier, one who was interested in personal gain. He had been poor when he was appointed Syria's
governor; he returned to Rome a rich man.[94]

   Varus's behavior before and during the campaign is a textbook example
of what generals should not do. He misunderstood the German attitude toward political subjection, overestimated their faithfulness to alliances and
friendships, and underestimated their style of warfare. He treated the Germans as if they were easterners (i.e., people who were comfortable with

Rome's supremacy); he dealt with them as slaves, says the historian Dio; and he asked tribute as if they were subject peoples. Moreover, he tried to quickly transform their lifestyle into his definition of Roman civilization, including policies that created great resentment among people who treasured independence and individualism.[95]

The German attack was launched in the vicinity of the Weser River. According to Hans Delbrück, there were three Roman legions, six auxiliary cohorts, and three cavalry squadrons—in all about 12,000–18,000 men.[96] Varus advanced without keeping his legions together.[97] He acted as if he were dispensing justice in Rome rather than leading an army in enemy territory, according to Velleius Paterculus, a man who knew Germany well, as he had fought there during the same period.[98] But the Germans were setting a deadly trap under the young Cheruscan leader Arminius, who had himself served under the Romans and received citizenship and the equestrian rank in reward.[99] He carefully hid his hatred of the Romans; with another German—probably his father, Segimer—he had become the constant companion of Varus, often sharing the Roman commander's mess, a sign of great trust.[100]

Varus was deaf to any suggestion of a trap. Yet his position was perilous: He was deep inside Germany, his troops spread through the countryside. The Roman commander even dismissed a warning from a member of Arminius's own tribe. And Arminius engineered another stratagem that ensured that the Roman forces became even more scattered: He asked Varus to act as arbiter of the quarrels among German tribes located farther in the interior. Varus complied and, even worse, allowed Arminius to leave the entourage when the German suggested that he would rally the allied forces in support of the main operation.[101] Thus at the time of the attack Varus was not on guard; his army was spread out; the terrain was unsuitable to legion warfare; and he had enemies on his rear.

The battle began with the Romans scattered in many groups across broken terrain marked by ravines and trees so dense that they had to be cleared for soldiers to proceed. The march was also encumbered by the presence of women, children, servants, and the supply wagons. At this stage, it was impossible to move as a cohesive body. Violent rains and winds worsened the terrain. The slippery ground, combined with the broken logs and roots, made walking treacherous. The winds broke treetops, which fell on the legionnaires.[102]

The Romans, hemmed in by forests and marshes and pummeled by bad weather, were surprised in an ambush.[103] The Germans surrounded them from all sides, launching javelins from a distance and then moving easily, for they knew the paths and were accustomed to the environment. Then they closed in for the kill; the Romans could keep no semblance of order because the soldiers were mixed with civilians, wagons, and beasts of burden. The first day of fighting seems to have ended when Varus's troops finally found a place where they could strike camp after abandoning or burning most of the wagons.[104]

The morning after must have brought some respite, because, as the Romans withdrew, they found open terrain where the legions could deploy and the Germans did not dare strike. But the Romans soon entered another forest in seeking the safety of the Rhine. They were an easy target. The forest was cramped; soldiers bumped into each other as they tried to repulse the enemy's attack. And it was here that Varus's men suffered the greatest casualties.[105]

The third day must have brought similar conditions, and by the dawn of the fourth day the situation was dire indeed. New rains and a violent storm weakened the remaining Roman resolve. Most of their weapons, soaked with water, had become useless. And as the Roman forces became smaller, the enemy was getting larger, for many joined Arminius once they realized that the Romans had reached the point of collapse and that plunder could be had.[106]

Varus and some of his officers decided that the end was near and took their own lives to avoid a more cruel death on the battlefield and torture should they be captured. It was "a terrible yet unavoidable act," says Dio; Velleius Paterculus adds with bitterness that this was a man who chose to die by his own hand instead of having the courage of fighting to the end.[107] And it is hard to disagree with Paterculus that Varus's suicide, although considered a noble act by the Romans, was premature, for resistance was still possible at that stage.[108] When the army realized that the commander had chosen suicide, some imitated him and some asked others to end their life; only a few were able to retire to a fortified place. The Germans were unable to take the fort: They were uninitiated in the art of siege, the Roman auxiliary archers mounted a tough defense from the ramparts, and looting became more important to Arminius's men. Finally, the Romans were able to trick the besiegers: Trumpeters sounded as if a relief army were coming to their aid. And a relief battle group coming up from the Rhine convinced the Germans to stop their pursuit.[109] Few of the 12,000–18,000 Roman soldiers survived. News of the disaster stunned Augustus. He cut neither hair nor beard for months afterward and sometimes, in utter desperation, would bang his head against a door crying, "Quinctilius Varus, give me back my legions!" And from then on, the defeat was observed every year as a day of "sorrow and mourning."[110]

Thus the debacle in the Teutoburg Forest was burned in the collective memory of the emperor and the Roman people; it also became an important symbol in the history of the German people. Yet the battle only partially explains why Roman expansion stopped where it did. The encounter was an oddity, for the serious logistical and environment difficulties caused the Romans to behave unlike themselves. Varus misjudged the nature of the opponent, ignored warnings from credible sources, stumbled into an ambush, split his army, trusted people he shouldn't have, and finally, losing his nerve—and any remaining hope for resistance—took his own life.

In contrast, Iulius Caesar Germanicus, a dashing man greatly loved by the Roman people and Augustus, would play a leading role during the Roman expeditions into Germany in A.D. 14, 15, and 16. His story exemplifies the strengths and liabilities of both the Romans and the Germans during this period in history.

Germanicus was the heir to Tiberius, his uncle. But he died mysteriously in the east—poisoned by a friend of Tiberius, people would allege. His father, Drusus, had been a brilliant general under Augustus and died in A.D. 13 after he fell from a horse. The father had gained the surname Germanicus after a series of successful campaigns in Germany, during which he had brought several tribes under Roman control, once even reaching the Elbe. His son followed in his footsteps, probably with revenge on his mind, for Varus's defeat in the Teutoburg Forest had nullified most of the conquests and weakened the hegemony that his father had established across the Rhine.

Germanicus led four campaigns into Germany, the first in the fall of A.D. 14, two more next year, and the last in A.D. 16. He inflicted serious defeats on the enemy in the second campaign. The last, and largest, campaign ended in failure of a sort, for he was unable to subdue the German lands. The elusive nature of his quarry and a change of mind of the newly crowned emperor, Tiberius, stopped him. The truth was that Rome faced insurmountable obstacles, some of its own making, in the drive to conquer Germany.

Unlike Gaul, the German territories were a logistical nightmare. food was scarce, so the Romans had to carry most of their supplies through difficult terrain—marshes, dense forests, and broken terrain. The Romans tried to overcome the problem by using the river system for transport—the Lippe, the Ems, and the Weser, for instance—and by building forts (e.g., at

Aliso at the source of the Lippe) as food depots. But in the end these did not work. Navigating the turbulent North Sea to reach the mouths of the Ems and Weser was difficult for the fleets, and the forts were easy targets for the tribes. Neither could the Romans live off the land; the economy in this region was based on livestock and hunting and only secondarily on agriculture.[111]

Gaul had presented an easy target, for it was a relatively developed urban civilization. Conquering their *oppida* (fortified urban centers) was enough to bring the Gauls to their knees, but Germans had no major urban centers. They congregated mostly in small villages that could be quickly evacuated if attacked or if lands elsewhere offered better resources. These villages provided minuscule incentive to Roman soldiers bent on looting, and the poor natural resources (even iron, which would make modern Germany formidable) were not enticing to Rome's ruling elites. Finally, the Germans' type of warfare baffled the Romans. The Gauls had always accommodated some sort of confrontation, either by seeking refuge in their *oppida*, where the Romans' sieges would eventually prevail, or in pitched battles, which invariably favored the Romans. The Germans, in contrast, cunningly refused face-to-face confrontations and usually attacked only where the terrain suited them and where they knew that the Romans were at a disadvantage—in a forest, in boggy terrain, on broken land.

This does not mean that the Roman troops could not win a war of attrition or that Rome was interested only in economic windfall. Conquest for conquest's sake or for security reasons (real or not) always remained an alternative. Yet the situation in Germany was somewhat similar to that in the Scottish highlands. The burdens of conquest were great, the gains minuscule, the danger serious. Germanicus's campaigns demonstrate this.

In the fall of A.D. 14. Germanicus led about 20,000 men into the area south of the Lippe, which flows into the Rhine's right bank opposite Vetera (near Birten), a major military base under Augustus. He divided his army into four groups, pillaging a region about 73 kilometers wide.[112] He returned to Germany the next spring, advancing from two directions; Germanicus personally led his soldiers from Mainz on the southwest, and his subordinate commander, Caecina, struck east from Vetera, following the Lippe, and then moved deeper into Germany. The operation was carried out with about 30,000 soldiers (legionnaires and auxiliaries) and about 10,000 support troops. It was a daring combined thrust, for Germanicus's target was the Chatti tribe near the upper Weser, and Caecina's drive threatened Arminius's Cheruscans on the middle Weser, thereby taking them out of the fight. Yet the campaign did not bring the expected results, for the Chatti refused to face Germanicus, and another tribe, the Marsi, attacked Caecina during his withdrawal. Still, the foray allowed the Romans to reconstruct the Aliso fort at the source of the Lippe River, an essential logistical location.[113]

Germanicus led another campaign before the year ended. It would be the most ambitious thus far, with eight legions and probably some 50,000 support troops. The target was twofold: Arminius's Cheruscans on the middle Weser, and their allies, the Bructeri, who were closer to the Roman lines north of the Lippe, near modern Münster. Germanicus kept the main body of soldiers in two battle groups, one under his command, the other under Caecina. The supplies were entrusted to a fleet that navigated the North Sea coastline and then penetrated the interior via the Ems River. Again, all the clever preparations brought limited gains. Arminius refused a pitched battle; supplies became scarce over time; and finally Germanicus was forced to withdraw. The return was more perilous, for it opened an opportunity for Arminius to counterattack. The cavalry, forced to follow the coastline, was on the verge of destruction; Caecina was suddenly attacked by Arminius, and for a while it seemed he was doomed to the same fate as Varus. His cleverness and bravery saved them, but an important role was played by Arminius's paternal uncle, Inguomerus, who convinced his own men to loot the Roman camps instead of inflicting the killing blow. Caecina took advantage of the situation and counterattacked, defeating the Germans.[114]

The next year, A.D. 16, opened with a short campaign to relieve the fort at Aliso, besieged by Arminius. The German leader, never willing to face the Romans in a pitched battle, withdrew, leaving Germanicus's six legions in control of the battlefield. Germanicus's quarry had again escaped with minimal damage. This time, however, Germanicus thought he had found the solution. He decided to strike into Cheruscan territory. He seems to have kept the army and supplies together, moving them with a fleet of 1,000 ships along the northern coast of Germany and then up the Ems or the Weser River. (Delbrück thinks that at least some soldiers marched overland.)[115] Apparently Germanicus defeated the Germans in two great battles, the first at Idistaviso near Minden; again, as the winter approached and supplies dwindled, he had to withdraw. Unlike Julius Caesar in Gaul, he did not have the luxury of wintering in Germany to continue the campaign the next spring.

Germanicus brought some luster back to the Roman military. Arminius had escaped, but he had also been wounded. Still, if the goal was to bring the

Cheruscans and other Germans under Roman supremacy, his endeavor was incomplete at best and a failure at worst. And the new emperor, Tiberius, recalled him to Rome either because he was worried about the rising popularity of the throne's presumptive heir or because he regarded the conquest of Germany not to be worthwhile politically or economically.

As they did with the Gauls, the Britons, and the easterners, the Romans could not establish a power base by making the Germans partners in power. Thus the German nobility escaped Roman domination. Yet this very situation also made the Germans a transitory threat to the Roman Empire, at least until the third century. The German tribes did have an aristocracy, and the noblemen were their natural leaders in wartime, but the German social structure did not provide a permanence for this group, especially during peace. Unlike in Rome, where the aristocrats' commonality of interests vis-à-vis other groups prevailed, within the German tribes factional conflict pitted aristocrat against aristocrat, thus preventing hegemony by any single faction. The Cheruscans, Arminius's tribe, provide the best illustration. Despite their great victory at the Teutoburg Forest and Arminius's cunning and charisma, the Cheruscan nobles rarely presented a united front against the Romans. Arminius's own father-in-law conveyed to Varus news of his son-in-law's plot, and there is reason to believe such was not an isolated incident. For instance, Arminius's great victory was followed by a series of intrigues and conflicts within his own tribe. His death was offered to Tiberius by another German tribe, the Chatti, but the emperor refused to accept the treacherous offer. Arminius's end would come soon enough; in A.D. 19 a kinsman killed him.[116]

The Stand at Masada

Roman military successes were often a combination of inflexible determination, relentless aggression, threatened reprisals of the cruelest nature, and unmatched engineering skill. Although their superior technology is illustrated by several engagements, none is more dramatic than the siege of Masada (see Figure 6.5).

In A.D. 73 (or more likely in A.D. 74) the last chapter in the Great Jewish Revolt (A.D. 66–73) against Rome was written with the fall of the Masada stronghold. The Revolt resulted in the most tragic consequences for the Jewish people—the destruction of the Second Temple, the burning of Jerusalem, ruthless repression throughout the land, and the most important stimulus for the Diaspora that would last for centuries.

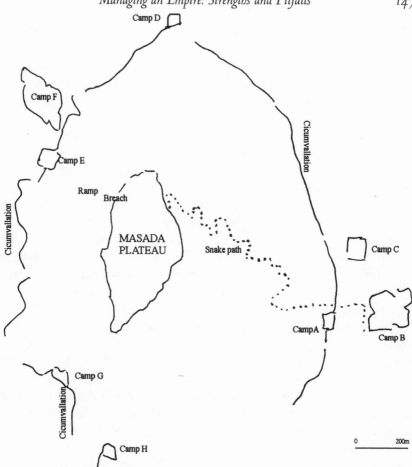

FIGURE 6.5   *The Siege of Masada, ca. A.D. 74*

Masada is a small episode within the context of the Revolt. It came long after Rome had firmly reestablished its rule (Jerusalem's capture in A.D. 70 being the key) and upon the completion of a mop-up operation that had squashed the remnants of the insurrection. Yet the story of 960 Jews who chose death at Masada to Roman rule and reprisal became a most powerful symbol during the formation of the modern state of Israel. To many Jews Masada became a metaphor for the historic voyage, resilience, and hope of Jewish people through the ages and thus is a powerful element in the Jewish identity. In the process, one can argue, the historical truth was distorted or falsified to ensure that an enigmatic mass suicide and a hopeless (and failed) military action would become a most heroic tale.[117]

For the Romans, however, the symbolic importance of Masada must have been much more pedestrian. They could certainly have ignored the presence of a few fighters atop a rocky plateau in the desert with no strategic importance whatsoever. The fighters in Masada were an oddity among most of the Jewish population, and they presented no threat to Roman power. Yet it was natural for the Romans to demonstrate to friend and foe alike that they were willing to go to the ends of the earth to crush the last symbol of a rebellion that began as early as A.D. 6, when the Jewish population resisted the Roman census. The Romans had to destroy Masada as a lesson to every corner of the empire: Resistance to the legions meant inevitable destruction.

There is only one source on Masada, the account given by Josephus Flavius (Joseph Ben-Matityahu), whose objectivity is suspect.[118] Josephus offers a brilliant reconstruction of the Revolt, but he was one of the Jewish fighters who switched sides. Born to a priestly family in Jerusalem in 37 B.C., he had been in command of the fortress of Jotapata (Yodfat) in Galilee during the Revolt. When the Romans were on the verge of capturing the Jotapata fortress, he at first agreed to take his own life instead of falling prisoner, then changed his mind, one of two men to do so. His account of Masada was written in Rome, but he had talked with one of the stronghold's seven survivors and probably had access to Roman sources in the capital. Yet he hated the defenders of Masada, the so-called Sicarii, who instigated the Revolt and were, in his mind, responsible for the catastrophe that befell the Jewish people.

There is no agreement on whether the Sicarii were an independent or a radical Zealot faction or indeed identical to the Zealots, the militant sect that opposed Roman domination. The renowned Israeli archaeologist Yigael Yadin, who was instrumental in digging the Masada site and establishing the parameters of the myth, identifies the defenders of Masada directly with the Zealots.[119] Josephus adds to the confusion. He consistently refers to them as the Sicarii, but he does not identify them as one of the four ideological factions in the Revolt.[120] They probably shared political ideas similar to the Zealots, in the sense that they connected their belief in God with an anti-Roman stand. But they added a radical element to the philosophy: the destruction of any opponent, whether Roman or Jew.

The Sicarii believed there could be no accommodation with the Romans. Their allegiance should be to God only, freed of any secular ruler. Assassination and indiscriminate terror became their weapons. Their name came from *sica*, the small dagger that they hid beneath their robes. In Jerusalem, for instance, they set fire to the high priest's house, killing him and his brother. The Sicarii played an important role during the earlier stages of the city's siege, but Jews who did not share their methods forced them to leave. They withdrew with their women and children to Masada, from which they had displaced a Roman garrison in A.D. 66.[121] There they seem to have continued their campaign against people who rejected their views, although the possibility of defeating the Romans disappeared after Jerusalem's destruction in A.D. 70. Josephus claims that they raided the Jewish village of Ein Gedi, about 17–18 kilometers from Masada, killing any person (man, woman, and child) who had not fled—more than 700 in all—and taking away "the ripest of the crops" to their refuge. They carried out similar raids against other nearby villages.[122]

- The Roman siege of Masada came about three or four years after Jerusalem burned. The most likely date is A.D. 74, for the Roman governor of Judaea, Flavius Silva, who ordered the operation, was appointed to his post that year. (In the spring of the previous year he was still a praetor, i.e., he did not possess the authority to command such an operation.)[123] Masada presented no danger to Roman security, but it certainly was an annoyance and a remaining symbol of the Revolt. Its capture, however, presented logistical problems. Located about 100 kilometers from Jerusalem, the fortress stands on the southwestern side of the Dead Sea, about 2 kilometers from the beach. It is hot, with temperatures reaching 33–40 degrees centigrade from May to October.[124] There were no food or water resources nearby at the time. The closest supply source must have been either Ebron on the west or Ein Gedi on the north. It is likely that teams of servants brought the needed provisions to the Romans from Ein Gedi.[125]

The rock rises dramatically, topped by a small plateau about 400 meters high, shaped like a diamond, about 645 meters by 315 meters.[126] The plateau drops precipitously on all sides, making any ascent possible in only two places, one being the so-called Snake Path on the eastern side, but even there the ascent was difficult and unsuitable for siege operations. The western side was also not favorable for a siege without extensive engineering. It was there that the Romans built their ramp.[127]

The Romans proceeded with typical care. Thirst or starvation would not bring Masada's defenders to bay; it was fortified under Herod the Great (ca. 73–4 B.C.), had large water cisterns, and extensive supplies of food, weapons, and metals. Moreover, the plateau's soil was soft enough to allow some cultivation. Herod had also increased the natural defenses by surrounding the plateau's perimeter with a rock wall. There was a splendid palace and other buildings, some of them used for military purposes.[128]

First the Romans surrounded the place with a 3.5-kilometer circumvallation, a wall that would protect them and prevent any of the besieged from escaping.[129] Building a circumvallation was usually the first task of most sieges. Eight camps, some of them integrated in the circumvallation, were placed to house Legio X Fretensis (Tenth Legion), which had taken part in the subjugation of two other fortified places, Herodium and Macherus.[130] Silva chose the western side for the ramp because it was the only place that could support earthworks.[131] On the basis of Yadin's excavations, the ramp was about 196.5 meters long and 73 meters high from the base to the top, which the Romans firmed up by compacting together stones, a good base for their siege engines. As a geologist has recently argued, it is likely that the ramp was built on an existing natural spur,[132] a conclusion that makes the Roman effort more understandable albeit no less impressive.

The siege took about four to five months at most—building the circumvallation and then the ramp. There is no record of a confrontation before the assault, no evidence that the Romans suffered any casualties. Once the ramp had been completed, the Romans took the installation with little opposition; many women and children must have been present. Silva's soldiers approached the plateau wall with a siege tower cased with metal, a ram, and heavy missile weapons like the *ballistae*, easily discouraging resistance atop the ramparts. They breached the wall, but the Sicarii had skillfully built another defensive barrier made of packed earth and wooden beams. Since the ram was less effective against the earthen barrier, the Romans set the wooden beams on fire. At first the wind blew the flames toward the Romans, but then it changed course, and the wall crumbled. The Romans were ready to storm the next morning.[133]

At this stage the Sicarii leader, Elazar Ben-Yair, decided that the only alternative was mass suicide. The other options—escape, surrender, fighting to the last—were impossible or unpalatable. If they fought until the end, for instance, what would happen to their children and women? One solution would be to kill the noncombatants, which a Jewish tradition claimed about 1,000 years later, then fight to the end.[134] But the decision was suicide, although it was reached with great difficulty, as Ben-Yair had to make his plea twice. Only seven people escaped—five children and two women who hid in a cave; the rest chose to die.[135]

Excavations have confirmed most of Josephus's account, although controversy still surrounds the interpretation of the event. Some do not trust

Josephus's veracity; some criticize the choice of suicide, because it is forbidden in Jewish law and permissible only in case of resistance to conversion; others feel that there was no suicide at all or that the number of suicides was inflated (Yadin found only twenty-five skeletons on the plateau); others attack the modern symbolic use of the event; others look at the Sicarii and the Zealots as the people who brought about a millenarian misery to the Jewish people by causing a war that they could not win, reserving the most terrible punishment for the defeated.

Some of these stand up to scrutiny, others do not, but Masada remains a powerful symbol in the Jewish heritage. Masada also has an important place in military history because its extensive siege works are strong evidence that the Roman art of war united the power of the *gladius* and the skillful labor of engineering.

How to Make Your Subjects Romans

Strategic and tactical superiority alone cannot explain the success of the Roman Empire in holding so many people together for such a long time in such a large geographical area. The menace of the *gladius* and the *pilum* fit hand in glove with the power and influence of Romanization, understood as the assimilation of the conquered nations to Roman culture and political worldview. The conquered became partners in running the empire. It was a selective process that applied directly only to the upper level of subject societies, but it trickled down to all classes, with benefits for some, negative consequences for others. It meant convincing or co-opting the non-Roman ruling groups to accept the primacy of Roman law, language, institutions, and lifestyle, together with the notion that the interests of Rome coincided with preserving its hegemony over the population. In the end, this was the main weapon for permanent conquest in places like Italy, Gaul, and Britain. Where it could not be applied because of the fractious nature of the local aristocracy (the unsubdued German lands, for instance), imperial conquest could be only sporadic, with failure inevitably following success.

According to St. Augustine, the Romans brought laws and peace and eventually partnership to the people they conquered, even if power was first projected through weapons. Virgil explains that peace and security are what the Romans established in the four corners of the world. Tacitus points out that his father-in-law, Agricola, used private money to build the amenities of civil life and to educate the British aristocracy. Yet the key to how the Romans viewed those actions and the way in which modern historians interpret them is seen in Tacitus's own poisonous evaluation: *idque apud imperitos humanitas vocabatur, cum pars servitutis esset* ("what those simpletons [the Britons] called civilizing mission, was instead a factor in their subjection").[136]

Traces of positive and negative definitions of Romanization are found in the modern debate, with many questions unresolved as to its meaning, application, extent, and characteristics. Yet common to all seems to be an acceptance that Romans exerted a certain influence over their subjects and that this influence—that is, their Romanization—was eventually another powerful asset in imperial control and safety.

There is no doubt that the Romans, relying on a limited number of troops, were able to establish an efficient security balance along the borders in the first two centuries A.D. Yet it was an equilibrium that could quickly career out of balance. For instance, the transfer of troops from northern Britain to the Danube frontier to face a recurring threat from across the river in the late A.D. 80s stopped the Roman advance into Scotland. A few years later, when Trajan recalled soldiers from Britain to support his conquest of Dacia, the Romans again had to curtail their ambitions in northern Britain, settling at the Tyne-Solway line, later strengthened with Hadrian's Wall.[137]

Roman supremacy was based on a masterful combination of violence and psychological persuasion—the harshest punishment for those who challenged it, the perception that their power knew no limits and that rewards were given to those who conformed. It was a role in which the army played a crucial role, because the assertion of power always suggested the use of military violence.[138] This brought powerlessness to many enemies and sometimes disorder even in the same family. During Germanicus's campaign to exact revenge for the destruction of Varus's legions, Arminius asked for a meeting with his brother, Flavus, who like him had begun serving the Romans but who, unlike Arminius, had kept his oath of loyalty to the emperor. Arminius asked his brother to switch sides in obedience to their nation, their gods, their ancestral liberty, and their mother's wishes that Flavus should not be regarded as a traitor and renegade. But Flavus, whose own body showed his years of service to Rome (he lost an eye fighting for the empire), refused his brother's entreaties. Rome had been good to him, showering him with rewards like increased pay and many military decorations. It was a lost cause to challenge the greatness of the empire and the power of the emperor, for the vanquished could expect heavy punishment; mercy would be granted to the individual who submitted.[139]

Romanization implied the introduction of taxation, the installation of military forces (at least temporarily), and the adoption of Roman customs by the local population. The culture never traveled in one direction only, that is, from Rome to the periphery. It was a two-way street in that the subjects became a partner in their own Romanization, and it was even more multifaceted in some parts of the empire.[140]

The extent to which the periphery internalized Romanization has been a matter of vigorous debate. In general, two trends emerged—one maintaining that Rome's influence was superficial, the other that it was so deep that it stamped out local culture.[141] Both theses, if stated inflexibly, miss the point. Those people who were co-opted to Roman ways must have been in the minority; the majority must have kept up with ancestral traditions and existing lifestyles. The people who were most influenced, and the ones who would shape the future, held power before, during, and after Roman occupation. It would always be, for until modern times those in power invariably shaped society. These transmitters of culture became the heralds of the Roman viewpoint. The most important question to ask is, How was the process of Romanization introduced, who were its agents, and why did the power groups in northern Italy, Gaul, Britain, and elsewhere make common cause with the Romans?

Military force, or the threat of force, was the most important factor. This could be carried by invasion, displacement, or diplomacy. After the Romans destroyed the German Eburones tribe on the left bank of the Rhine, they brought in another German tribe from across the river, the Ubii, to settle there—a population that seems to have identified with the Roman way of life.[142] Under Augustus, the Thracian Getae were moved across the Danube; on at least two occasions during Nero's reign more barbarian tribes were displaced in the same region; Marcus Aurelius brought the German Quadi tribe to Pannonia, the area south and west of the Danube; and Commodus distributed lands within the borders of the empire to the free Thracians.[143] This approach dated to the republican period.

Diplomacy also played a role. In the initial stages of the imperial period, peoples at the periphery were often granted treaties of friendship. As long as they kept order in their kingdoms—understood as crushing unrest within and acting as a barrier against the outside invader—they also retained the appearance of independence. This was the case for some tribes on the Danube frontier and in Armenia. Later, however, this system was dropped, and once-friendly territories were formally annexed as provinces. Judaea, a kingdom, was changed into a province; the same applied to Galatia and Cappadocia in Asia Minor and Commagene in the upper Euphrates.[144]

Promise and denial of trade was another way to extend control. For instance, the friendly German Hermunduri tribe was allowed to trade across the frontier and thus was free to cross the Danube without supervision.[145] Less trustworthy peoples were either prevented from trading or, like the German Tencteri, were granted limited commercial rights with the Romans. They had to cross the river without weapons, under guard, during daylight—and they had to pay a fee.[146] Trade was thus a closely regulated activity. In the eastern empire, trade provided revenues to the state (the customs duty reached 25 percent); in the west, specifically on the Rhine and the Danube, the situation was much more complex.

Eastern trade consisted of high-value goods like silk, spices, and perfumes. The only concern of the state was to avoid draining too much gold from Europe to the east, a problem that continued to plague Europe until the early modern period. Trade in Europe was less a source of revenue than a strategic measure to convince a volatile entity or a hostile or unstable neighbor to sign or respect peace treaties. The Romans compelled tribes across the Rhine and/or Danube to trade only through designated locations—the *portoria*, through which traders had to pass to pay customs and tolls. It was a difficult system to enforce; efficiency varied according to the state of military supremacy. Easy to enforce if the Romans were there in force, it became fragile and inefficient following a Roman defeat.[147]

The process of Romanization quickened once peace was established. The first agents were the soldiers and imperial administrators. Sometimes Rome's representative (e.g., Agricola) must have taken a personal interest in spreading the precepts of Romanization—the knowledge of the law, education, and rhetoric, that is, the art of speaking and writing well in the language of the empire (Latin) and the involvement of the individual in political life.[148]

The centers of Romanization were inevitably the cities founded after occupation. As Whittaker writes, the city was the major cultural construct and the conveyer of Roman imperialism abroad. Cities were the centers of the imperial administration, places that symbolically and visually fostered the value system of the empire, the cult of the emperor, and the social structure of the commonwealth.[149] On the frontier, aspects of urban life were reflected in the soldiers' behavior and, physically, in the forts, posts, and other constructions that became increasingly prevalent, reproducing Rome on a smaller scale. However, a major difference existed between life at the frontier and life in the city. Frontiers tended to sharpen the warlike ethos, not just of the soldiers but of potential recruits. The emphasis on city life, in contrast, was to create communities of peace-loving, law-abiding citizens.[150]

The landscape itself could be reshaped to reflect and consolidate the military and economic interests of the empire. For instance, the integration of Gallia Cisalpina in northern Italy, roughly from Ariminum (Rimini) to the Alps, offers a good example of how the Romans dealt with their conquests and how the new territories adopted the value system of their conquerors. The area was of particular concern to Rome. Fairly large, it was inhabited by people—the Celts—who had a long and sometimes successful history of enmity against Rome, who kept up contacts with Celts on the other side of the Alps (modern-day France), and who were blessed with a particularly rich and fertile plain irrigated by Italy's largest river, the Po. Its conquest was completed only when Augustus finally subjugated the tribes controlling the mountain passes to Gaul. Yet integration came not by new garrisons and military repression but by the slow and inexorable erosion of the foundations of native culture. It began with modifications to the rights and statutes of indigenous communities, it continued with the foundations of new cities—the embodiment of the Roman value system—and it ended by organizing the landscape in a manner that suited the interests of the conquerors.[151] In the process, erstwhile enemies became not just friends but partners in Rome's imperialistic ventures. Gallia Cisalpina would be a precious source of food, minerals, and soldiers for the legions.

Another interesting example is the Roman conquest of Iberia. Here, too, new constructions tended to erase the ancient, sacred connections of the local populations to the land. Again, it was not implemented by force. As long as the local population did not rebel, it could build any way it saw fit. Yet the cultural hegemony of the imperial power won in the end, and native connections to the landscape were lost and forgotten. The people who introduced Romanization were the local elites—the most prominent native groups and Roman citizens who had settled the peninsula in the past.[152]

In the long run, then, power and force would not have been enough to retain control over the new acquisitions. The key was to rely on the local ruling groups. It was a process that came naturally to the Romans, whose society was marked by a hierarchical structure, reflected in most aspects of their civilization visually and symbolically. As P. Zanker has shown, Romans consciously manipulated the power of images to convey their value system. Rome was a "permanent architectural stage"[153]—a process that seems to have been repeated in most of the major imperial cities. Theaters were a symbolic restatement of the social order, with a rigid separation of the seats according to the social and political status of the theatergoers. Statues in the forum were placed according to size, most of them (about 60 percent) being images of the emperor.[154] The Iberian statues reflected social reality. "At the top was the Emperor, represented by his cult; around him the highest echelons of society who formed the flaminate [Roman priests drawn from the aristocracy with both religious and secular duties]; below them the wealthy free and freedmen; below them the citizens; and lower the slaves. All had a place in the Imperial plan. All had a place in architecture."[155] In other words, "at every stage in Rome's history the aristocrats that ruled Rome found it most natural to support men like themselves elsewhere."[156]

The integration of the formerly hostile aristocracies had a long history by the time of Augustus's rule.[157] The empire was built with Italian, not just Roman, hands. Rome, even before the Social War, had made the local aristocracies of the Italian cities partners in its rise to dominance. In exchange, after a final struggle, the rest of the Italians were granted citizenship and all its benefits.[158] This largesse was not extended elsewhere, at least at first, and then only to the ruling classes. For every aristocrat like Vercingetorix, who bravely held out against the Romans, there would be dozens of other Gauls who accepted the principles of Romanization and who became its messengers and arbiters.[159] The upper classes, even among the Jews who clashed with their Roman invaders, seem to have preferred the Romans to the xenophobia among the lower social groups.[160] The most successful in retaining their identity were peoples who did not oppose Rome outright, like the Greeks.

Rome's rule brought peace and the promise of dominance over the rest of the population. Thus in most cases the acceptance of Roman rule must have strengthened the local elites' social and political hold over others. Moreover, it opened opportunities to them and their children—a world of learning and career possibilities as shareholders in the imperial government. They made Latin their language and Rome "our common motherland" *(communis nostra patria)*. And if the interests of the ruling groups corresponded with Rome's interests, soldiers would not be needed. The process was quicker in the west than in the east, where Rome had to compete with Hellenism. Yet in the end the people west of the Adriatic Sea found their political identity best reflected in Rome. They too became Rhomaioi (Romans). And although Greek remained the language of the people, knowledge of Latin was mandatory for people aspiring to a career in the army or the imperial administration—a very attractive proposition.

Of course, such developments benefited male elites, the urban population, and those involved in public administration. Commoners, women, and rural inhabitants were not included.[161] They were unaware of what had happened to their land or accepted the perpetuation of old abuses by the same masters, who merely had adopted the conquerors' speech, dress, and architecture. Resistance to the original and new agents of Romanization may have existed, but it was increasingly less frequent and less important. The enemies were no longer in their midst but came from outside, from across the heathen frontiers. And although the resilience and persistence of native lifestyles should not be discounted, in the long run the future pointed to Roman dominance—the civilization of all, rich and poor, powerful and powerless. Until a few centuries ago, the civilization best transmitted to future generations came naturally from the ruling classes—the very few representing so many according to their own principles and biases. It was so in ancient Greece, so in the Hellenistic countries, so in Rome, and so in the Renaissance. It is fascinating and only fair to recall the world of the dispossessed and inarticulate. But in the end we must admit that the old civilizations are the heritage of those who dominated politics, society, and the economy.

There is no doubt that Roman control could be oppressive, regardless of the ethnic background of the agents. Ramsay Macmullen presents the tyranny of the new masters; taxation was merely the first burden.[162] Yet Rome's hegemony may have been positive overall, and at times the benefits trickled down to most everyone, not just the native ruling groups. First of all, taxation was regular, severely imposed, but relatively mild; administration remained in the hands of locals; peace became the reality; and the rule of law was applied with fairness. Moreover, some regions clearly benefited. Gaul, for instance, became richer and more prosperous following Roman conquest. It shows in the rapid growth of villas in the Somme region, the invention of the Gallic harvesting machine, the growth in the urban network, and the increasing density of the population (roughly twenty persons per square kilometer, a figure not matched until the High Middle Ages). Moreover, the taxes that were raised in Gaul were spent for the troops stationed there and for articles and goods originating in Gaul proper.[163] As a rule, tax money flowed more from the center to the periphery, not vice versa.[164]

All this does not lead one to conclude that Romanization was a cold, deliberate process. The Romans intended to make the ruling groups become Roman, and everything else developed from there. The process suited the interests and eventually the value systems of native ruling groups. It would never have succeeded if there was opposition, for in fact the Romans lacked the machinery to impose their worldview on so many different peoples.

Notes

1. Tacitus, *Annales* I.11; Dio lvi.33.1–5.
2. Dio lvi.33.5–6.
3. See P. A. Brunt, "Laus Imperii," in his *Roman Imperial Themes* (Oxford, 1980), pp. 288–297. The quotation is at p. 295.
4. Ibid., pp. 96–109, 297–300, 433–440.
5. Brunt, "Roman Imperial Illusions," in ibid., p. 477.
6. A. Ferrill, *Roman Imperial Grand Strategy* (Lanham, MD, 1991), pp. 45–47.
7. E. L. Wheeler, "Methodological Limits and the Mirage of Roman Strategy," *Journal of Military History* 57 (1993): 215–240.
8. W. S. Hanson and G. S. Maxwell, *Rome's North West Frontier: The Antonine Wall* (Edinburgh, 1983).
9. D. J. Breeze and B. Dobson, *Hadrian's Wall* (London, 1987).
10. Fergus Millar, *The Roman Empire and Its Neighbours* (New York, 1967).
11. A. V. Matei, "Limes Prolissensis—A New Defensive Line (Ditches, Wall, and Towers) Discovered in Front of the Military Site of Porolissum, in Dacia," in *Roman Frontier Studies 1995: Proceedings of the XVIth International Congress of Roman Frontier Studies*, edited by W. Groenman-van Waateringe et al. (Oxford, 1997), pp. 92–95.
12. Hugh Elton, *Warfare in Roman Europe, A.D. 350–425* (Oxford, 1996), p. 155.
13. N. Hodgson, "Relationship Between Roman Frontiers and Artificial Frontiers," in *Roman Frontier Studies 1995*, edited by Groenman-van Waateringe et al., p. 61.
14. All the data on the legions' location are from Y. Le Bohec, *L'esercito romano: Le armi imperiali da Augusto a Caracalla* (Roma, 1992), pp. 218–236.
15. See the table of the legions, deployment from Augustus to Valerian in ibid., p. 236.
16. Tennes Bekker-Nielsen, "*Terra Incognita:* The Subjective Geography of the Roman Empire," in *Studies in Ancient History and Numismatics Presented to Rudi Thomsen* (Aarhus, 1988), pp. 148–161. For the ratio of transport costs, see Richard Duncan Jones, *The Economy of the Roman Empire*, 2nd ed. (Cambridge, 1982), p. 368.
17. C. R. Whittaker, *Frontiers of the Roman Empire: A Social and Economic Study* (Baltimore, 1997), p. 66.

18. C. R. Whittaker, "Where Are the Frontiers Now?" in *The Roman Army in the East*, edited by David L. Kennedy (Ann Arbor, 1996), p. 38.

19. B. Isaac, *The Limits of Empire: The Roman Army in the East* (Oxford, 1990), p. 395.

20. Particularly influential on this topic has been Benjamin Isaac's work on the Roman army in the east.

21. See Whittaker, *Frontiers of the Roman Empire*, p. 59, summarizing Isaac's view; Isaac, *The Limits of Empire*, p. 373.

22. Isaac, *The Limits of Empire*, p. 391.

23. Brunt, "Roman Imperial Illusions," in his *Roman Imperial Themes*, pp. 435–437.

24. Whittaker has been particularly strong in espousing this thesis. See *Frontiers of the Roman Empire*, p. 59, containing a much different assessment.

25. Ibid., pp. 58, 56, 36. See also N. Hodgson, "Relationship Between Roman River Frontiers and Artificial Frontiers," in *Roman Frontier Studies 1995*, edited by Groenman-van Waateringe et al., p. 61.

26. J. Kunow, "Relations Between Roman Occupation and the *Limesvorland* in the Province of Germania Inferior," in *The Early Roman Empire in the West*, edited by T. Blagg and M. Millett (Oxford, 1990), pp. 86–96.

27. Ibid., p. 90.

28. Ibid., pp. 90–93.

29. Ibid., pp. 93–95.

30. William V. Harris, *War and Imperialism in Republican Rome, 327–370 B.C.* (Oxford, 1985).

31. Cicero, *In Pisonem* 38.

32. B. Bartel, "Culturalism and Cultural Responses: Problems Related to Roman Provincial Analysis," *World Archaeology* 12 (1980–1981): 19; see also L. A. Curchin, "Roman Frontier Concepts in the Spanish Interior," in *Roman Frontier Studies 1995*, edited by W. Groenman-van Waateringe et al. (1997), pp. 67–68.

33. Curchin, "Roman Frontier Concepts," pp. 69–70.

34. Whittaker, *Frontiers of the Roman Empire*, pp. 10–18.

35. Isaac, *The Limits of Empire*, p. 386.

36. Harris, *War and Imperialism in Republican Rome*, pp. 50–53.

37. See Isaac, *The Limits of Empire*, pp. 380–381. The specific examples are in Josephus, Svetonius, and Tacitus.

38. P. A. Brunt, "Augustan Imperialism," in his *Roman Imperial Themes*, pp. 96–109.

39. Ibid., pp. 446–454.

40. Peter Connolly, *Greece and Rome at War* (Englewood Cliffs, NJ, 1981), pp. 226–239.

41. Ibid., p. 233.

42. Le Bohec, *L'esercito romano*, pp. 162–163.

43. Adrian Goldsworthy, *The Roman Army at War, 100 B.C.–A.D.200* (Oxford, 1996), pp. 216–218.

44. Connolly, *Greece and Rome at War*, p. 233.

45. Tacitus, *Agricola* 36.

46. Tacitus, *Annales* xiv.36.

47. Vegetius i.12.

48. Peter Connolly, "The Roman Fighting Technique Deduced from Armour and Weaponry," *Roman Frontier Studies 1989*, edited by V. A. Maxfield and M. J. Dobson (Exeter, 1991), pp. 358–363.

49. Goldsworthy, *The Roman Army at War*, pp. 218–219.

50. Ibid., pp. 217–218.

51. Antonio Santosuosso, *Soldiers, Citizens, and the Symbols of War from Classical Greece to Republican Rome, 500–167 B.C.* (Boulder, 1997), p. 15.

52. Le Bohec, *L'esercito romano*, p. 163.

53. Ibid., pp. 168–172; Connolly, *Greece and Rome at War*, pp. 239–242.

54. J. Brian Campbell, *The Roman Army, 31 B.C.–A.D. 337: A Sourcebook* (London, 1994) , p. 89.

55. See the concluding comments in Goldsworthy, *The Roman Army at War*, pp. 283–286.

56. See Goldsworthy's excellent discussion in *The Roman Army at War*, pp. 133–139.

57. Caesar, *De bello civili* i.83.

58. Frontinus, *Strategemata* ii.22.

59. Caesar, *De bello Gallico* i.52.

60. Caesar, *De bello Gallico* i.49; 3.24.

61. Pollio, *De bello Africo* 13.

62. Hans Delbrück, *History of the Art of War Within the Framework of Political History*, 2 vols., translated by W. J. Renfroe Jr. (London, 1975–1980), vol. 1, p. 416.

63. Tacitus, *Agricola* 11.

64. Frontinus, *Strategemata* ii.15.

65. Josephus, *De bello Judaico*, i.22.

66. Ibid., iii.72–75.

67. Tacitus, *Annales* ii.45.

68. Goldsworthy, *The Roman Army at War*, pp. 180–181.

69. On the approach to battle of the Romans, see Goldsworthy, *The Roman Army at War;* Lawrence Keppie, *The Making of the Roman Army from Republic to Empire*

(Norman, OK, 1984); G. Webster, *The Roman Imperial Army* (London, 1985); and Santosuosso, *Soldiers, Citizens, and the Symbols of War*, pp. 148–200.

70. Tacitus, *Annales* xiv.29–30.

71. Tacitus, *Agricola* 14.

72. Tacitus, *Annales* xiv.31.

73. Dio lxii.22.2.

74. Tacitus, *Annales* xiv.32.

75. Dio lxii.2.3–4.

76. Ibid., lxii.2.3; lxii.8.2.

77. Tacitus, *Annales* xiv.33.

78. Dio lxii.7.2; Tacitus, *Annales* xiv.33.

79. Tacitus, *Annales* xiv.34.

80. Dio lxii.8.1.

81. Tacitus, *Annales* xiv.34.

82. Ibid., xvi.37.

83. Ibid., xiv.34.

84. Ibid., xiv.36–37; Dio lxii.12.

85. Tacitus, *Annales* 37; but the cause was sickness, according to Dio lxii.12.6.

86. Tacitus, *Agricola* 16.

87. Ibid., 13.

88. Velleius ii.105–106.

89. A. Passerini, *Linee di storia romana in età imperiale* (Milano, 1972), pp. 235–236.

90. Velleius ii.119.5.

91. Ibid., ii.108–109.

92. Passerini, *Linee di storia romana*, p. 236; cf. Velleius ii.114.4; also lvi.12–16.

93. Velleius ii.71.2.

94. Ibid., ii.117.2–3.

95. Dio lvi.18.4.

96. Delbrück, *History of the Art of War*, vol. 2, pp. 74–75.

97. Dio lvi.19.1.

98. Velleius ii.118.1.

99. Ibid., ii.118.2.

100. Dio lvi.19.2.

101. What follows is based on Dio lvi.18–21 and Velleius ii.117–119.

102. Dio lvi.20.

103. Velleius ii.119.2.

104. Dio lvi.21.1.

105. Ibid., lvi.21.1.

106. Ibid., lvi.21.3–4.

107. Dio lvi.21; Velleius ii.119.3.

108. Passerini, *Linee di storia romana*, p. 236.

109. Dio lvi.22.

110. Svetonius, *Divus Augustus* 23.2.

111. E. A. Thompson, *The Early Germans* (Oxford, 1965), pp. 3–8.

112. Delbrück, *History of the Art of War*, vol. 2, p. 99.

113. Ibid., pp. 99–101.

114. Ibid., pp. 102–106.

115. Ibid., p. 113.

116. On the German aristocracy in general and on the Cherusci in particular, see Thompson, *The Early Germans*, especially pp. 72–88.

117. Nachman Ben-Yehuda, *The Masada Myth: Collective Memory and Mythmaking in Israel* (Madison, WI, 1995).

118. Josephus, *De bello Judaico* vii.8–9.

119. Yigael Yadin, *Masada: Herod's Fortress and the Zealots' Last Stand* (Jerusalem, 1966).

120. Cf. Louis H. Feldman, *Josephus and Modern Scholarship, 1937–1980* (New York, 1984), pp. 665–667; also Arich Kasher, ed., *The Great Revolt* (Jerusalem, 1983), pp. 299–388.

121. Ben-Yehuda, *The Masada Myth*, pp. 35–36.

122. Josephus, *De bello Judaico* iv.7.2.

123. W. Eck, "Die Eroberung von Masada und eine neue Inschrift des L. Flavius Silva Nonius Bassus," *Zeitschrift für die Neutestamentliche Wissenschaft* 60 (1960): 282–289.

124. Ben-Yehuda, *The Masada Myth*, p. 32.

125. Mireille Hadas-Lebel, *Masada: Una storia e un simbolo*, translated by Claudia Maria Tresso (Genova, 1997), p. 41.

126. Ben-Yehuda, *The Masada Myth*, p. 32. He describes the mountain height as 320 meters; Yigael Yadin says that it measures about 1,300 feet (about 400 meters) on the eastern side in the direction of the Dead Sea. "The Excavations at Masada," in *Masada and the Finds from the Bar-Kokhba Caves: Struggle for Freedom,* by the Jewish Theological Seminary of America (New York, 1967), p. 19.

127. Josephus, *De bello Judaico* vii.8.3.

128. Ibid., vii.8.3; on the result of modern excavations, see Yadin, *Masada*.

129. Yadin, *Masada*, p. 214.

130. Edward Dabrowa, *Legio X Fretensis: A Prosopographical Study of Its Officers (I–III c. A.D.)* (Stuttgart, 1993), pp. 14–15.

131. Josephus, *De bello Judaico* vii.8.5.

132. Dan Gill, "A Natural Spur at Masada," *Nature* 364 (1993): 569–570.

133. Josephus, *De bello Judaico* vii.8.5.

134. This was in a Hebrew document originating from southern Italy called the *Yosippon*. See Hadas-Lebel, *Masada*, pp. 60–62.

135. Josephus, *De bello Judaico* vii.8.6–7; 9.1–2.

136. St. Augustine, *De Civitate Dei* 5.17; Virgil, *Aeneid* 6.851ff; Tacitus, *Agricola* 21; all are discussed in D. B. Saddington, "The Parameters of Romanization," *Roman Frontier Studies 1989*, edited by V. A. Maxfield and M. J. Dobson (Exeter, 1991), pp. 413–414.

137. W. S. Hanson, "Forces of Change and Methods of Control," in *Dialogues in Roman Imperialism: Power, Discourse, and Discrepant Experience in the Roman Empire*, edited by D. J. Mattingly (Portsmouth, RI, 1997), pp. 68–69.

138. Ibid., p. 68.

139. Tacitus, *Annales* ii.9–10.

140. D. J. Mattingly, "Introduction," in his *Dialogues in Roman Imperialism*, pp. 8–9.

141. For short summaries of these positions in regard to Britain, see Martin Millett, "Romanization: Historical Issues and Archaeological Interpretation," in *The Early Roman Empire in the West*, edited by Thomas Blagg and Martin Millett (Oxford, 1990), pp. 35–41; Mark Grahame, "Redefining Romanization: Material Culture and the Question of Social Continuity in Roman Britain," in *Trac 97: Proceedings of the Seventh Annual Theoretical Roman Archaeology Conference, Nottingham 1997*, edited by C. Forcey et al. (Oxford, 1998), pp. 1–10. Grahame also emphasizes a different approach. He argues that the problem should be examined from the interplay of the personal bonds used to establish control over society.

142. J.H.F. Bloemers, "Introduction to the Section on 'Roman and Native,'" in *Roman Frontier Studies 1989*, edited by V A. Maxfield and M. J. Dobson, p. 412.

143. Hanson, "Forces of Change and Methods of Control," p. 72.

144. Brunt, "Roman Imperial Illusion," p. 435.

145. Tacitus, *Germania* 41.

146. Tacitus, *Historiae* iv.64–65.

147. William G. Kerr, "Economic Warfare on the Northern Limes: *Portoria* and the Germans," in *Roman Frontier Studies 1989*, edited by V. A. Maxfield and M. J. Dobson, pp. 442–445.

148. For this definition of Romanization, see Saddington, "The Parameters of Romanization," pp. 413–418. cf. Bloemers, "Introduction to the Section on 'Roman and Native,'" in *Roman Frontier Studies 1989*, p. 412.

149. C. R. Whittaker, "Imperialism and Culture: The Roman Initiative," in *Dialogues in Roman Imperialism*, edited by D. J. Mattingly, pp. 145–148.

150. Ibid., pp. 143–144.

151. Nicholas Purcell, "The Creation of the Provincial Landscape: The Roman Impact on Cisalpine Gaul," in *The Early Roman Empire in the West,* edited by Blagg and Millett, pp. 7–29.

152. William E. Mierse, *Temples and Towns in Roman Iberia: The Social and Architectural Dynamics of Sanctuary Designs from the Third Century B.C. to the Third Century A.D.* (Berkeley, 1999), pp. 1–53, 298–304.

153. Zanker, *The Power of Images in the Age of Augustus* (Ann Arbor, 1988), pp. 273, 299.

154. Whittaker, "Imperialism and Culture,"pp. 145–148.

155. Mierse, *Temples and Towns in Roman Iberia,* p. 304.

156. Brunt, "The Romanization of the Local Ruling Classes in the Roman Empire," in his *Roman Imperial Themes,* p. 276.

157. What follows is mainly based on Brunt, "Did Imperial Rome Disarm Her Subjects?" and "The Romanization of the Local Ruling Classes in the Roman Empire," in his *Roman Imperial Themes,* pp. 254–266, 267–281.

158. Brunt, "The Romanization of the Local Ruling Classes in the Roman Empire," p. 274.

159. Mierse, *Temples and Towns in Roman Iberia,* p. 303.

160. Brunt, "The Romanization of the Local Ruling Classes in the Roman Empire," p. 272.

161. On the Romanization of different groups, see the table in Nicola Terrenato, "The Romanization of Italy: Global Acculturation or Cultural *Bricolage,*" in *Trac 97 (1998),* p. 24.

162. Ramsay Macmullen, *Roman Social Relations, 50 B.C.–A.D. 284* (New Haven, 1974).

163. J. F. Drinkwater, "For Better or Worse? Towards an Assessment of the Economic and Social Consequences of the Roman Conquest of Gaul," in *The Early Roman Empire in the West,* edited by Blagg and Millett, pp. 210–219.

164. K. Hopkins, "Taxes and Trade in the Roman Empire, 200 B.C.–A.D. 400," *Journal of Roman Studies* 70 (1980): 101–125.

7

Enemies on the Borders, Violence at Home: Soldiers as the Makers of Emperors

In the long period that followed [the reign of Septimius Severus], no good came to the state from his sons, and after them, when many invaders came pouring in upon the state, the Roman Empire became a thing for thieves to steal.

Historia Augusta, "Severus" 19.6

Septimius Severus's reign began in A.D. 193. He was elevated to emperor following a period of great civil disorder. When he died in York in 211, his last advice to his children was, "Get along together, enrich the soldiers, scorn all other men."[1] It was a cynical but politically wise admonition, intended to make sure that his sons retained the purple colors reserved for the emperor. It is also indicative of how different the army had become since Augustus and Tiberius. These first two emperors excluded the troops from political decisions, a situation that lasted until the later part of the second century A.D. despite difficult moments under Claudius and Nero and brief anarchy following the death of the latter. But by the end of the second century and for most of the following hundred years, the soldiers' political influence, especially that of the praetorians, increased so much that the armed forces became the makers of emperors, not the servants of the state.

Blood on the Praetorians' Swords

Events similar to those surrounding Septimius Severus's rise to power in
A.D. 193 had happened once before in Roman history. During A.D. 68–69 violence and disorder preceded the suicide of Nero. He was abandoned by the
praetorian guard because they thought he had fled the city; and someone
whom they regarded a more useful pretender to the throne, Galba, bribed
them. For a time three men vied for the crown—Galba, Otho, and Vitellius.
Galba, the primary opponent of Nero, was discarded by the army once he
threatened to reestablish strict discipline and, worse, failed to pay the large
donative that he had promised the praetorians. Otho, a puppet in the hands
of the praetorians, took his own life after being defeated by Vitellius. Vitellius desperately tried to hang on to the throne—but not for long. When a
new claimant, Vespasian, appeared, the end came for Vitellius, too. As the
Roman mob favorable to Vitellius attacked those who sided with Vespasian,
burning even the temple of Jupiter to the ground, Vespasian's army stormed
the city, dragged Vitellius through the streets as if he were an animal, then
tortured, humiliated, and executed him.[2] An even better example of the emperor's humiliation and praetorian power is seen in the events befalling the
previous emperor, Otho, soon after his proclamation. The praetorians,
afraid that a plot was being hatched to deny them the large donative, forcefully broke into the palace, where Otho was holding a banquet. The emperor's guests fled in all directions, while Otho in tears stood on a couch
desperately beseeching the soldiers to be patient and trust him.[3]

After the events of A.D. 68–69, no emperor could disregard the power of
the praetorians and soldiers. Even a strong individual like Vespasian (who
ruled during 69–79) recognized this reality: He dated his reign from the day
his troops proclaimed him emperor, not from the day the Senate had accepted his choice, as was the custom.[4] During subsequent years Vespasian,
an able soldier and administrator, restored discipline and a more peaceful
lifestyle in the center of the empire. And even though no emperor for the
next century ignored the fact that his rule was dependant on the allegiance
of the armed forces—especially the praetorian corps—emperors generally
controlled the soldiers, not vice versa.

This situation changed during the last four decades of the second century
A.D. when violence, bloodshed, treason, and the disintegration of political
harmony followed the reign of a most remarkable individual—Marcus Aurelius (161–180). Marcus held the throne during a period of great danger,
for the empire was being attacked on its frontiers. There was trouble in

Britain, in Germany near the sources of the Rhine and the Danube, along the Danube itself, and in the east, where the Parthians seized Armenia, a region within the Roman sphere of influence. Marcus was a philosopher, not a soldier, but bravely took on the burden of restoring Roman power and even attempted to extend it. He was the perfect emperor, in the judgement of his contemporaries.[5]

His son and successor, Lucius Aurelius Commodus (180–192), was unlike his father. He was a cruel, unbalanced man whose everyday behavior brought shame to the throne. His expression was dull, as "is usual in drunkards," according to the *Historia Augusta*, his speech uncultivated, his hair always dyed and sprinkled with gold dust.[6] He would dress up as the god Mercury or perform in the arena as a common gladiator, a despicable profession that Romans enjoyed watching. If such appearances were inappropriate for an emperor, Commodus's behavior was even worse. He was a homicidal maniac.

Dio, an eyewitness (he was a senator at the time), describes in great detail one of the games that Commodus organized in the arena and to which all the senators, except one, felt obliged to attend, for doing otherwise would have placed their life in danger. In the games' first day Commodus killed many bears (one hundred, says Dio, with obvious exaggeration), shooting at them from the safety of the balustrade and taking respite, when tired, by drinking chilled sweetwine from a cup shaped like a club (Commodus proclaimed himself the "Roman Hercules"), while the senators, in fear of their lives, shouted the customary good wishes, "Long life to you!"[7] In the following days (the games lasted two weeks) Commodus slaughtered more wild beasts, including a tiger, a hippopotamus, and an elephant.[8] Then, dressed like a gladiator, he went into the arena's center, performing against professional gladiators, who made sure that they lost to him. After such exertions, he would withdraw to his customary place in the stands, leaving the arena only to gladiators. Such child's play ended with many men killed.[9] The senators were prompted to shout: "You are the lord, you are the first, you are the most fortunate of all men. You are the winner and you shall always be the winner."[10]

The humiliating display demonstrated the emperor's lack of respect for the Senate, in theory the highest body of the empire after the ruler. Commodus followed this up with real or implied threats. One time he cut the head off an ostrich and, grinning, brought it to where the senators stood.[11] The correlation between the life of the animal and those of the senators was obvious. Facts followed suggestion, for he "turned to murder and killing off the prominent men."[12] All this came during a time of economic problems (prices doubled in a period of ten to twelve years.[13] And a new plague brought misery to the capital, with up to 2,000 persons dying in a single day.[14] And Commodus, jealous of the achievements of his father, Marcus, tried to erase most traces of him and to remake Rome in his own image, renaming it "Colonia Commodiana."[15]

The senators' hatred for Commodus was deep, but they had little recourse. Everything depended on the praetorians. The moment came when the praetorian prefect (the leader of the guards), assisted by Commodus's own chamberlain and the widow of a man slain by Commodus, united in a plot. First they poisoned Commodus, but when it failed to work immediately and Commodus was struggling on the ground in pain and vomiting, they sent in an athlete to strangle him.[16]

Commodus's body was barely cold when the praetorian prefect and his accomplice offered the crown to a sixty-year-old senator, Pertinax; a corpulent man with a regal bearing, he was honest and had a good military record (still a mandatory qualification for an emperor).[17] Pertinax accepted it with some reluctance, yet he promised 12,000 *sesterces* apiece to the praetorians, an enormous amount, representing years of pay. Pertinax did not last long either. The praetorians soon hated him, for they feared that he would restore the old discipline, and they resented that they had been paid only 5,000 of the promised 12,000 *sesterces*.[18] After three months a group of praetorians broke into Pertinax's house. The new emperor tried to calm them, and many hesitated. One approached him and sunk a *gladius* into his body, exclaiming, "The soldiers have sent you this sword." The rest followed suit. They cut off Pertinax's head, fastened it atop a spear, and paraded it through the streets.[19]

The events that followed were indicative of the anarchy in Rome and the power of the military, especially the power of the praetorian guard. The crown was offered at a type of auction, with two bidders. Didius Julianus won, offering 20,000 *sesterces* to each praetorian. But soon thereafter the crown was offered to Septimius Severus, the commander in Pannonia.[20] When Severus arrived in Rome, the senators obligingly ordered that Julianus take his own life or that a soldier kill him.[21] Julianus was fifty-six; he had reigned two months and five days.[22]

Commodus's reign began a period of military anarchy—which was interrupted by the elevation of Septimius Severus—setting off a trend of violence, lack of discipline, and turmoil until the end of the third century A.D. Coupled with problems on the frontiers, this trend inevitably changed the nature of the Roman Empire. After Severus's death at York in 211, the praetorians and/or the soldiers murdered most of the succeeding emperors until the accession of Diocletian in A.D. 284. Thus the imperial guard and the rank and file in the field made and unmade emperors through violence and murder. They held the real power, standing behind the often weak rulers. All this happened while important changes were occurring within the new Roman army. Most of these changes were implemented during 193–211—the reign of Septimius Severus.

The Emperor from Africa

Some contemporaries were not kind to Severus, accusing him of weakening Rome's military system. But such criticism came from proponents of the party, the Senate, which opposed most of his reforms. Modern scholarship has been more generous. Before leaving for Rome from his post as governor of Pannonia to claim the purple, Lucius Septimius Severus made sure that each soldier received a donative of 1,000 *sesterces* (nine to ten months' pay).[23] Then, with the political backing of all sixteen legions located on the Rhine and Danube frontiers, he moved into Italy. His entrance into Rome was an ominous sign of his intentions and the sort of power he was planning to use to retain his office. He first disbanded the praetorian guard, which had murdered Pertinax, then entered the city in the fashion of a conqueror. He dressed in civilian clothes, but his whole army followed him in battle attire.[24] When he addressed the Senate the next day, few soldiers accompanied him, but he was armed, and many more troops patrolled the perimeter. Meanwhile, his other men were camped in the city's most important locations, stirring hatred and fear among the citizens.[25]

Severus was born on April 11, 145, at Lepcis Magna, a city on the North African coast. It is not clear whether both paternal and maternal ancestors were of Italian origin; his father may have been of Carthaginian background.[26] He spoke Latin, if we believe the *Historia Augusta*, with an African accent.[27] He was small in height but sharp of mind and physically powerful (although he would be afflicted with gout later in life). A man of few words but many ideas, Severus was generous with his troops, friends, and capable subordinates; he was ruthless and without pity toward his enemies. His reign, almost eighteen years, was marked by impressive but transitory military successes.[28] He died at age sixty-five. His successors, the Severans, were a failure: "In the long period that followed [Septimius Severus], no good came to the state from his sons, and after them, when many invaders came pouring in upon the state, the Roman Empire became a thing for thieves to steal."[29]

The newly increasing power of the army was apparent even before the Senate ratified Septimius's appointment. The new emperor, his army at Rome's gates, fulfilled the promise that had initially justified his march on Rome—to punish Pertinax's murder. It was a measure that reasserted the emperor's image as a sacred figure, satisfied his soldiers' desire for revenge (they had been well treated by Pertinax), and was the first stage of a new structure of the guard. Punishing the killers was easy. The praetorians had quickly surrendered the comrades guilty of the murder.[30] But that was not enough. Severus enticed the rest of the guard out of Rome, asking them to pay homage in ceremonial uniforms and thus without their weapons. He surrounded them when they arrived, ripped off their belts, uniforms, and military decorations, commanded them never to set foot in Rome again, and sent them away naked. Simultaneously, he had instructed other legionnaires to march to the praetorian camp and sequester their weapons (the praetorians were wearing only the ceremonial short dagger to greet the new emperor).[31]

Soon after disbanding the old guard, Severus opened the praetorian ranks to the most deserving men from the frontier legions.[32] Under Augustus and Tiberius, only citizens born in central Italy and in the older colonies were eligible to enroll in the guard. Later, Claudius opened the ranks to citizens from Cisalpine Gaul, the region south of the Alps. The Italian-born, according to A. Passerini, comprised 86.3 percent of the praetorians; those originating from outside the peninsula included 9.5 percent from the European regions west of Rome and 4.2 percent from the east. After Severus, there were no Italians among the praetorians: 60.3 percent came from the west, 39.7 percent from the east. The majority of the western praetorians were Dalmatians and Pannonians, some perhaps of distant Italian origin.[33] A praetorian assignment was a great prize, for it provided greater career possibilities, better pay, and the advantage of living in the center of the empire in a more comfortable environment.

The historian Dio harshly criticized the emperor's changes at the time: They "ruined the youth of Italy," he said, for without the enticement of the praetorian guard many now made their living by becoming gladiators or by brigandage, a plight of the Mediterranean lands. Moreover, the new praetorian recruits walking Rome's streets were disgusting because of their violent attitude, barbarous speech, and uncivilized behavior.[42] It is likely, as Dio claims, that in some cases Latin was not the language of birth of the new praetorians and that some disbanded members of the old guard may have become brigands or gladiators.[35] It is also likely that the new recruiting regulations chilled Italian youths' aspirations for becoming a soldier.

Yet all this did not mean that Italian-born men were excluded from other military careers. There were several options: the regular army (Severus recruited in the cities of Italy before marching east to confront a pretender);[36] urban troops located in Rome or nearby, that is, the urban cohorts; and the *vigiles*, who accepted all free-born Italians besides freedmen. Actually, if we count Severus's increase of the strength of the urban cohorts and the *vigiles*, the soldiers located in or nearby Rome rose from 10,500 to 23,000 (10,000 praetorians, 6,000 members of the urban cohorts, and 7,000 *vigiles*). Added to this were 1,000 mounted troops for the imperial bodyguard *(equites singulares)* and 5,000–6,000 for the permanent legion at Alba Longa, near Rome. In all, some 29,000–30,000 men were stationed within Italy—a threefold increase.[37]

The action against the old praetorian guard demonstrated the new emperor's strength, yet the praetorians continued to play a role in the emperor's appointment. In fact, later events would prove that they were indeed the makers of emperors. It began under Severus, with the strange career of the prefect Gaius Fulvius Plautianus, the new praetorian leader; he is a good example of the enormous power that had accrued to the guards, whether of the old type or new.[38] Plautianus, also born in Africa, had probably known Severus as a child, related through the latter's mother.[39] Plautianus was such a close friend that Severus did not notice (or pretended not to notice) the misdeeds he committed.[40] First appointed prefect of the *vigiles* in A.D. 195 and then prefect of the praetorians around 197,[41] Plautianus amassed enormous wealth and power—more, some people thought, than the emperor himself. In one instance Plautianus was sick in bed, and the emperor came to visit him in his tent; Plautianus prevented the emperor's escort from entering. In another instance, a man refused to present his legal case to the emperor because Plautianus had not asked him yet.[42]

Plautianus's ambition must have been not so much to gain the throne for himself but to position his daughter's children for ascension to the throne, for he intrigued to have her marry Severus's son, Antoninus (later called Caracalla), who was emperor from 211 to 217. It was a mistake. The vicious Antoninus hated his fourteen-year-old wife, probably never consummated his marriage, and had her killed soon after he succeeded his father.[43]

Plautianus "had power beyond all men." He put to death many prominent men, used—on the emperor's order—the children of Severus's opponents to blackmail their parents into acquiescence, and castrated several boys, youths, and married men in his daughter's service in order to avert any threat to her chastity. He even dared to inquire about and censure the probably loose behavior of the empress.[44] His greed was limitless: "He wanted everything, asked everything from everybody, and would take everything."[45] Even his private behavior, according to the hostile Dio, was appalling. He would gorge himself so much at banquets that he vomited as he ate, and he would use boys and girls for his pleasure but was insanely jealous of his wife, whom he kept isolated from everybody, even from the imperial couple.[46]

Plautianus, strong in his position as prefect of the praetorians, felt confident that the emperor would not curtail his actions. After all, Severus was a relative, an old friend, and, according to Herodian, a homoerotic companion.[47] Moreover, the emperor had appointed him *comes* (companion) in all his war campaigns,[48] an honorific title of great social importance.

But all this influence and power came to naught when Severus's dying brother finally convinced the emperor to face his close companion's misdeeds. The emperor first deprived Plautianus of some of his honors and then summoned him to the palace. There he accused Plautianus of plotting to murder him (something concocted by his son, Antoninus, to turn his father against Plautianus). As Plautianus desperately denied any guilt, Antoninus knocked him down with a punch and ordered one of the guards present to slay him, probably with the emperor's consent. Someone cut a few hairs from Plautianus's beard and took them to a nearby room, where the emperor's wife was staying with Plautianus's daughter (Antoninus's ill-fated wife). "Here, he said, is your Plautianus." The empress expressed joy, her daughter-in-law horror.[49]

This episode demonstrates that a strong emperor could still command supreme authority. Yet in the years after Severus the power of the praetorian leader, his men, and the legions increased. After his death, there is a long list of emperors whose careers were cut short by the sword. The average reign from Septimius's death (211) to Diocletian's accession (284) was three years; all others (except for three) died at the hands of their own soldiers or in civil wars. Of the three that escaped this fate, one was killed in battle against German invaders, another died while imprisoned by the Persians, and the third succumbed to the plague.[50]

The new structure of the praetorians and the growth of the troops stationed in Italy were not Severus's only military reform. There were twenty-five legions at Augustus's death in A.D. 14. By 211 the Roman army consisted of thirty-three legions (three being added by Severus), with a likely increase as well in the auxiliary units. One of the legions, the II Legio Parthica, was stationed permanently about 34 kilometers from Rome.[51] The location of the II Legio Parthica so close to Rome was of great concern to contemporaries: It defied the old principle that no legion should be stationed in Italy and constituted an implied threat to the capital.

Establishing three new legions meant a substantial growth in the military budget when the state's purse was actually depleted, especially when combined with the large increase in the soldiers' pay and the generous donatives.[52] Soon after entering Rome, Severus, somewhat under pressure, gave 250 *denarii* to each soldier (the troops had requested ten times that amount)—about ten months' pay.[53] Moreover, the legionnaires' pay was raised for the first time since Domitian, from 300 to 450 *denarii*, the auxiliary infantry from 100 to 150, the legionnaire cavalry from 400 to 600, and the auxiliary cavalry from 200–266 to 300–400 if part of the cohort and from 333 to 500 if detached at the wing. Severus's son, now known as Caracalla, roughly doubled the pay from before his father's accession.[54]

The increase was needed badly, for pay had remained stagnant for about a century despite inflation and the decreased value of the *denarius* (which affected all groups, especially common workers and peasants). Favoring one group must have deepened the civilians' antagonism toward the soldiers and cemented the gap between the enforcers and the rest. The military budget increases also meant that the emperor had to impose higher and higher taxes, even during the declining economies in the late second and third centuries.[55]

Soldiers were also granted other privileges. Severus gave them the right to marry while in service and probably the right to live with their wives outside military lodgings. He allowed them to wear the symbol of the equestrian class—a gold ring—although Severus excluded common soldiers. Finally he granted them a larger and better food supply. According to Herodian, this changed the quality of the Roman soldier himself, who discarded the harsh but healthy diet of the past and adopted a more comfortable lifestyle. The result was to weaken the strict discipline and reduce efficiency.[56]

The idea of deprivation—in food, clothing, and luxuries—is a leitmotiv among the Greeks and especially the Romans. Hardships, they thought, were essential to shaping a responsible citizen, whose main duty was to be a soldier. We can recall the raising of Spartan children.[57] We can also see the constant refrain in many Roman biographies: Outstanding individuals trained their bodies by a strict and harsh training regimen or the tolerance of an unduly harsh lifestyle. The recognition of marriage during service legalized a reality (cohabitating) that must have been widespread.

Yet the reforms may have weakened the war machine by making it more dependent on the frontier and, eventually, alienating soldiers from the central authorities, who must have seemed self-absorbed and profligate. What had made Rome powerful in the past had been, among other things, the sense that the troops' most important tie was with the capital. But now several factors diluted that link, strengthening instead the relationship of the frontier soldier to the frontier lands.

Caracalla's extension of citizenship to all free people of the Roman Empire in 212 must have diluted Rome's standing even more (although his action must have been inspired by the need for recruits as well as a half-hearted desire to return to the ancient ideal of soldier-as-citizen). But this did not solve the recruiting problem (additional measures were soon needed) or reestablish the link with Rome.

The manpower needs were met by opening the ranks of the army to frontier populations, that is, non-Roman citizens (settlement did not necessarily imply army service). A process, which steadily increased in the third century after Severus, permitted barbarian families to settle in imperial territories with the understanding that they would provide soldiers for the army *(laeti)*. Then larger groups of barbarians were allowed to relocate on the Roman side of the frontier, again with the understanding that the new settlers would be recruited to serve. This so-called barbarization of the imperial forces had an enormous and deleterious impact on the empire. The newcomers were often effective fighters, but many lacked the crucial ingredient—the understanding that being a soldier for Rome required complete loyalty to a man and city far away. The main problem was probably not the origin of the recruits, however; it was the change in the military command structure.

The Roman army had always been complemented by non-Romans, first allied troops, then Italians living in the peninsula or settled throughout the empire, and finally their children and children's children, often the result of intermarriage with the indigenous population. (Septimius Severus may have had Roman blood only from his mother's side.) Yet the army's command structure—mainly in the hands of people adhering to imperial principles for generations—cemented the troops' loyalty to a distant city and the ideal of cosmopolitan society. Leadership was the privilege of senators, then the equestrians, and then the provincials born and raised in cities settled by

Romans. And the transition of most praetorians (before Severus) from their post in Rome to centurion at the frontier must have reinforced this strong sense of allegiance to the capital.

Thus the command structure itself—that is, the military leaders in charge of the legions—believed in the supremacy of imperial Rome as a result of ideology, class, tradition, and personal interest. This suited anyone who could claim Italian origin and, even more so, the upper classes, whether aristocrats or equestrians in Rome or aristocrats among the subject populations. It was also an ideal that provided peace in the empire and a milder sort of exploitation of the lower classes. This all crumbled in the third century A.D. as the process for becoming a praetorian changed: The new guards would came from the outside into Rome. In time the senators were excluded entirely from the army. The only remnants of cohesion were the equestrians and the emperor, who was often murdered in office.

Many ancient and modern writers contend that Severus deliberately excluded senators from the army. Certainly the number of aristocrats serving in the army declined during his reign, a trend that continued until they were legally forbidden to serve by statute under Gallienus in 261. It is likely that the number of candidates declined following the executions of many senators. It could also be that aristocrats were reluctant to serve in faraway locations (much like commoners, especially after their exclusion from the praetorian guard and the increasing difficulty in gaining a centurion's post). It is hard, however, to maintain that Severus undertook a deliberate policy. Yet Augustus before him had solved the problem by increasing the number of senators and by financially helping those in danger of losing their status. Severus probably lacked the means to do this, yet he never even tried this approach. Regardless of the reasons for the elimination of aristocrats, the last tie to the old imperial system had broken. In theory the Senate was still the highest institution of the empire. But after Severus the real power would be in the hands of one group—the army (at least until Diocletian).

A good example is the accession of Maximinus in A.D. 235. He was a giant man born in a Thracian village from a Gothic father and Indo-European mother.[58] The army proclaimed him emperor, breaking tradition, as he was not yet a senator. Maximinus, a brutal and accomplished soldier, never cared to visit Rome, spending his time fighting Germans, Sarmatians, and Dacians. He also persecuted the Roman upper classes and preyed on richer men. At the beginning, the Senate tried unsuccessfully to install an alternative candidate. The Senate's first legally appointed emperor (Augustus) was murdered by soldiers in Africa; the next, Gordian II, was killed in battle. Each had ruled three weeks. Maximinus's reign ended in 238 after his own soldiers assassinated him; the Senate proclaimed two other emperors, Balbinus and Pupienus. Yet the praetorians had different ideas. They assassinated the Senate's choices and acclaimed a new emperor, a ten-year-old (Gordian III).[59]

Augustus, the first *princeps*, recognized that support from the military was essential. That changed radically with Severus and succeeding emperors as new assumptions became acceptable in choosing the emperor. Normally two institutions—the army and Senate—confirmed any new appointment. Thus heredity gave way to merit in union with two republican ideals: the power of the Senate and the will of the people as embodied by the soldiers. It was a reflection of the military structure, with command going to the two highest social groups—the senators and the equestrians—in alliance with the rank and file, commoners who had citizenship. After Severus the Senate's approval became increasingly meaningless even in appearance; the soldiers became the makers of emperors.

All this played out under unrelenting pressure from invaders along most frontiers. In the past Rome would survive by shifting soldiers from peaceful to threatened areas. That policy worked as long the attackers were not numerous or attacking simultaneously along different frontiers. But by the third century A.D. Germanic populations along the Danube came under pressure from Asiatic peoples pushing from the east. Moreover, the brave but isolated tribes of the past banded together to form stronger alliances. On the Euphrates a new Persian dynasty took over the rather ineffectual Parthian throne. Now Rome faced stronger, well-organized, and in some cases better-disciplined enemies. If they poured over the frontiers simultaneously, local forces would be left to fend for themselves. Thus men stationed on the frontiers inevitably became more interested in their own survival and shifted their loyalty from a distant emperor to the local commander. In truth, Rome's enemies had taken the initiative.

Enemy forces crossed the Rhine, the Danube, and the Euphrates; major Greek cities, including Athens, were besieged; the northern Italian plains were invaded; Gaul was sacked twice (255 and 276). The Franks, a Germanic population, started to spread across the Rhine, capturing several dozen towns before being pushed back to the right bank after suffering many casualties. But they felt confident enough to sack the Spanish coast and even to launch a pirate enterprise in the Mediterranean. In 258 the Alamans (another Germanic tribe) reached the gates of Rome before being driven back (roughly twenty years later they were within sight of Rome's hills before being annihilated).[60] At one point Emperor Gallienus's power was limited to the central part of the empire, leaving lands in the east and the territories from Gaul eastward to self-styled rulers. Gallienus even buckled under to the Marcomanni by assigning them lands across the Danube and marrying the king's daughter.[61]

Along the Danube the Goths had moved in from the Baltic areas. Rome abandoned Dacia, the province across the river (a good strategic move, for Dacia stretched the frontier and weakened defense in the area), but even that was not enough. Yet somehow Rome defeated all the barbarians and pushed many back with terrible casualties. Still, they attacked from outside, and to add to the troubles the plague affected Roman territories for about fifteen years during the middle of the third century.[62]

Eventually Rome overcame both the external and internal threats. Military anarchy ended when a strong and capable man, Diocletian, a soldier from a peasant background in Dalmatia, gained the throne in 284. Civil order was restored, and the frontiers became relatively secure. But a new type of society also emerged: The emperor claimed his right to rule directly from the gods; the old social structure was in shambles and partially destroyed; and new people with new customs and new ideals—the barbarians—were allowed to settle permanently within the borders of the empire. In theory, allowing erstwhile enemies to become imperial subjects was a good solution. It relegated them to vacant territories; it assigned them the humble condition of peasant; and it provided a new pool for recruiting soldiers. It all fit neatly with tradition, when the empire would assimilate the conquered and transform them into loyal Roman citizens.

This time around, however, the outcome would be far different.

The Field Army and the Cavalry

There is solid evidence that the Roman Empire adopted a defensive posture after Septimius. Septimius himself was belligerent, strengthening borders and annexing new territories (e.g., Parthia, which became the new province of Mesopotamia, the last conquest of the Roman Empire; along the Dacian frontier across the Danube; and Britain). The Romans also extended control farther south, from the border with Egypt to the Atlantic.[63] But Rome's main interest thereafter was to defend, not to acquire (except in exacting revenge on an invader across the frontier).

Caracalla tried to emulate and surpass his father's military success, but the Romans were soon forced to adopt a more cautious approach—the beginning of elastic defense and, later, defense in depth. In the first case, best exemplified by Gallienus, Rome abandoned the concept of border defense and relied instead on mobile forces to hammer invaders once they had penetrated the frontier. In the second case defense came in stages, combining strong points (forts, walled towns, fortified farmhouses) with mobile forces. This meant a renunciation of the earlier policy of forward defense, which was based on meeting the threat before it reached the border. The problem with elastic defense and defense in depth was that the border populations would be poorly defended, a radical departure from the past.

This required a different type of army. The events of the third century made clear that the legions stationed at the frontiers were not enough to defeat simultaneous invasions. In the past the solution was to gather detachments from different legions and transfer them to the threatened areas. Marcus Aurelius did raise entirely new legions, but the traditional recruitment pools were depleted over time. (Not even the recruitment among the *laeti* and *foederati* solved the problem.) Thus the solution came in remaking and rethinking the army's structure. What Rome needed were more mobility and stable forces without depleting the frontier.

The mobile army—the *comitatus*—was not created overnight. The process came in fits and starts and the goal was finally achieved under Constantine (emperor, 312–337) in the fourth century. Some historians, however, attribute its beginning to Septimius Severus, either as creator or as the person who provided the nucleus. He increased the soldiers stationed in or around Rome and settled the II Legia Parthica permanently at Alba Longa, on the hills nearby the city. Yet it is impossible to claim with certainty that he intended to create a mobile field army. The troops' location in central Italy could hardly have been efficient for a quick strike against enemies across the Alps or to relieve the frontier.[64] Although it is difficult to determine Severus's real motivation, the most logical explanation seems to be that a man who had to fight three civil wars may have thought it necessary to keep a strong weapon of interdiction near the capital. In other words, the new troops in Italy were for personal security and a projection of the emperor's power. Future rulers would use these men as the nucleus of a large mobile army.

Emperor Gallienus (emperor, 253–268) was more likely the creator of the mobile field army. A depraved individual, he is reviled among the ancient sources; he spent his time in taverns and places of ill repute or made love to his wife and mistress while the barbarians laid waste to the empire.[65] Regardless of his personal behavior, Gallienus (he held the throne jointly with his father, Valerian, from 253 to 258, then alone until 268 after his father died a captive in Persian hands) was clever and valiant. Gallienus is also credited with other innovations: the formation of a professional officer staff; the tendency to promote candidates on merit, not social background; and the exclusion of senators from military duties.[66] He also increased the legionnaire cavalry from 120 to over 700, eventually separating them "more or less permanently" from the legion.[67]

In this time of peril, internal turmoil had split the territories in three: Gallienus remained in control of the central empire—Italy, the Danube provinces, and Greece in Europe, and North Africa and Egypt across the Mediterranean; another individual, self-styled as the emperor's subject but in reality an independent ruler, controlled the east; and another proclaimed himself emperor of Gaul, Britain, and Spain.[68] After 255, Gallienus faced another major threat in the west from the German Alamans. After piercing the frontier in the middle Rhine and upper Danube and spreading to Raetia (modern-day Tyrol and parts of Switzerland and Bavaria), they threatened to strike south. Mobility was essential, as there were no buffer troops to protect the imperial core.

Gallienus surrounded himself with a considerable body of cavalry, likely from different sources—Dalmatia, Mauretania (the region including modern Algeria, Morocco, and part of Tunisia), Mesopotamia, and Italy. He stationed the forces in Milan, an excellent location from which to meet any threat from the west and north; it was also a transportation center rich in supplies.[69] Yet the evidence does not confirm that this became a permanent cavalry force. [70] Regardless, Gallienus's action indicated two ideas that would become fundamental to the army of the Late Roman Empire: a large body of soldiers ready to strike invaders or provide relief to a threatened area; and troops led by horsemen, not footmen. Moreover, Gallienus's attitude toward the two usurpers in the west and east (i.e., noninterference) was praiseworthy, for they provided a barrier against enemies threatening the frontiers.[71] But like so many emperors of the third century, he died at the hands of his own officers while besieging Milan, where a pretender to the throne had taken refuge.[72]

Diocletian (emperor 284–305) may well have established a permanent mobile field army. Yet his *comitatus*, mentioned for the first time in 295, was "a very small body," according to A.H.M. Jones. When this emperor needed a large personal army, he gathered troops in the manner of the past, that is, in detachments from frontier troops and auxiliaries.[73] However, he fundamentally reshaped the Late Empire (see Figure 7.1). He ended the military anarchy and the bloody accession of transitory emperors. But he had started in the old fashion. In 283 a praetorian prefect named Aper killed the reigning emperor, Numerianus, and offered the crown to Diocletian, a man from Dalmatia who had risen from a humble background to command the emperor's bodyguard, the *domestici*. Diocletian accepted it but soon killed the man who had made him emperor. For the next seventy years rulers died in ways other than assassination—from natural causes, suicide, or battle. The next imperial assassination did not take place until 350.[74]

Diocletian was a conservative, hardworking man and a skillful organizer. He rearranged the administrative structure of the empire, reassessed its frontier policy, and introduced important changes in the army's structure. His most important reform was the establishment of the tetrarchy, a type of collegiate government. He split the empire between two coequal emperors (the Augusti), one in charge of the west (with the capital in Rome) and the other of the east (with the eventual capital in Constantinople, founded by Constantine in 324 on the site of Byzantium, an ancient Greek colony dating from 688 B.C.). Diocletian also clarified the problem of succession by appointing two coequal junior emperors (the Caesares), who would ascend to power after the Augusti. Finally, he returned to the old method of choosing emperors, that is, merit with ratification by the people through the Senate and army.

These reforms were bound to fail, and Constantine (306–337) returned to the dynastic system of succession. The weakened Senate, in theory the ultimate power and the ratifier of any new emperor, led to failure as well. Thus the army remained the only meaningful institution in electing the supreme commander. In any case the tetrarchy seemed to be an improvement, for the administration was now shared by a foursome with two senior and two junior partners. In addition, the ability to tap four supreme commanders may have rendered the defense more manageable, as they could support one another in the field. In reality, the system did not always work smoothly. Among the Augusti, theoretically coequal partners, there was inevitably a more senior partner, and at times there were more than two.[75] And the rivalry between the Augusti and the Caesares could cripple the workings of the state, as demonstrated by the Battle of Adrianople in 378. Finally, the unity of the empire was broken. Except for brief periods (e.g., the latter part of Constantine's reign), no single ruler emerged after Theodosius I (emperor, 379–395) until well after the fall of Rome in 476 with the emergence of Justinian (emperor, 527–565).[76]

Another significant reform was Diocletian's separation of administrative roles from military functions. He divided the provinces into smaller units,

FIGURE 7.1   Roman Empire under Diocletian

almost doubling them from fifty to 100, and differentiated the function of the civil administrator from that of the military commander assigned to the area. The leaders appointed to the command of the *limitanei* in the various legions went by a new title—*duces*. For example, there were seven *duces* on the eastern frontier in command of fourteen legions and fourteen cavalry formations.[77] Constantine appointed other provincial commanders at a higher level, the *comites*, senior in command to the *duces*.

And finally, Diocletian tried to reestablish the traditional style of border defense. As was his nature, he continued Gallienus's policy in the territories across the Rhine and the Danube and abandoned them permanently to barbarian hands. The rivers thus delimited Roman lands from those of the German and Sarmatian tribes and made it easier to pay the troops (Gallienus had established mints in their vicinity).[78] But in keeping with previous approaches, Diocletian projected the power of Roman arms by stationing troops in barbarian lands on the left bank of the rivers at important transit points. He also restored old forts, built new ones, strengthened barriers, and constructed at least one new barrier in Syria. Yet the border policy remained fragile, for the state did not possess the power to strike the enemy before it reached the frontier. This was a potentially dangerous trade-off. For if the invaders won a battle at the frontier (as opposed to beyond it, from the Romans' point of view), then nearby territories would be open to attack before the relief could arrive, and that could take days, weeks, even months. Moreover, the army had roughly doubled in size since the Severans.[79] Under Septimius Severus the army was around 350,000; under Diocletian it had ballooned to 400,000–500,000.[80]

Constantine, who had been chosen Augustus in 306, rose to the throne in most dramatic fashion. Heavily outnumbered by a rival pretender, he won the Battle of the Milvian Bridge in 312 with the sign of the cross on his soldiers' shields. Later in life he claimed that before the encounter he had seen a vision in which a cross had appeared inscribed with words signaling his triumph—"Be victorious in this." Soon the new emperor, who had shown tolerance toward Christians a year earlier, ending their persecution, would adopt Christianity as the state religion; paganism would decline. Diocletian had persecuted the Christians, but he also fostered a theocratic conception of imperial power, that is, the gods anointed the emperor, which meant that as long as he could count on the army the emperor had absolute power over his subjects. Constantine followed in Diocletian's footsteps, but with one major difference: The pagan gods of the past were dropped in favor of Christianity. Under both, the concept of imperial rule broke with the past. Scipio Africanus, Caesar, and August linked their office to the divine, but the ultimate sanction remained always in the hands the people, as embodied in the Senate and in the army. Despite all the changes, neither Diocletian nor Constantine nor the following emperors would become absolute sovereigns.[81]

Constantine's frontier policy was different from that under Diocletian. Both emphasized defense, but whereas Diocletian's soldiers shouldered most of the burden at the frontiers, Constantine relied on defense in depth. The latter was based on the assumption that the invaders would first encounter the frontier troops but, as they moved into imperial lands, would contend with troops lined behind various fortifications. The intention was to slow them down until the mobile army could arrive to deliver the killing blow.

Continuous deployment of large forces at the frontier was probably impossible. In any case in the long run it was probably a bad strategy.[82] Yet the new emphasis on mobility undermined the failing prestige of the infantry, sacrificed the frontier population, and dispelled the myth that the state provided absolute security to all. The tensions between the two policies is well illustrated by the fact that infantry, despite the emphasis on cavalry, still determined the outcomes of the great battles.[83] Moreover, the soldiers were divided into two camps: the "superior" mobile field army, and the "inferior" border troops. Over time the border troops, often undermanned, would develop closer ties to their locations at the expense of the center; in contrast, the mobile troops were less exposed to immediate danger, were probably better paid, and enjoyed better career prospects.[83]

The events of the third century give the impression that the Roman Empire's very survival was in the balance. Yet the western empire lasted for some 150 years after Constantine. Even so, by examining the important reforms undertaken from Septimius through Constantine, we can clearly see that they were harbingers of greater problems ahead. During the late fourth and fifth centuries, the Roman Empire would face its ultimate crisis.

Notes

1. Dio lxxvii (epitome).15.2.
2. On the 68–69 crisis, see Charles L. Murison, *Galba, Otho, and Vitellius: Careers and Controversies* (New York, 1993).
3. J. B. Campbell, *The Emperor and the Roman Army* (Oxford, 1984), p. 369.
4. Ibid., p. 367.
5. Anthony Birley, *Marcus Aurelius: A Biography* (London, 1987), p. 224.
6. *Historia Augusta*, "Commodus," xvii.3.
7. Dio lxxiii (epitome).18.1–2.
8. Ibid., 20.1.
9. Ibid., 19.
10. Ibid., 20.2.
11. Ibid., 21.
12. Ibid., 14.1.
13. A. Passerini, *Linee di storia romana in età imperiale* (Milano, 1972), pp. 693–694.
14. Dio lxxiii (epitome).14.4.
15. Ibid., 15.
16. Ibid., 22.4–6.
17. Ibid., lxxiii.
18. *Historia Augusta*, "Pertinax" 14.1.
19. Dio (epitome) lxxiv.10.1–3.
20. Ibid., lxxiii.
21. *Historia Augusta*, "Julianus" viii.6–8.
22. Ibid., viii.9.3.
23. *Historia Augusta*, "Severus" 5.2.

24. Dio lxxv (epitome).1.3.

25. *Historia Augusta*, "Severus" 7.1–5; also Herodian ii.14.1. Dio (epitome).lxxv.1.3–5, cautiously claims that instead the citizens accepted Septimius with joy.

26. Anthony Birley, *Septimius Severus the African Emperor* (London, 1971), p. 35.

27. *Historia Augusta*, "Severus" 19.10. Birley thinks that this was unlikely; see *Septimius Severus the African Emperor*, pp. 73–74.

28. See Dio lxxiii (epitome).16.17.

29. *Historia Augusta*, "Severus" 19.6.

30. See Dio lxxiv (epitome).17.3.

31. Herodian ii.13; also Dio lxxv (epitome).1.1–2.

32. Dio lxxv (epitome).2.4–6; Herodian ii.14.5.

33. A. Passerini, *Le coorti pretorie* (Roma, 1939), pp. 141–189; M. Durry, *Les cohortes prétoriennes* (Paris, 1938), pp. 239–257; Y. Le Bohec, *L'esercito romano: Le armi imperiali da Augusto a Caracalla* (Roma, 1992), pp. 126–127.

34. Dio lxxv (epitome).2.5–6.

35. Eric Birley, "Septimius Severus and the Roman Army," in his *The Roman Army: Papers, 1929–1986* (Amsterdam, 1988), pp. 22–23.

36. Herodian ii.14.6.

37. Birley, *The Roman Army*, p. 65; Birley, *Septimius Severus the African Emperor*, pp. 283–284. Cf. Durry, *Les cohortes prétoriennes*, pp. 81–89, on the pretorians' numerical strength.

38. For Plautianus, see Dio lxxvi (epitome).14–16; lxxvii (epitome).1–6; also Herodian iii.10.5–7; 11; 12.10–12. His account differs somewhat and seems less reliable.

39. Birley, *Septimius Severus the African Emperor*, pp. 10, 282, 294–295.

40. Dio lxxvii (epitome).2.3.

41. On his career, see the evidence summarized by Birley, *Septimius Severus the African Emperor*, p. 294.

42. Dio lxxvi (epitome).14–15.

43. Ibid., lxxvii (epitome).6.3; lxxviii (epitome).1. On Antoninus's marriage, see Birley, *Septimius Severus the African Emperor*, pp. 231–232. On the hatred for his wife, beside Dio, see Herodian iii.10.5, 8.13.2.

44. See Dio lxxvi (epitome).14.1, 4, 6.15.6. On the children, see Birley, *Septimius Severus the African Emperor*, p. 171.

45. Dio lxxvi (epitome).14.3.

46. Dio lxxvi (epitome).15.7.

47. Herodian iii.10.6. Cf. Birley, *Septimius Severus the African Emperor*, p. 62.

48. Birley, *Septimius Severus the African Emperor*, p. 294.

49. Dio lxxvii (epitome).1–4. Herodian, iii.12.10–12, gives a slightly different version of Plautianus's end. Cf. Birley, *Septimius Severus the African Emperor*, pp. 231–235.

50. Edward N. Luttwak, *The Grand Strategy of the Roman Empire from the First Century A.D. to the Third* (Baltimore, 1976), p. 128.

51. Le Bohec, *L'esercito romano*, p. 43.

52. See, e.g., Dio's remarks in lxxv (epitome).2.3.

53. Birley, *Septimius Severus the African Emperor*, p. 167.

54. Le Bohec, *L'esercito romano*, p. 283.

55. Milan, *Le forze armate nella storia di Roma antica*, pp. 179–180.

56. Herodian iii.8.5.

57. Antonio Santosuosso, *Soldiers, Citizens, and the Symbols of War from Classical Greece to Republican Rome, 500–167 B.C.* (Boulder, 1997), p. 85.

58. *Historia Augusta*, "The Two Maximini" 1.5; 6.8. His height is described as over 8 feet, 6 inches. The Roman foot, divided normally into 12 inches, was equivalent to 24.6 centimeters.

59. Passerini, *Linee di storia romana*, p. 167.

60. Ibid., pp. 465–470.

61. Ibid., p. 465.

62. Ibid., p. 168.

63. D. L. Kennedy, "The Frontier Policy of Septimius Severus: New Evidence from Arabia," *Roman Frontier Studies 1979*, pp. 879–880.

64. Moving troops from Rome to Cologne could be a matter of two months, according to Ferrill, *The Fall of the Roman Empire*, p. 46.

65. Sextus Aurelius Victor, *De Caesaribus* xxxiii.6; *Historia Augusta*, "Valeriani Duo" 16.1.

66. On Gallienus's military reforms, see Lukas De Blois, *The Policy of the Emperor Gallienus* (Leiden, 1976), pp. 23–47; also see the summary in Le Bohec, *L'esercito romano*, pp. 262–264; and Southern and Dixon, *The Late Roman Army*, pp. 11–15. For the senators' exclusion from military service, see Sextus Aurelius Victor, *De Caesaribus* xxxiii.34.

67. Southern and Dixon, *The Late Roman Army*, p. 12.

68. The self-styled "dux of the East" was Septimius Odenaethus of Palmyra, the "emperor" of the West Marcus Cassianius Latinius Postumus.

69. Southern and Dixon, *The Late Roman Army*, pp. 13–14.

70. De Blois, *The Policy of the Emperor Gallienus*, pp. 29–30; Southern and Dixon, *The Late Roman Army*, p. 14.

71. Cf. Le Bohec, *L'esercito romano*, p. 263.

72. *Historia Augusta*, "Valeriani Duo" 14.8–9.

73. Jones, *The Later Roman Empire*, pp. 53–55.
74. The emperor was Constans, who reigned for about a year and a half.
75. Jones, *The Later Roman Empire*, pp. 321–324.
76. Ibid., p. 182.
77. Milan, *Le forze armate nella storia di Roma antica*, p. 196.
78. On Gallienus and Aurelian's policy, see Lawrence Okamura, "Roman Withdrawals from Three Transluvial Frontiers," in *Shifting Frontiers in Late Antiquity*, edited by Ralph W. Mathisen and Hagith S. Sivan (Aldershot, 1996), pp. 11–19.
79. Jones, *The Later Roman Empire*, p. 60.
80. Ferrill, *The Fall of the Roman Empire*, pp. 41–42.
81. Jones, *The Later Roman Empire*, p. 321.
82. Ibid., p. 100.
83. Ferrill, *The Fall of the Roman Empire*, pp. 46–47.
84. Milan, *Le forze armate nella storia di Roma antica*, pp. 199–201.

8

Rome Is No More: The End of the Empire

When the brightest light on the whole earth was extinguished, when the Roman empire was deprived of its head, when, to speak more correctly, the whole world perished in one city, then "I was dumb with silence. I held my peace even from good, and my sorrow was stirred."

Jerome, *Comm. In Ezech* i.pref.

In 410, about eight centuries after it was sacked by the Gauls, Rome fell again to barbarians. This time, Gothic troops broke through the gate, having taken imperial lands about three decades earlier. As Jerome lamented from Palestine (see epigraph above), the whole world perished in one city.[1] But this event was not the beginning of the age of troubles. The troubles had begun three decades earlier, but after the sack of Rome the political landscape in western Europe would shift. Fifteen years afterward, Britain was no longer part of the empire. Barbarian kingdoms under the Vandals, Suebians, Visigoths, and Burgundians would be established throughout western Europe and North Africa. Rome was lucky to keep a tenuous hold on the Italian peninsula and the Balkans, but these territories would also fall to the invaders. Forty-five years later a new barbarian army—the Vandals—would sack the city again; twenty-one years after that—in A.D. 476—the Western Roman Empire came to its official end.

The Late Roman Army

The Roman military forces of the Late Empire were formidable, at least on paper, about 600,000–645,000 by 425. Some 250,000 troops were stationed in the west, 352,000 in the east. The *comitatenses* (mobile field troops) numbered 113,000 in the west, 104,000 in the east. The majority were *limitanei* (border troops), 135,000 in the west and 248,000 in the east (which included not just the eastern frontier, but a portion of the Danube and all of North Africa).[2] Those figures are based on the *Notitia Dignitatum*, an important document of the Late Empire, the interpretation of which is uncertain (among other problems, not all sections were compiled at the same time). Yet the information could be fairly accurate. If we assume an increase of 33.5 percent in about a century, the 600,000 figure found in the *Notitia Dignitatum* makes sense, as there were 435,266 men (including the fleet) under Diocletian and at least 286,000 in the 312 confrontation between Constantine and Maxentius.[3] Yet establishing the numerical strength of the Roman army in the Late Empire remains an educated guess.[4] The problem is complicated by the practice of commanders who inflated their troops' numerical strength by counting the deceased or nonexistent so that they could pocket the extra wages. As a fourth-century intellectual put it, the dead were "kept alive so that their rations could still be drawn."[5]

Eventually the mobile armies split into different components: one army directly under the emperor's control (the *palatina* or *praesental*), and several regional armies. In time that would also change, as most regional armies became static, with cadres spread throughout the frontier and functioning mainly as garrisons (and thus like the *limitanei*). That arrangement may have been the major weakness. Although the legionnaires had from the very beginning performed various roles—soldier, engineer, farmer—it seems reasonable to assume a decline in military proficiency occurred if soldiers were interested more in their civilian occupation than their military function. It led emperors to rely on quantity, not quality, and thus to recruit more men to face the oncoming emergencies. This implied higher taxes, an increasing financial strain on the population, and no guarantee of capable fighting troops.[6]

The mobile field army included both cavalry *(vexillationes)* and infantry *(legiones, auxilia)*. At times from the fourth century onward, another term *(numeri)* was used for both footmen and horsemen.[7] Usually cavalry regiments reached 500–600 men, infantry 1,000–1,200. The field army's most prestigious units were the *comitatenses palatini*, originally the emperor's escort, although in time there seems to have been no differentiation between the *palatini* and the other cavalrymen (the *comitatenses*). Seniority probably played a role in both.[8]

Roman citizens and erstwhile barbarian enemies served in the mobile army. The barbarians usually were referred to as federates *(foederati)*, although they should be distinguished as two separate groups. Some were hired only for certain campaigns and then disbanded; others became a permanent feature of the army. The *foederati* regiments, apparently mostly cavalry, were deliberately recruited from barbarians, although Roman citizens from outlying colonies must have participated. Hugh Elton has shown that in the period 365–440 the federates came from Germanic tribes as well as a variety of other ethnic populations like the Alans, an Indo-European people originally from the Iranian plains and long settled in the Ukrainian steppes, and the Huns, a nomadic people originally from Central Asia.[9] The mobility of the troops was heightened within the Mediterranean as well, as the emperor could shift soldiers about using warships and merchant vessels. The main ports in the west remained Ravenna and Misenum, although other bases existed (e.g., Como and Arles). The fleet's main task was, it seems, the North African coast, especially after the Vandals conquered that region.

The border troops had small fleets on the Rhine and the Danube. They were moored in fortified places along the rivers, where both cavalry and infantry were stationed. The *limitanei* regiments of both armies were probably smaller than their counterparts in the *comitatenses*. They were in the range of about 500, called generally *cohortes* and *legiones* (infantry) and *alae* (horsemen). They repeated on a smaller scale the *comitatenses*, although they differed in organization, deployment, physical specifications, period of service, and benefits at retirement, all which were less stringent or less generous compared to the *comitatenses*.[10] Moreover, there seems to be no doubt that the *limitanei* were held in low esteem. One bishop, for instance, complained bitterly to the emperor about the transfer of a unit of his regular troops in Cyrenaica to a new role as *limitanei*. It would be a demotion, he wrote, deprived as they would be of their donatives, with no remounts, no military equipment, and not enough resources to fight the enemy.[11]

At least until the fifth century the Roman army also included units that accompanied the emperor during a campaign (the *domestici*), who with the so-called *protectores* provided officers to the army's units, or specific bodyguards for generals (the *bucellarii*). All of them seem to have disappeared or lost importance in the later years. One of the weaknesses of the empire eventually would be the lack of militia, probably out of habit but also because the general population was prohibited from owning arms. This meant that when barbarians attacked only makeshift forces of retired veterans and untrained slaves could be raised, often with dismal results.[12]

The soldiers of the Late Empire differed from the troops of the Early Empire in several ways. Cavalry increased, probably to an average of one cavalryman for every three footmen.[13] (In the legion of the first century A.D. the ratio was closer to one per forty.) Long-distance missile units (archers and slingers), rare in the early period outside the auxiliaries, now accounted for as much as a third of all troops, performing specialist and perhaps combined functions. Moreover, they were armed with a variety of short-distance missiles, from darts (probably only in the infantry) thrown from a distance of 30–65 meters to several types of javelins (both infantry and cavalry). Footmen seem to have carried at least two javelins, one heavier and longer (1.6 meters), the other about 1 meter. The javelins remind one of the old *pila* (the term is sometimes still used), but in reality both the shape and the function were different.

There were differences in the basic equipment of the infantry. The *gladius* was substituted in some units by a longsword *(spatha)* 0.7–0.9 meter long. The *spatha* could be used for thrusting and cutting. And although the infantry still fought in close order, the primary weapon was not the sword but a spear 2–2.5 meters long. Also, the rectangular shield of the earlier republic was dropped in favor of large oval shields probably 1–1.2 meters high and 0.8 meter wide. The cavalry also used the spear as its main weapon, together with the longsword and the bow and javelin in the case of the lighter units.[14] Vegetius suggests that certain elements of armor protection were dropped in the Late Empire, but Elton, mainly on the basis of visual representations, argues otherwise. Besides shields and helmets, the cavalry and footmen used at least three types of body armor: mail, scale corselet, and, in the case of officers, bronze or iron cuirasses. This equipment was not standard for all units. Missile units and light cavalry may have worn little or no armor—including no helmet.[15]

Except for light cavalry and certain missile units, main units conformed to the old model of heavy infantry and heavy cavalry. Elton calculates that about 76 percent of the horsemen in the field army were shock cavalry (15 percent very heavily armored, the remainder less so), to which we should add at least two-thirds of the close-order infantry. The proportion among the *limitanei* in Europe was different, with the emphasis on units that could move quickly; light cavalry, for instance, constituted about 47 percent and shock cavalry decreased to 51 percent.[16]

By this time citizens and barbarians were recruited from within and outside the borders of the empire. Some people were automatically excluded: slaves, freedmen (slaves who have been given their freedom), and some lower occupations (e.g., bakers, innkeepers, cooks). Among the middle classes, the *curiales*, that is, members of city councils, were also excluded.[17]

Rome needed at least 30,000 soldiers per year during peacetime to maintain 600,000 troops. Demand grew during periods of conflict.[18] And even though many signed on for their own reasons—adventure, alienation from society, poverty—Rome had to rely on conscription to fill the rolls. Whereas some groups were not eligible to serve in the regular army, others were required to do so. These included soldiers' sons (even if their fathers were officers), vagrants, and general conscripts (although at times recruits could avoid service by paying a certain amount of money). The ability to buy out of one's service filled the state's dwindling coffers and provided cheaper recruits.

Obligations to serve paralleled the land tax, which meant that the burden fell on landowners, small and large. Landowning citizens were assessed on the value of their land and charged accordingly. The levy was also imposed on the holders of high administrative offices *(honorati)*, although in their case the required service was normally commuted if they paid out the equivalent of a soldier's value.[19]

Military service must have remained attractive to poor peasants with weak community ties. The pay was low, although legionnaires, whose regular salary was 600 *denarii*, still averaged 12,500 a year (a more than 2,000 percent increase over the base pay) when we count the donatives they received, usually every five years and at the accession of the emperor (the Augustus) and his junior colleague (the Caesar). The situation was less satisfying for the lower troops, who averaged about 1,250 *denarii* a year. If we account for the high inflation rate, soldiers' wages were of minuscule value in the later years of the empire.[20] Yet even the lowest pay was attractive to peasants in preindustrial societies. Soldiers received considerable and good-quality food rations *(annona)* for themselves and fodder for their horses *(capitus)*. The individual ration likely included bread, meat (veal, pork, or salt pork), and wine. The food supply was carefully arranged throughout the year, especially during a campaign, when large supplies of biscuits and sour wine were included.[21]

The state, though not always consistently, also provided shelter on location for soldiers' families. The *limitanei* must have found lodging in the constructions at the frontier, and the *comitatenses* were billeted with the local population (but only with the lower classes, who were obliged to provide one-third of their living quarters). The policy created all kinds of abuses, as in 396 when a soldier allegedly forced his host (a widow) to let him marry her young daughter, whom he later abandoned. He had already been married to another woman, and he was tried and executed for his transgression.[22]

Promotion was always a possibility. One of the few paths to upward mobility, it was usually based on years of service (besides, that is, merit and graft). Upon discharge veterans enjoyed several other privileges. If he became a trader, he received goods or cash from the emperor. He was also exempt from the poll tax.[23] Thus the benefits of military service were considerable, even accounting for dishonest officers who appropriated benefits due their men.[24]

By the fourth and fifth centuries A.D. imperial agents found their best recruiting grounds among barbarians living inside and outside the empire.[25] The government could force prisoners of war to join the Roman forces, an ancient tradition used by the Egyptians and Assyrians in the last two millennia before the Christian era. Others were recruited from the barbarians who were forcibly resettled to Roman territories, Gaul, and northern and southern Italy, where many had settled (e.g., the German Alamans and Indo-European Sarmatians).[26] Many barbarians crossed the border of their own volition to take part in civilized and easy living. For a person coming from a primitive economy, the reward must have been enticing indeed, and many barbarians rose to the highest positions in the army.[27] As a policy, then, Rome actively encouraged its former barbarian enemies to sign up. In fact, formal treaties (following war and during peace) between the empire and a tribe could include the obligation to provide soldiers for a certain period. In consideration for providing personnel, the tribe received gold, supplies, or the promise of peace.[28]

Many have claimed that hiring so many outsiders "barbarized" the Roman army, leading to a decline in fighting spirit and allegiance to Rome. There is little evidence to support this theory. The new breed of soldier usually fought well and was prone to betrayal neither more nor less than Roman citizens.[29] Some even claim that the "barbarian intrusion" has been overexaggerated and that "the majority of the regular Roman regiments continued to be composed mostly of non-barbarians."[30] Yet this did not necessarily mean that soldiers, regardless of heritage, absorbed Roman customs and ideals. In fact the ideal of citizenship had been diluted by Caracalla's edict of A.D. 212, allowing every free individual in the empire to become a citizen. The point is that the differences in values were not very great after most everyone enjoyed the benefits of citizenship.

In any event, these new armies did not compare very well to the mighty armies of the Early Roman Empire.[31] Still, they were formidable and defeated most adversaries. The basic structure and policies were intact, and they had good supplies, logistical support, and transportation. The campaigns in the second half of the fourth and the first half of the fifth centuries continued to be organized to punish outsiders, but in most cases only in response to an invasion. If the campaign was in enemy territory, preparation took a long time (e.g., eighteen months for Emperor Valens's campaign against the Goths in 366, three months for Emperor Valentinian I's campaign against the German Quadi in 375). The strategy was always to strike the enemy with as much force as possible, ensure adequate supplies of food and weapons, and withdraw only after completing the defined goal. This meant operating across the border only when the weather was favorable (July in Gaul and on the Danube, May in Italy, late winter and very early spring against nomadic peoples like Huns and Alans, who needed pastures for their horses). The campaign was complete only when the enemy had been punished enough and had signed a treaty recognizing Rome's sovereignty.[32]

As A.H.M. Jones writes in one of his classic works on the Late Roman Empire, "In the West the Roman army disintegrated in the middle of the fifth century, being gradually replaced by bands of barbarian federates. In the East there was no such break of continuity, but the army which emerges into view after the obscure period of the mid-fifth century is markedly different from that of the fourth."[33] The process had become irreversible after the changes following the crisis of the third century. The problem was that the assaults on the frontiers never stopped. Rome nested its adversaries within their own territories. And ambitious Roman leaders often considered their internal rivals to be much more dangerous than barbarians crossing the imperial border.

The Invaders

The Greeks began to use the term "barbarian" in the aftermath of the Persian expansion in Asia Minor and as a result of the Persians' invasion of Hellas. Originally it meant people who did not speak Greek or cherish Greek institutions. Thus the term differentiated those who were part of a familiar political and social commonwealth from outsiders who were disruptive and

FIGURE 8.1   *The Fourth-Century Frontier*

potentially dangerous. The Romans inherited the Greek meaning and extended it to all people who were not part of the empire, as well as those living in imperial territories who had not been granted citizenship. Thus we should understand "barbarian" to refer simply to people who geographically and/or politically lived outside the empire.

By the fourth century A.D. certain tribes emerged as serious threats along the Roman frontiers (see Figure 8.1). Across the northern section of the Rhine there were the Franks and the Saxons behind them. On the upper course of the Rhine and near the source of the Danube were the Alamans with the Suebians behind them and the Burgundians on the northeast. Across the Danube, we find, moving eastward, the Quadi and the Sarmatians (Sarmatae), with the Vandals on their back. The Goths spread across what is now Romania and the Ukraine, with the Alans on their left flank. Except for the Sarmatians and the Alans, the other peoples spoke some form of German. The Sarmatians were nomadic Indo-Europeans of Iranian origin related to the Scythians. The Alans were nomads from Asia who had moved to the northern edges of the Black Sea. Other barbarians would move south and west, including the Longobards, originally from Scandinavia but now living in central Europe, as well as the Asiatic Huns. The Huns would play a major role in the collapse of the frontier, moving first against the Eastern Empire then against the Western Empire with greater success. They in fact forced the Goths to cross the imperial border. But the Romans faced adversaries throughout the frontier, from Britain to North Africa: the Picts and Irish in Britain; Persians on the Syrian border; desert people (Saracens) living in tents east of Egypt and south of Palestine. Peoples within the empire included the Isaurians in Asia Minor and the Moors (Berbers) in North Africa.[34]

These peoples were not new to the scene. The Romans had been fighting German tribes for almost four centuries, beginning at least with Marius's confrontation with the Cimbri and Teutones at the end of the second century B.C. It continued in the waning days of the republic and through the first two centuries of imperial rule. It is probable, however, that alliances had by now grown, even if a single alliance did not span the collective whole. The Goths were no brothers of the Quadi, the Saxons no brothers of the Franks. There was, in other words, no German "nation" at this time.[35]

The German numbers were small, with invading armies, except in a few cases, numbering 20,000–40,000 soldiers, and never more than 100,000.[36] We find an 80,000-man Burgundian army in 373, according to Jerome, and the same number for a Vandal army in 428–429. But likely only 25 percent were of fighting age. But the Goths, who came across the Danube in the 370s, must have numbered some 200,000 if we include both Visigoths and Ostrogoths. On paper the Roman Empire should have had no problem; the western army, which took the brunt of most invasions, numbered about 250,000. Yet the imperial forces were spread thinly along a massive frontier. In Britain there was a tiny army of 3,000. In Spain 10,000–11,000 men had to confront both Suebians and Vandals when they invaded the Iberian peninsula. There were only two major armies against two Roman armies, 35,000 in Gaul and 30,000 in Italy. Rome's Gallic contingent had to match forces against Visigoths, Burgundians, Franks, and Armoricans, who sometimes acted in alliance. Four barbarian armies assailed the Gallic army in 406–407, and a barbarian leader in 405 led many more against Italy, the only place that could spare personnel for reinforcements.[37]

The problem was compounded during the second half of the fourth century by Themistius, a Constantinople philosopher and member of the ruling group (he was a senator of the Eastern Empire). He questioned why the majority should waste lives and money to defend a few people at the frontier. He argued that peace was the ideal, but that peace could be kept only if the Romans abandoned the defense of the borders.[38] Themistius's suggestion was a radical reversal from Diocletian (about fifty years earlier), who assumed the throne when the frontiers were a sieve. Diocletian's reaction was traditional: The Roman army marched to the frontier, pushed the invaders back, and reestablished the traditional boundary.[39] This would not happen in A.D. 378, when the Romans suffered a horrible defeat at Adrianople to the Goths who, in fear of the Huns, had forced their way across the Danube two years earlier. The reaction of the eastern emperor, Theodosius I, was not to push them back across the river but to grant them autonomous status within the empire. In A.D. 408 the outcome was even worse after a coalition of Alamans, Suebians, and Vandals spread across the Rhine and eventually established a kingdom in Spain.

Defeat at Adrianople

The most dangerous invaders were the Goths. By the middle of the third century A.D. the Goths inhabited the eastern section of the Danube frontier, but their ancestral home seems to have been Scandinavia and the area nearby modern Poland (see Figure 8.2). They had moved southward along the Vistula River (there are traces of their culture in modern Poland and Belorussia) to settle finally on the lower Danube and Black Sea, east and south of the Carpathian Mountains; they divided into two branches, separated by the Dniester River.[40] They moved into an area that had been mostly under Roman control, but in the third century A.D. the Romans had decided to move back to the southern side of the river, creating a vacuum in the north.

There the Goths found three other civilizations: the Dacians, integrated into the empire at the turn of the second century A.D. under Trajan; the Sarmatians, a nomadic Indo-European population that had appeared on the lower Danube around the second and first century B.C.; and on their left the Indo-European Alans. There was a certain tolerance, especially between Dacians and Sarmatians (they exploited different resources). The archaeological evidence shows a peaceful coexistence in the area annexed to Rome and even on the border area north of Transylvania and east of the Carpathians (which the Romans had left as a buffer zone against other invaders).[41] Moreover, finds in the region in Wallachia, Dacia, Bessarabia, and Moldavia suggest some blending between Goths and Sarmatians.[42]

The Goths were settled agriculturalists, not nomads. Yet they suffered from chronic food shortages, a situation the Romans exploited by cutting or

FIGURE 8.2   Adrianople Campaign, A.D. 376–378

awarding supplies from the empire.[43] This policy was effective, for the Goths could be dangerous indeed. In the past, compelled by hunger or adventure or greed, they had created trouble for the empire in Asia Minor and the Balkans. But nothing compared to the events of the 370s.

The problem began when the Asian Huns appeared on the Russian steppe behind the Gothic lands. These new invaders were different.[44] Their appearance was shocking to many.[45] Excellent horsemen, their heads covered with round caps and their legs with goatskins, the Huns galloped through the territory followed by their wagons, where the women and children remained. They were the "most terrible of all warriors," according to Ammianus. Moving quickly, often in a wedge formation, they scattered into smaller bands, shouting savagely as they moved to strike.⁴⁶ Their first victims were the Alans, then the Goths as they advanced westward. They seized and destroyed everything they could, finally driving the Visigoths (Theruingi) away from their homes.

With the Huns menacing them on their rear and probably suffering their usual food scarcity, the Goths moved toward the Danube, requesting refuge across the waters among the Romans in the fertile lands of Thrace. They hoped the great river would provide safety from enemies.⁴⁷ The traditional Roman response would have been to refuse the request and push them back to the opposite bank. Valens (emperor, 364–378), however, preoccupied with the eastern frontier and perhaps hopeful that these new agriculturalists would provide additional income,⁴⁸ gave them permission to move across the river, ordering that they be given food and fields to cultivate.⁴⁹ Valens's decision was the "ruin of the Roman world." Several Gothic groups were ferried across the river in boats, rafts, and hollowed-out tree trunks. But the waters were turbulent, especially when sudden rain raised the water level. During the crossing to the opposite bank several tried to swim, and many drowned.⁵⁰

The Battle of Adrianople develops like a Greek tragedy in which greed, arrogance, ambition, and jealousy move the players toward disaster. Allowing in outsiders known for their warlike spirit was not the only mistake that the emperor and his associates made. With so many thousands on Roman land, the immediate priority was to disperse them. A large group of refugees was moved away from the crossing area; others were hired as soldiers and sent to the eastern frontier; and a third group was settled in the countryside near Adrianople to winter there. But the majority was kept in the area bounded by the Danube on the north and the Haemus Mountains on the south.⁵¹ There Roman officers, especially Lupicinus, the commander in chief of the province, preyed upon them. The provisions promised by Valens either did not arrive or were pilfered by corrupt officials; with few other resources, the refugees soon began to starve. Lupicinus, described as an associate of "slave merchants and dealers," found the situation to his liking. He or people under his command robbed the refugees of the only valuable commodity they had—freedom. He traded them for dogs at the barter rate of one dog per man or child, then sold them elsewhere as slaves.⁵²

Guarding the Goths on the riverbanks north of the Haemus Mountains must have loosened up the defenses upstream. Not even the usual flotilla of patrol boats was active on the Danube. The Ostrogoths (Greuthungi), who had been refused entry into the province earlier, took advantage and crossed the Danube.[53] Now there were two major groups of Goths in Roman territory; they would be joined by the Huns and Alans soon thereafter. The leader of the first refugee wave (the Theruingi) started to march toward the newly arrived Goths (the Greuthungi), probably in search of an alliance to force the Romans to pay off on their promises. The treacherous Lupicinus, probably worried about such an alliance, invited two Theruingi leaders to a banquet, intending either to kill them or confirm their loyalty to Rome. In a series of confusing events the barbarian escort was massacred, but the two chiefs escaped, one of them being the leader Fritigern.[54] There is no reason to assume that the Goths were seeking a fight with the imperial troops.

To echo a famous description, the Goths were so numerous that counting them was like trying to count the grains of sand in a desert.[55] Yet many were children, women, and elderly persons, and the Romans had forbidden anyone to cross the river with weapons. But some must have carried weapons during the crossing,[56] and the Romans continued to compound their mistakes.[57] When Fritigern escaped the banquet ambush, the only logical solution may have been to challenge the Romans. His men spread through the Thracian countryside, pillaging and burning, an action that Lupicinus tried to stop with "more haste than discretion." When he came face-to-face with Fritigern his men were slaughtered (he escaped to the nearby town while his men were engaged in combat).[58]

Valens ordered the Goths wintering near Adrianople to leave immediately for the province of Hellespont across the straits between Europe and Turkey. This faction had shown no desire to join the revolt, but they could still be dangerous if they changed their mind. Still, the emperor's orders were carriedout in atrocious fashion. When the Goths demanded a two-day delay, provisions, and money for the journey before the march began, the local administrators ordered them to leave immediately. It was a poor decision, for Fritigern's men too were not far from the town's walls.

The heretofore peaceable Goths rose up in arms, killed many citizens, and then joined forces with Fritigern. They besieged Adrianople but were unable to make headway until Fritigern, apparently now the leader of the united Goths, decided to strike the softer targets of the countryside, wryly commenting that he could not make war against walls. The barbarians spread over every quarter of Thrace, their numbers growing daily. Even some citizens of the empire, Thracian gold miners, made common cause with the rebels, for they felt that their lifestyle and tax burden were so harsh that life among an alien people was preferable.[59] In many ways the revolt became a war of the dispossessed and poor against the powerful and rich.

The situation was dire, for Rome now had to confront the rebels in force. The emperor, who was in Antioch, dispatched two new generals, Profuturus and Trajanus, to the front in the fall of 376. He also requested help from Gratian, his nephew and the emperor in the west, and the troops of two other generals, Frigerid and Richomer, also from the west. The emperor's strategy was to destroy the Goths with a large army, but in the manner of an irresolute neophyte, his choice in leadership was poor. Profuturus and Trajanus, sent immediately to the war front, were ambitious but unfit to wage war; there were also problems with two generals called from the west: Richomer hurried but with depleted troops (most had deserted); Frigerid, afflicted by gout, advanced slowly.[60]

While waiting for the arrival of the troops from east and west, Profuturus and Trajan bottled up Fritigern's troops in the defile of Mount Haemus, hoping to starve them into submission. But the Goths had apparently fanned out into Thrace and nearby Moesia on the west. Upon his arrival Richomer took command of the entire force and decided to strike one of the enemy contingents before the rest of the troops under Frigerid had arrived. The battle was fought at Ad Salices—the prologue to Adrianople. In the end the barbarians survived with heavy losses on both sides.[61] The trap set by Profuturus and Trajanus had failed, as did Richomer's premature attack. The Romans had to withdraw behind the walls of nearby Marcianopolis on the border of eastern Moesia, a province adjacent to Thracia; the Goths, fearful of a new Roman attack, did not leave the protection of their wagons for seven days. Richomer reverted then to Profuturus and Trajanus's plan: He closed every exit from the mountains in order to starve the enemy. He returned to the west, intending to bring reinforcements.[62]

Blind to the military principle of leaving the enemy an out, the Roman generals made a valiant people desperate. As they consumed their meager food supplies, the Goths, "driven alike by ferocity and hunger," tried to fight out of the trap (they failed) but managed to strike an alliance with bands of Huns and Alans. The acquisition of "immense booty" was the rebels' hope.[63] Valens sent another general named Saturninus to replace Richomer toward the latter part of 377. Saturninus changed policy yet again. He retreated, afraid that the longer the Goths were entrapped, the more dangerous they would become. It was a gamble that did not pay off. The Goths, free to escape, brought devastation and death to Thrace. They ended up storming a small town, where they slew a tribune of the bodyguard after a harsh struggle.[64]

The new successes must have increased the barbarians' confidence. Although most of them were still divided into pillaging bands, some moved forward to intercept Frigerid, who had returned to Thrace. But Frigerid, , became the hunter instead of the prey. He surprised the barbarians marauding western Thrace upstream from the main body and quickly fell upon them, slaughtering their leader. When the rest pleaded for mercy, he spared them and deported them to Italy, near Mutina, to toil in the fields.

Frigerid proved his worth, yet Valens dismissed him (probably jealous of his relationship with the emperor's nephew Gratian) and appointed Sebastian to lead the army in late 377 or early 378. It seemed that Sebastian, a man with a good military reputation, would follow Frigerid's example, for he too decided to defeat the enemy in detail: He surprised a group of Goths during a night attack and came away with so much booty that some had to be kept outside the city walls of Adrianople, for there was not enough space to house it in town.[65]

Sebastian's and Frigerid's successes indicated the road to success: defeat the roving bands of Goths in detail until the arrival of Gratian's reinforcements. But the Romans underestimated the leadership qualities of Fritigern, the leader of the Theruingi Goths, while overestimating their own, especially after Valens arrived in Thrace. Realizing that as long as his bands were scattered throughout Thrace they were open to surprise attack and destruction in detail, Fritigern recalled all his men near Adrianople, making sure the location would provide enough provisions for his warriors.[66] By this time the Greuthungi Goths had joined Fritigern,[67] as the Romans had been unable to keep the two groups separated.

Valens reached Thrace by the spring or summer of 378. He was almost fifty years old and had reigned the Eastern Empire for almost fourteen years. Physically he was far from striking: With a cataract, knock-kneed, and pot-bellied, he had a dark complexion and was of average height. He had neither a liberal education (a must for the times) nor good knowledge in the art of warfare. It was in the hands of this man—irresolute and often swayed by his courtiers—that the destiny of the eastern army rested.[68]

Gratian's triumph against the Alamans troubled Valens instead of pleasing him. Gratian's letters that he was speedily proceeding by boat on the Danube must have added to his jealousy: Now he would have to share any triumph. But other factors caused him to join battle with the assembling Goths. Sebastian's night raid and the general's insistence that it was time to inflict the killing blow inclined Valens toward confrontation despite the fact that during the war council a general urged him to adopt a more cautious approach. The most decisive element must have been poor intelligence. His skirmishers informed him that the Gothic forces numbered 10,000 or a few more. Many generals would have delayed the confrontation until Gratian arrived with his reinforcements. Instead Valens decided to strike, committing error after error while marching into battle.

Fritigern first gave the impression that he could cut the imperial troops' supply line, then played a game of psychological warfare with Valens, proposing peace even until the very beginning of the battle. Finally, he made sure that his opponent would have to face battle in the most uncomfortable conditions.

Fritigern let Valens come to him, and Valens did so. It was a hot day, August 9, 378.[69] The emperor left Adrianople around noon in the heat; the Goths were deployed a good distance from the city on rough ground.[70] The march must have fatigued the imperial troops. They reached the enemies around two in the afternoon. When they arrived, they found the Goths protected behind their customary tactical arrangement, a circle of wagons (the laager). It was their custom to build an impregnable fortification with a double moat defended by stakes, their wagons rigged with oxhide all around like a wall.[71] The wagons were joined together in a circle. The discomfort of the imperial troops, probably wearing cuirasses, must have increased because of the delay before battle and because the barbarians had started and maintained fires around themselves. Their throats dry from the heat and march, Roman men and beasts were thirsty and hungry. They had left their baggage and packs near Adrianople's walls.[72]

Valens had already made enormous mistakes: He had not waited for reinforcements; trusted inaccurate intelligence; played into the hands of the enemy; sought battle on a day when soldiers laden with armor would inevitably be at a disadvantage; marched a long distance and in the heat to the battlefield; and made no arrangement to satisfy the hunger and thirst of his men.[73] The enemy was rested and secure behind their laager (see Figure 8.3). Moreover, the Roman emperor continued to consider the compromises offered by Fritigern, who quite certainly sought delay to allow the fires to add to the oppressive heat and discomfort of the imperial troops; his cavalry had also not yet arrived from foraging. Although the barbarian horsemen played a key role in the ensuing battle, there is no reason to presume that they were particularly numerous.[74] The Roman cavalry was likewise small.

The battle opened by mistake—an indication that Valens's chain of command was not functioning properly. While the emperor was considering Fritigern's last proposal, the Roman *sagittarii* (archers) and *scutarii* (elite cavalry) rushed forward to engage the enemy. Their charge, Ammianus says,

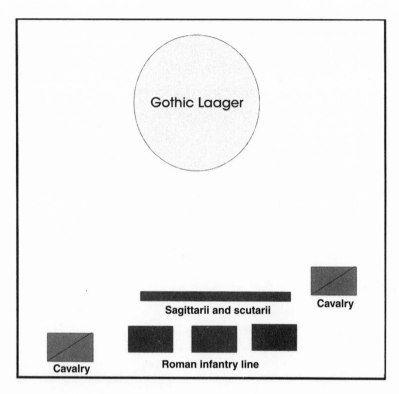

FIGURE 8.3   Adrianople, A.D. August 9, 378: The Initial Deployment

was untimely, their failure and ultimate retreat cowardly.[75] Moreover, their dash forward added to the confusion. It stopped the last effort at negotiation and gave time for the Gothic cavalry to attack while the Roman forces were in disorder. The Gothic cavalry, combined with Alan horsemen, under the command of the Greuthingi Alatheus and Saphrax, dashed forward like a "thunderbolt" and slaughtered all the Romans along the way (probably the *scutarii* and *sagittarii* and very likely the cavalry on the right; we do not know if the cavalry on the left was also hit).

The Roman horsemen on the left had great difficulty in taking their proper place; scattered along the same roads the troops took to the battlefield, they were arriving in small groups.[76] In any case, if they were hit, they survived with minimal damage since we find them later supporting an aggressive action of the left infantry.[77] The disorder of the rest of the Roman

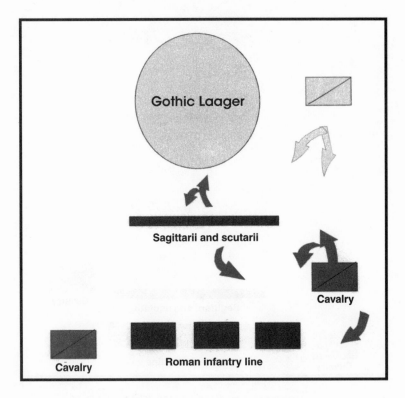

FIGURE 8.4   Adrianople: Defeat of the Roman Right Cavalry

line, center and right, must have been severe due to the Gothic cavalry strike and because it had not deployed properly yet (see Figure 8.4). For instance, as right-wing horsemen arrived on the battlefield, they took a position ahead of the infantry, which stood as if it were a reserve. When the Roman cavalry was routed, the right flank was left unprotected. Then the left flank was overturned.[78]

Valens's soldiers had some initial success on the left as the left infantry wing pushed the enemy back to the laager. But the left's forward move must have opened a gap in the Roman infantry line, and the Goths' superior numbers soon crushed them, routing the horsemen on its flank (Figure 8.5).[79]

The struggle continued mainly with infantry against infantry as all horsemen left the battlefield, the Romans being routed with the Goths in pursuit. The Gothic infantry left the laager and moved forward to meet the

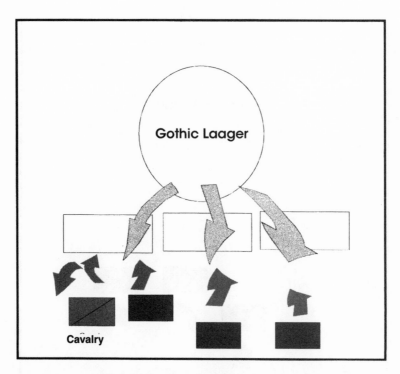

FIGURE 8.5   Adrianople: Defeat of the Roman Left Cavalry

Roman infantry. The Romans, with their flanks unprotected and their left wing destroyed, were hit on the left flank of their center by the enemy's "huge hordes" and routed again (Figure 8.6). They had little space to fight, their spears broken or ineffective, their swords being the only useful weapon.[80] The struggle lasted until night.[81] It closed with the Roman line broken; the survivors (barely a third) fled the battlefield as best as they could.[82] The emperor perished, and even the crack unit of Batavian soldiers were lost (they either fled or were destroyed).[83] The emperor's body was never found, unnoticed among the casualties or, more likely, incinerated when the barbarians (probably unaware Valens was inside) set fire to a refuge he had entered.[84]

Adrianople was not the greatest massacre suffered by the Romans.[85] Yet if we assume that Valens had about 15,000–18,000 troops at his disposal and Fritigern about 18,000–20,000,[86] the 10,000 casualties suffered by the Ro-

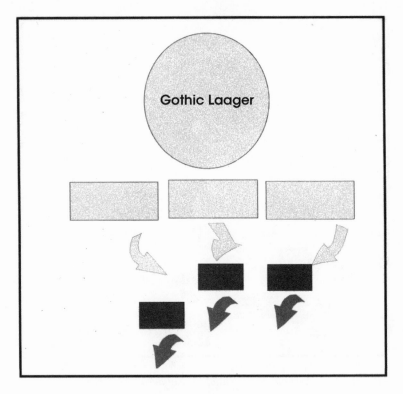

FIGURE 8.6　Adrianople: The End of the Battle

mans must have been a tremendous blow to their recruiting efforts, not to mention their confidence.

The tactical details as described by Ammianus are vague, perhaps mere rhetorical devices. Yet at least two fascinating themes surface: the brutal "face of battle," and Valens-as-symbol—the personification of Roman corruption and decline. Once the battle begins, we see a hallucinatory view of the common soldier. He arrived tired, famished, his throat burning, terribly uncomfortable in his heavy armor. The "savage and dismal howls" of the barbarians greet him, soon lost amid more fearful noises and images and sensations—whirring arrows obscuring the sky, the crash of the spears, axes, and arrows into flesh, the shrill of splitting metal, the cry of the wounded and dying, the clouds of burning dust, the odor of human and animal sweat, the stench of urine and excrement, spraying blood, heaps of bodies and streams of blood making the ground slippery and his equilibrium unstable. Fear, fear, fear all around, friend striking friend in the confusion of the battle. Yet Ammianus cannot but praise the bravery of the participants.[87]

But the core of the eastern army was destroyed, with the greatest repercussions in the Western Empire. Until the late fifth century A.D., the eastern emperors did not consider it their task to defend the Western Empire; even worse, they granted autonomy to the Goths within imperial territories. Soon those same Goths would descend upon the Balkans and Italy. Alaric's men or their descendants, who in A.D. 410 sacked Rome, had crossed the Danube on the eve of the Battle of Adrianople.

Yet this did not mean that the barbarians could outfight the Roman army in a pitched encounter. As Arther Ferrill maintains, "The defeats [Rome] suffered in Persia [in 363 when the emperor Julian was killed] and at Adrianople were the result of a failure in leadership, not a lack of training, discipline or *esprit*."[88] Elton echoes this sentiment: The defeat, he says, "lay in the impatience of Valens, in his desire to win a victory before the arrival of Gratian, then, as a result of his impatience, a faulty interpretation of an intelligence report, and finally commitment to battle before the army had come out of line of march."[89] Much better examples of the military efficiency of both Romans and Germans are found in the Battles of Ad Salices and Strasburg.

The Battles of Ad Salices and Strasburg

The smaller engagement at Ad Salices, fought before Adrianople, ended in a draw. Both sides were bloodied, but the barbarians probably gained the psychological edge.

Ad Salices (literally, "By the Willows") was a Scythian town located in Thrace. The Roman commander Richomer was in pursuit of Goths who had stopped over nearby, their booty and lives protected by a laager. He intended to defeat the enemy in detail, striking their rear as they evacuated. His objective was the booty, acquired through depredations on the Roman territory. But the Goths were not fooled. They stood their ground and recalled all the bands nearby; these bands joined by nighttime.[90]

Both sides spent the night in fear. At first light the two armies stood ready, the barbarians trying to reach the higher ground. The Romans, probably also on high ground (the two sides must have been separated by a valley) but inferior numerically, answered by keeping their ranks in order but refused to advance. The two sides moved forward cautiously. The Romans' *barritus* (elephant's cry) grew louder, and the barbarians, shouting the greatness of their forefathers, sent skirmishers forward, exchanging javelins, arrows, and slingshots. The two main lines clashed, the Romans protected by their shields held close like a tortoise shell, the Goths throwing clubs hardened in fire and beating their swords on their shields and at times armor.[91] The Goths' first charge broke the Roman left. But a strong body of reserves stopped the impending catastrophe, moving forward to meet the rush. The battle continued for the entire day. It ended with heavy casualties on both sides—a draw.[92]

Ad Salices demonstrated that the Roman infantry could still hold its own and probably beat greater barbarian numbers. After the debacle at Adrianople they won many successes under Theodosius (emperor, 379–395) against enemies crossing the borders. Yet casualty figures like those suffered at Ad Salices took their toll. Unable to man punitive expeditions and thus deter the enemies, the empire, at least in the west, was doomed. The waning days saw a melancholic series of disasters small and great until, in 476, the barbarian Odoacer, probably a member of the Germanic Scirian tribe, deposed the last official emperor of the Western Empire, a young boy named Romulus Augustulus ("Little Augustus"). More than a thousand years had passed since the foundation of Rome.

Around A.D. 350, a confederation of German tribes, the Alamans (or Alemans—both names are correct) invaded the Roman territory known as Agri Decumates, roughly the area including the Black Forest, the Neckar Basin, and the Swabian Alps. The region, annexed by the Flavian emperors, provided an easily defended border in the triangle formed by the upper Rhine and upper Danube. Archeological exploration of the area (lacking evidence of burning and devastation at the time) has shown that the invasion was not a sudden event but the intrusion of small groups over time. Thus we see "a long and gradual process of change from a landscape dominated by the Roman military and administrative apparatus to one transformed through interaction with and migration by peoples from across the frontier."[93]

The Alamans' emergence was symptomatic of the fundamental ethnic changes that were occurring across the entire length of the Roman frontier in the third century A.D.: the Alamans in 231, the Goths in 238 in the lower Danube, the Franks in 257 in the lower Rhine, and the Saxons in 286 east and north of the Franks. They radically altered the ethnic complexion of western Europe—the Saxons in Britain; the Goths in the Balkans, Italy, southern France and Spain; the Franks in France; and the Alamans briefly in southwestern Germany, northern Switzerland, and France.[94] They were different from the populations that the imperial troops had encountered in the past: They belonged to larger communities, showed a more complex political structure, and produced more wealth. This meant that in a period of Rome's increasing military weakness they represented a serious threat. In addition, the Romans were training many young warriors in the Roman army, establishing and supporting kings across the Rhine and the Danube, and encouraging the development of trade centers that they could exploit.[95] Thus in a way the Romans created the machine of their own demise.

The Alamans, along with all Germans, shared a suspicion of towns (tombs surrounded by nets, they said)[96] and were sedentary agriculturalists spread in the rural cantons of a territory ranging from Mainz to Basel in the west, to the northern shores of Lake Constanz in the south, and, following the old Roman fortifications of the Agri, from south of Frankfurt-am-Main to south of Regensburg, behind which the Burgundians had settled.[97] Physically they showed a particular fancy for long hair and were reputed to be stronger and taller than the Romans.[98] They were formidable enemies, but they were not unbeatable, for the Romans were disciplined and well trained, poised, attentive, and with stamina; the Alamans were "savage and uncontrollable" and trusting too much in the power of their huge size.[99] Like all barbarians, they lacked the staying power of the Roman armies.

The Battle of Strasburg concluded an ambitious Roman campaign that had gone wrong. The Roman commander was Julian, who had been elevated in A.D. 355 to the rank of Caesar and who had been sent by Constantius (emperor, 337–361) to the Gallic provinces, where a dangerous situation existed. In 350 the Alamans had broken through the Rhine frontier and established control on the left bank of the upper Rhine, taking advantage of civil war in the empire. Julian's mission was to drive them across the river and then to conduct a punitive expedition in German territory. In other words, he was entrusted with what by then had become the classical Roman response to aggression on the frontier.

Julian began his task successfully in a dual operation with the emperor in 356. Constantius pinned down the Alamans by attacking from Raetia (roughly Switzerland); Julian, first poised for an attack from the west from Gaul, moved north in relief of the besieged Cologne.[100] A year later Constantius did not take personal command of the imperial army, delegating leadership to Barbatio. The task would again be to undertake another pincer movement, with Julian marching from the northwest, Barbatio north from

Raetia. But Julian carried out the plan half-heartedly, wasting time in secondary but financially fruitful operations along the Rhine. His delay was disastrous. In the end Barbatio had to remain in Raetia, engaging the Alamans in minor operations. Moreover, he felt compelled to burn the supplies gathered for the expedition in fear that they might fall into enemy hands. This also meant that Julian could not rely on those supplies; Julian's Rhine operations had placed supplies and Barbatio's men in danger.[101]

At this stage Julian's options were few and unappealing, but in Roman fashion he decided that something had to be done because Alaman reinforcements were pouring into Gaul from the Rhine's eastern bank.[102] Yet Julian's failure to cooperate with Barbatio meant that instead of the 25,000 or so troops at his disposal he had only 13,000 soldiers, some of them in elite units. The Alamans were under the dual leadership of "kings" Chnodomar and Serapio, who enjoyed higher authority over the remaining five tribal leaders and ten "princes" present. They amounted to 35,000 troops, which included many nobles and some mercenaries.[103] Hans Delbrück has challenged these figures, assigning 6,000–10,000 men to the Alamans and 13,000–15,000 to the Romans.[104] N.J.E. Austin has argued that it was "perfectly possible" that the Alamans could raise a large army, although it is likely that they were about 30 percent less than Ammianus's estimate, that is, 20,000–25,000. The exact battle location has not been identified with certainty; the terrain around Strasburg could allow the deployment of about 50,000 soldiers.[105]

The Roman army arrived in the proximity of the Germans around noon.[106] Their Rhine crossing lasted three days and nights.[107] Julian was unwilling to engage them immediately and tried to delay the encounter to the next day, for he thought that it would be to his men's advantage to do so. But the war council, included people with higher decisionmaking power than Julian (clearly the emperor did not trust his Caesar), and his own soldiers decided otherwise.[108]

The Roman cavalry deployed on the right wing; the Germans countered by lining up their horsemen, intermingled with light troops, on their left. Opposed as they were to a unit of armored cavalry *(clibanarii)*, the Alamans feared that their own horsemen would have a rough time. Thus they intermingled light troops with the animals so that the foot soldiers, while the horsemen engaged the enemy, could stab the *clibanarii's* horses from the ground and throw the riders. Once on the ground they could be killed.[109] The decision to deploy all the cavalry on the right suggests that the Roman left could count on some kind of protection so that its flank could not be turned.

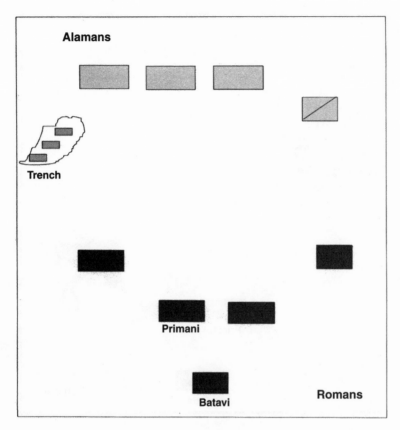

FIGURE 8.7   *Strasburg, A.D. 357: The Initial Deployments*

The rest of the Roman line—center and left—was all infantry in very close order, similar to "an impregnable wall."[110] Behind the center Julian placed at
least one or, more likely, two detachments in reserve, the Batavians and the
Regii in one group and the Primani in another group. Julian was on horseback
escorted by 200 cavalrymen slightly ahead of the first line (see Figure 8.7).[111]

The Alamans had set a trap: They hid several soldiers in trenches and other
obstacles on their extreme right so that they would surprise the Romans and
hit them in the flank if Julian's left advanced.[112] Chnomodar and most of the
other leaders dismounted after their own soldiers complained that while they
were on horseback they could always save their lives, whereas those on foot
risked much more.[113] The Aleman infantry deployed in wedge formation.[114]

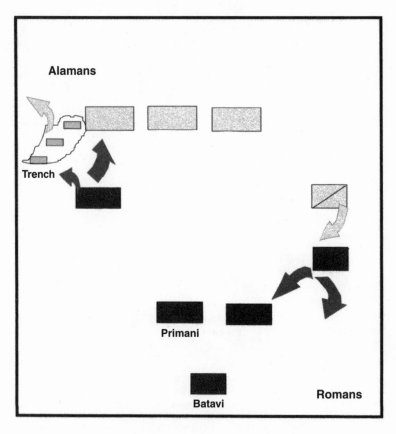

FIGURE 8.8   Strasburg: Roman Victory on the Left, Defeat on the Right

The battle would be decided in the center, but initially disaster struck the Roman right (see Figure 8.8). The Roman cavalry, including detachments of armored horsemen and mounted archers, was defeated and started to flee from the battlefield.[115] Although Ammianus is unclear on what follows and Delbrück rightly argues that a fleeing cavalry cannot be easily rallied, what likely happened is that some horsemen must have left the battlefield.[116] However, some also found refuge in the midst of the legions, and others found it impossible to escape or seek refuge when, in total disorder, they came face-to-face with their own infantry firmly standing in close order. It is here that Julian intervened and rallied at least some of the horsemen, who would fight mixed with the infantry from then on.[117]

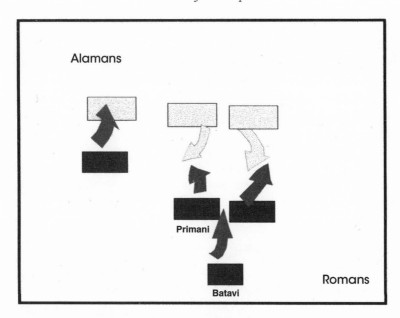

FIGURE 8.9   Strasburg: The Final Phase

While the cavalry was going down to defeat, the Roman left pushed the enemy back as it sprung the ambush, then proceeded to challenge the Aleman right.[118] The enemy trap failed because the Roman left must have been aware of it from the beginning. During the initial deployment of the battle line, it had cautiously but firmly advanced ahead of the rest of the line probably because it was aware of the trap and wanted to entice the Alemans out of their hiding places. Another goal would have been to allow the center, where most of Julian's soldiers stood, to line up in safety.[119]

The struggle and success see-sawed, but in the end a fearsome Aleman charge got the upper hand. They penetrated the Roman center. It is here that two Roman units, the Batavi and the Regii, probably held in reserve, intervened, but even those elite soldiers could not stop the barbarians. The intervention of another unit, the Primani (in reserve), turned the tide (Figure 8.9). The barbarians did not have the staying power of the Roman soldiers. This was the main reason the Romans gained an edge over enemies who were as strong or stronger than they.

Once the Alemans retreated, the grim work of slaughter began, but even here Julian made sure his soldiers did not overpursue, for that would open his army to counterattack.[120] By the end of the day 6,000 Alamans died on the battlefield; many others died while trying to cross the Rhine to the safety of the opposite bank.[121] The last stage closed with the capture of the Aleman leader, Chnodomar. A proud man of great size and strength at the battle's onset, he was a humble, beaten individual at the end, pale, bewildered, and speechless. He was sent to Rome, where he died, his mind gone, without memory of the past.[122]

Julian was not finished. The Romans carried the offensive into the barbarians, lands so that the fear of punishment would deter a future invasion. He sacked and burned a few Aleman villages and returned to Roman territory after dictating a ten months' truce to the barbarians.[123]

The Illnesses of the Empire

In one of history's surprises, an empire as powerful as Rome raised an army of only a half-million (with mobile armies in support) to guard an enormous frontier and was unable to meet the barbarians' concerted attacks. The truth is that the empire could recruit no more than 600,000–650,000 men. The total recruiting pool was relatively small, the mortality rate was high, and financing and administration were a crushing burden.[124] Any tax increase could not be implemented unless the state taxed the people that tradition, power, and prestige made untouchable.[125] Even maintaining this army on the field disrupted society and stressed the Western Empire so much that it fell to the barbarians.

Although the figures are debatable, there are several factors indicating a demographic decline in the Late Empire. Cultivated lands decreased as much as 50 percent in Africa and perhaps 10–15 percent elsewhere due to lack of manpower, land erosion, deforestation, soil exhaustion, and a logical tendency to abandon areas prone to barbarian attack. The Roman Empire was essentially a primitive subsistence peasant society. The lower classes must have been weakened by chronic malnutrition, which prevented prodigious childrearing. The economic situation was so dire that peasants and the urban poor sold their children. Plagues struck the Roman Empire under Marcus Aurelius and Commodus in the second century and then in repetition in the third century (251, 261, and 271) before subsiding in the fourth century. Farmers abandoned their lands under the tax burden, unable to make a living. The "landlords were perennially short of tenants to cultivate their land," and the government tried to meet the demand by tying agricultural workers to their occupation by law—a policy implemented for most essential activities, including the armed forces. All this limited the labor force and thus the ability to recruit more soldiers. Even worse, the state and the rigid class and religious structure excluded many adults from serving in the army.[126]

Roman technology was low, and the manpower (i.e., the lower classes) had to provide for consumers who paid either no or few taxes. The senatorial order, which continued even after being spoiled of most political power, was one of the wealthiest groups of the empire; besides gaining enormous wealth and building large estates, this class was able to avoid fiscal obligations by way of privilege. The civil service was another group that was supported by the state and thus sucked resources from the economy with minimal benefit to the rest. The Christian Church created a new group that provided spiritual guidance but no economic gain. The situation became more serious because the new church accumulated wealth to a degree unknown in pagan religions. The 600,000–650,000 soldiers cost too much but created no new wealth once being placed on the defensive for more than a century.[127] (The last large territorial acquisition had been the brief control of Mesopotamia under Septimius Severus.) Finally, the soldiers (who could barely hold their own against the increasing waves of barbarians) needed a large administrative machine that was inefficient, corrupt, and nonproductive.[128]

A decline in civic spirit spread throughout the social system and touched all classes. The official defenders of the state, the soldiers, became isolated from the civilian population, the butt of ridicule and scorn or the object of fear. As Jean-Michel Carrié points out, the situation had reversed since the first two centuries A.D.[129] The new army was divorced from society because so many soldiers came from behind the frontiers, spoke languages that the rest could not understand, brought alien customs that were reprehensible, and were considered as barbaric as those who pressed at the gates.

Christianity, in the words of Friedrich Nietzsche, "was the vampire of the *imperium Romanum*—in a night it shattered the stupendous achievement of the Romans."[130] But surely he exaggerates. The old pagans and the new Christians were attached to the empire just the same.[131] And both looked in horror at the "savage nations" pressing the empire's defenses.[132] In any case, Christianization of the military was a slow process, and those who subscribed to the Christian God could hardly be viewed as inferior soldiers.[133] Yet it is hard to deny that Christianity emphasized peace, not war, and that several reluctant recruits tried to avoid military service for religious reasons. The old gods were part and parcel of the army and the state; the Christian God praised peace and brotherhood and encouraged many new believers to

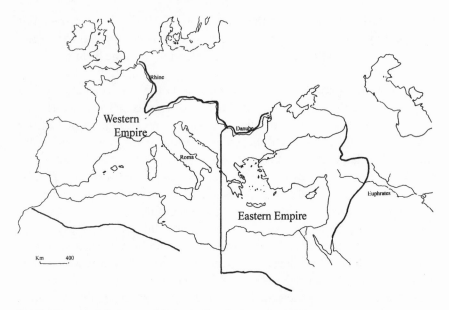

FIGURE 8.10   Western and Eastern Empires, ca. A.D. 400

choose a life removed from the battlefield. The Christian God would provide a martial function in time in the form of the Crusades.

The major problem was the lack of manpower. More than 50 percent of
the soldiers became "second-class troops"; the recruits were men of inferior
quality organized under the greatest administrative abuses. Even if we
downplay this negative interpretation, the *limitanei* seemed undisciplined
and undermanned in comparison to their fighting peak under Diocletian.
The elite was the mobile field army, and the idea behind it was effective.
Even the later development, when mobile armies were stationed in the west
and the east, was a step forward, for a single mobile army could not hope to
cover the length of the frontier (see Figure 8.10). Then regional reserves
mushroomed in the Western Empire, Africa, Spain, and Britain, and the
huge army in the Eastern Empire remained idle, poised against Persia while
providing no relief to the Rhine and the Danube frontiers.[134] The Roman
empire was fragmented, stretched, and about to break down.

In time the problem would become insurmountable. Enemies roamed
about at will. Stopping one threat was not enough, for another would
emerge; if that new threat was pushed back, another popped up elsewhere.

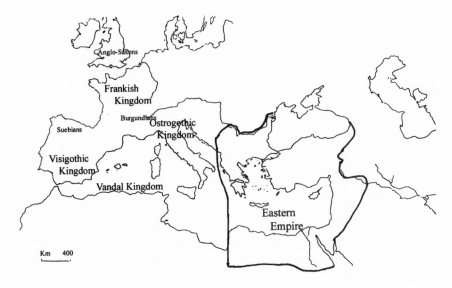

FIGURE 8.11   The End of the Western Empire

This was an epidemic of violence, yet contenders to the throne fought one another as much as they fought the enemy. Invasions often took advantage of civil war in the empire. As with the German tribes during the first two centuries A.D., the empire had fractured into factions that were impossible to unite in common cause. The Western Empire was a "nursery" of pretenders to the throne, (see Figure 8.11) and the armies of Britain and Gaul were the real threat to the security of the emperors.[135] This meant that Roman generals sometimes had to rely more on barbarian soldiers. They were cheaper and more trustworthy than Roman citizens, who were quick to back a different pretender to the throne.[136] The emperor and the pretenders alike did not hesitate to employ recruits from across the northern frontier to attack their rivals.[137]

Still, the Eastern Empire—the "Romans of Constantinople"—continued for another thousand years. Why did they remain so strong? The western frontiers were too long, the resources too few, the coffers empty, the population smaller, civil wars more common, the enemy more intrusive and persistent. But the Roman army created the stresses, throwing society and the economy off balance. It required huge taxation, which in turn caused a decline in agriculture and population. It also required the establishment of a large civil service to gather and administer the tax revenues.[138] But the real key was the decision of the Eastern Empire not to support the Western Empire. When the emperors of Constantinople like Justianian had a mind to, they successfully defeated the barbarians in the west. By that time, however, it was too late. Rome lay in pieces.

Notes

1. Quoted in A.H.M. Jones, *The Later Roman Empire, 284–602* (Oxford, 1964), p. 1025.
2. Ibid., pp. 679–686.
3. Ibid., pp. 679–682.
4. See Terence Coello, *Unit Sizes in the Late Roman Empire* (Oxford, 1996); Ramsay MacMullen, "How Big Was the Roman Imperial Army?" *Klio* 62 (1980): 451–460; Hugh Elton, *Warfare in Roman Europe, A.D. 350–425* (Oxford, 1996), pp. 106, 210–211, 244–245.
5. Quoted in Coello, *Unit Sizes in the Late Roman Empire*, p. 62. The writer was a Greek rhetorician from Antioch, Libanius (314–ca. 393).
6. Jones, *The Later Roman Empire*, pp. 685–686.
7. Ibid., p. 610.
8. Elton, *Warfare in Roman Europe*, p. 94.
9. Ibid., p. 93.
10. Ibid., pp. 99–101.
11. Synesius, Ep. 78 in *Patrologia Graeca*. See also Jones, *The Later Roman Empire*, pp. 653–654.
12. Elton, *Warfare in Roman Europe*, pp. 101–103.
13. My figures are a rough calculation of the evidence in Elton, *Warfare in Roman Europe*, pp. 103–107.
14. Ibid., pp. 107–117.
15. Ibid., pp. 111–114.
16. Ibid., pp. 106–107.
17. Jones, *The Later Roman Empire*, p. 614.
18. Elton, *Warfare in Roman Europe*, p. 130.
19. Jones, *The Later Roman Empire*, pp. 615–616.
20. Ibid., pp. 623–626.
21. Ibid., pp. 626–630.
22. Ibid., pp. 630–633.
23. Ibid., pp. 633–636.

24. Ibid., pp. 644, 646–649.

25. Ibid., pp. 617–619.

26. Ibid., pp. 620–621.

27. Ibid., pp. 619–623.

28. Ibid., pp. 619–623; Elton, *Warfare in Roman Europe,* pp. 134–145.

29. Jones, *The Later Roman Empire*, pp. 621–622.

30. Elton, *Warfare in Roman Europe*, pp. 151–152.

31. See Arther Ferrill, *The Fall of the Roman Empire: The Military Explanation* (London, 1986).

32. Elton, *Warfare in Roman Europe*, pp. 224, 235–237.

33. Jones, *The Later Roman Empire*, p. 607.

34. John Matthews, *The Roman Empire of Ammianus* (London, 1989), pp. 304–382.

35. One may have appeared in very weak form in the ninth century during Carolingian times. Walter Goffart, "Rome, Constantinople, and the Barbarians," in **his** *Rome's Fall and After* (London, 1989). The article first appeared in the *American Historical Review* 86 (1981): 275–306.

36. Goffart, "Rome, Constantinople, and the Barbarians," pp. 10–11.

37. Jones, *The Later Roman Empire*, pp. 194–199.

38. See the comments in Goffart, "Rome, Constantinople, and the Barbarians," pp. 16–17.

39. Ibid., pp. 10–11.

40. Matthews, *The Roman Empire of Ammianus*, pp. 318–322.

41. Linda Ellis, "Dacians, Sarmatians, and Goths on the Roman–Carpathian Frontier: Second-Fourth Centuries," in *Shifting Frontiers in Late Antiquity*, edited by R. Mathisen and H. Sivan (Aldershot, 1996), pp. 105–119.

42. Matthews, *The Roman Empire of Ammianus*, p. 322.

43. Ibid., pp. 321, 328–329.

44. Ammianus xxxi.2.21.

45. Ibid., xxxi.2.2.

46. Ibid., xxxi.2.3–11.

47. Ibid., xxxi.2–3.

48. Ibid., xxxi.4.4.

49. Ibid., xxxi.4.7.

50. Ibid., xxxi.4.1–6.

51. Ibid., xxxi.4.9; 4.9; 6.1; 16.8.

52. Ibid., xxxi.4.11. The senator was Themistius as quoted in Jones, *The Later Roman Empire*, p. 153.

53. Ammianus xxxi.5.3.

54. Ammianus xxxi.5.1–7. On Lupicinus's motivation, see N.J.E. Austin, "Ammianus' Account of the Adrianople Campaign: Some Strategic Observations," *Acta Classica* 15 (1972): 78–79.

55. Ammianus xxxi.4.6.

56. The fact that they needed more equipment or that they preferred the equipment worn by the Romans is shown in at least two instances where they spoiled the defeated Romans of theirs; ibid., xxxi.5.10; 6.3.

57. Ibid., pp. 602–603.

58. Ammianus xxxi.5.8–9.

59. Ibid., xxxi.6.1–6.

60. Ibid., xxxi.7.1–4; 14.1–7 (on Valens's description).

61. Ibid., xxxi.7.5–16.

62. Ibid., xxxi.8.1–2.

63. Ibid., xxxi.8.3.

64. Ibid., xxxi.8.3–9.

65. Ibid., xxxi.10.21; 11.1; 11.4.

66. Ibid., xxxi.11.5.

67. Ibid., xxxi.12.12. The two leaders were Alatheus and Saphrax, who had taken control of the Greuthingi after the death of their king before crossing the Danube.

68. For a portrayal of both merits and defects of the emperor, see ibid., xxxi.14.

69. Ibid., xxxi.12.10.

70. F. Runkel, *Die Schlacht bei Adrianopel* (Berlin, 1903), pp. 33–36.

71. Claudianus, *In Rufinum*, ii.127.129.

72. Ammianus xxxi.12.10.

73. For a less negative view of Valens, see Austin, "Ammianus' Account of the Adrianople Campaign," pp. 82–84.

74. Thomas S. Burns, "The Battle of Adrianople: A Reconsideration," *Historia* 22 (1973): 341.

75. Ammianus xxxi.12.16.

76. Ibid., xxxi.12.11–10.

77. Ibid., xxxi.12.17.

78. Ibid., xxxi.13.2.

79. Ibid., xxxi.13.2.

80. Ibid., xxxi.13.5.

81. Ibid., xxxi.13.11.

82. Ibid., xxxi.13.7; 13.18.

83. Ibid., xxxi.13.9.

84. Ibid., xxxi.13.10–17.

85. Ammianus claims it was the worst since their defeat at the hands of Hannibal at Cannae in 216; ibid. xxxi.13.19.

86. There is no complete agreement on the numerical strength of the two armies. It is 15,000–18,000 for the Romans and 12,000–15,000 Goths according to Hans Delbrück, *History of the Art of War Within the Framework of Political History*, vol. 2, translated by W. J. Rinfroe Jr. (London, 1975–1980), pp. 269–284; a similar strength is accepted by Austin in "Ammianus' Account of the Adrianople Campaign," pp. 82–83. Austin specifies that the 18,000 Goths included 10,000 Visigoths and 8,000 Ostrogoths. Thomas Burns, *Barbarians Within the Gates of Rome: A Study of Roman Military Policy and the Barbarians, ca. 375–425 A.D.* (Bloomington, IN, 1994), p. 33, thinks that the Romans numbered 15,000–20,000 men and the Goths 20,000. Unless Ammianus does not tell the truth, which is unlikely, the Goths, however, must have been fairly stronger than the Romans. At least this is the impression that the reader receives from his account, although the only figure that he mentions is the incorrect intelligence report of 10,000 Goths (xxxi.12.3).

87. Ammanius xxxi12.10–17; 13.1–11. Matthews, *The Roman Empire of Ammianus*, pp. 296–297. Ammianus is a good, fair historian. Yet his veracity at times is doubtful, for he had a personal axe to grind. His account of the subsequent slaying of all Goths by the Romans as the only solution to the barbarian problem is especially suspect.

88. Ferrill, *The Fall of the Roman Empire*, p. 65.

89. Elton, *Warfare in Roman Europe*, p. 266.

90. Ibid., xxxi.7.6–8.

91. Ibid., xxxi.7.8–12.

92. Ibid., xxxi.7.12–16.

93. Peter S. Wells, *The Barbarians Speak: How the Conquered Peoples Shaped Roman Europe* (Princeton, 1999), pp. 259–260.

94. Ibid., pp. 259–261.

95. Ibid., p. 261.

96. Ammianus xvi.2.12.

97. Matthews, *The Roman Empire of Ammianus*, pp. 306–310.

98. Ammianus xvi.12.26, 12.47.

99. Ibid., xvi.12.47.

100. Ibid., xvi.2–4.

101. Matthews, *The Roman Empire of Ammianus*, pp. 299–300.

102. Delbrück, *History of the Art of War*, vol. 2, p. 261.

103. Ammianus xvi.12.26.

104. Delbrück, *History of the Art of War*, vol. 2, p. 262.

105. N.J.E. Austin, "In Support of Ammianus' Veracity," *Historia* 22 (1973): 333–335.

106. Ammianus xvi.12.12.

107. Ibid., xvi.12.19.

108. This episode's inclusion shows that Ammianus, despite his association with Julian, was quite concerned to base his account on accurate information, even if it deflated Julian's reputation; ibid., xvi.12.9–14; see also Barnes, *Ammianus Marcellinus*, pp. 152–153.

109. Ammianus xvi.12.21–22.

110. Ibid., xvi.12.20.

111. Ibid., xvi.12.28 (on Julian's escort). The role of the units as reserves is suggested by the battle's development (xvi.12.45, 12.49).

112. Ibid., xvi.12.23, 12.27.

113. Ibid., xvi.12.34–35.

114. Ibid., xvi 12.20.

115. Ibid., xvi 12.7.

116. Delbrück, *History of the Art of War*, vol. 2, pp. 263–265.

117. Ammianus xvi.12.37–41.

118. Ibid., xvi.22.37.

119. Ibid., xvi.12.27–28, 12.34.

120. Ibid., xvi.12.51–55.

121. Ibid., xvi.12.63.

122. Ibid., xvi.12.58,12.24, 12.66.

123. Ibid., xvi.17.1–14.

124. Jones, *The Later Roman Empire*, p. 1041.

125. Elton (*Warfare in Roman Europe*, pp. 118–127) argues instead that despite some difficulty the empire could financially support the army. This is also the opinion of C. R. Whittaker, "Inflation and the Economy in the Fourth Century A.D.," in *Imperial Revenue, Expenditure and Monetary Policy*, edited by C. E. King BAR S76 (Oxford, 1980), pp. 1–22. Yet the problem is not that in emergencies the emperor could not find the money but that the existing taxation, already very oppressive, could be increased only with great difficulty unless he canceled the traditional exemptions and privileges.

126. Jones, *The Later Roman Empire*, pp. 1038–1045.

127. Ibid., pp. 1045–1048.

128. Ibid., pp. 1048–1058.

129. Jean-Michel Carrié, "L'esercito: trasformazioni funzionali ed economie locali," in *Istituzioni, ceti, economie*, edited by Andrea Giardina (Bari, 1986), p. 461.

130. Quoted in Goffart, "An Empire Unmade: Rome, A.D. 300–600," in his *Rome's Fall and After* (London, 1989), p. 34.

131. A.H.M. Jones, *The Later Roman Empire*, pp. 1061–1064; Goffart, "An Empire Unmade," in *Rome's Fall and After*, pp. 34–35.

132. Roger Tomlin, "Christianity and the Late Roman Army," in *Constantine: History, Historiography, and Legend*, edited by Samuel N.C. Lieu and Dominic Montserrat (London, 1998), p. 41.

133. Ibid., p. 35.

134. Jones, *The Later Roman Empire*, pp. 1035–1038.

135. Goffart, *Rome's Fall and After*, p. 18.

136. Ibid., p. 21.

137. Ibid., p. 9.

138. Jones, *The Later Roman Empire*, p. 1067.

Epilogue

Melancholy pervaded the last years of the Roman Empire and it never disappeared. The Empire gave future generations their sense of destiny. It survived for another thousand years in the East, it was ever-present in most of the barbarian kingdoms. New people emerged, the borders were different.

Rome shaped the past and the future of western Europeans and through them most of the world. After a dramatic entrance following the Second Punic War, Rome would teeter on the edge of collapse but always reemerged. The first century B.C. would set Rome down another path. Marius's reform of 107 B.C. made sense, for the ranks of the army were difficult to replenish as long as the old eligibility requirements were maintained. Marius opened the army to everyone as long as they held Roman citizenship. But over time this would upset the republic's stability. For the next seven decades or so, until Augustus's victory at Actium in 31 B.C. against the fleet of Marcus Antonius and Cleopatra, the glorious armies of the past became hosts of pillagers.

With the military ranks opened to all, the new army no long longer served as the depository of values for upper-class and propertied families; potentially it could become the representative of the poor. In reality, however, the leadership core was unchanged. And the new soldiers—the rank and file—simply wanted to improve their lot, to gain immediate wealth, material goods and improve their condition. Overthrowing the privileged classes was not on their mind, and the "war managers" of the past—the aristocrats—remained in command. If one can identify any innovation, it was probably in the appearance of the new leader, the obvious case being Marius. But even he did not come from the dregs of society; he was an equestrian who had married into a distinguished family. The most radical change was seen in the soldiers' behavior. The troops became the enemy within; pillage and slaughter of fellow citizens was indiscriminate; loyalty was pledged not to the republic but to their leaders—as long as they provided the booty.

All this played out amid external and internal disorder. New invaders, the Cimbri and the Teutones, had to be thwarted; then the *socii* (non-Roman

Italian allies) united and requested citizenship; finally Spartacus and the slaves threatened the very idea of Roman domination. It is remarkable that the slave rebellion never mushroomed into class warfare, with the lower classes making common cause with Spartacus and his men. Even the *socii* episode was not a class conflict for, with few exceptions, all social orders shared similar goals—to have the same rights, not just the duties of Roman citizens. In spite of the immense bloodshed that it caused, the integration of all peninsular Italians south of the Rubicon, that is, central and southern Italy (not the islands, however), made Rome stronger and laid the basis for extending its power even farther. Yet for decades afterward Romans slaughtered Romans, and troops felt little loyalty to society. The situation changed during the last stages of the Roman Civil Wars, and certain events made the reestablishment of social harmony mandatory: In part it was the work of a remarkable individual—Julius Caesar; in part it was the realization among the generals and their followers that killing friends and enemies alike led nowhere; and in part it was the massacre of members of the highest aristocratic order—the senators.

The new army, forged under Caesar and refined by his successor, Augustus, reacquired the traditional sense of destiny. It was Rome's duty to conquer all and to bring civilization to all corners of the earth. But it was also a matter of material gain and the fulfillment of a sense of violence and lust for power that had distinguished the men of Rome from the very beginning. Caesar and Augustus were pivotal in shaping the Roman Empire that followed. By Augustus's time the borders had reached almost their farthest expansion; the army finally was brought under control.

But Augustus went much further than did Julius Caesar (his great-uncle). The army finally received fair rewards for its services, but he also ensured that the emperor was the one who held the purse strings. This made the army reluctant to listen to anyone other than the commander in chief, it spoiled the troops from any political ascendancy that they may have acquired in the last stages of the civil wars. Augustus monopolized military power by controlling most of the far-flung provinces where the army was stationed, leaving the Senate to control few soldiers. Moreover, he made certain that generals kept military control only for short periods to prevent the emergence of rivals to the throne. The imperial forces were his army, his soldiers, his fleet.

The reorganization of the state went hand in glove with a reformulation of the "Roman man" and its symbols. As the republic neared its final days and the army's rank and file transformed, Roman intellectuals, foremost Cicero, felt it necessary to restate the traditional virtues first articulated following the Second Punic War. The highest orders—senators and equestrians—were depicted as separate from the lower classes and provincials just as they were making their impact on society felt. This attitude was reflected in the emergence of the Principate: The emperor became the highest symbol of the state through Roman literature, art, and architecture, and the capital became his city. Soon this became the deliberate policy of the emperor, his family, and his troops and was mirrored in places throughout the frontier.

Augustus also added a new dimension to the commander in chief. Like his great-uncle Caesar, he would become worshipped as a god. Scipio Africanus was the first to undertake a process toward divine status, but Augustus perfected it. The idea that the supreme commander was a deity in death if not in life became a fixture of imperial power. Beginning with Diocletian, the association with the gods became stronger. Before him, the emperor's selection was based on merit and reflected the will of the people through the Senate. It was not a hereditary right (even though succession was often kept in the family). As we move toward the end of the third century A.D., however, it was understood that imperial authority rested in the will of the gods, a policy repeated under Constantine a few decades later (although the pagan gods of the past had given way to the Christian God).

Like all emperors, Augustus realized that his power rested on the support of his soldiers, for the emperor had become the exclusive manager of war. Yet he kept them at a distance from the center of power, a policy that worked for about two centuries (excepting a brief period in the aftermath of Nero's death). In the waning years of the second century A.D. things changed, ironically in the aftermath of the death of the ideal emperor, Marcus Aurelius, under his son Commodus. The praetorians, the emperor's guard formed by Augustus and stationed in and near Rome, became, sometimes with soldiers stationed at the frontier, the makers of emperors.

The third century A.D. was a most turbulent period. Barbarian tribes—more numerous, better organized, and more proficient in the art of war than in the past—pierced the empire's border (although this was a problem that Marcus had to face already in the second half of the second century A.D.). Emperor Septimius Severus, who finally brought some order to the anarchy following Commodus's death, was compelled to deal with this threat. And where Marcus and Septimius succeeded, others did not, and the remainder of the third century saw a series of barbarian strikes and Roman defeats.

Septimius was the greatest reformer since Augustus. He increased the number of legions and opened their ranks to more and more non-Romans.

By then the armed forces had changed their nature. Senators were apparently discouraged from serving—a policy that became permanent about half a century later under Gallienus; Italian-born men, except in moments of great emergency, practically disappeared from the rank and file (although they still held higher commands); the old praetorian guard, the exclusive reserve of Italians, was disbanded and then refashioned using the best legionnaires from the frontier. This weakened the central tenet of the imperial army: Rome's dominance. Yet the soldier-citizen ideal would be renewed in 312 A.D when the next emperor, Caracalla (Septimius's son), extended citizenship to all freemen within the Roman Empire. By extending such privileges to practically all imperial subjects, this policy diluted the Roman military ideal.

Disorder followed. After Septimius, every ruler and pretender (except for three emperors) fell victim to the sword until Diocletian in 284 A.D. returned stability to the center; no emperor was murdered during the next seventy years.

Augustus made certain that legions were never located within Italy. Nearly all of them would be stationed in the most dangerous frontier hot spots—the Rhine, the Danube, and the Euphrates. Despite Augustus's last instructions, neither he nor his successors intended to switch over to a defensive policy, for the Roman mind believed in aggression. All territories, even those beyond the Roman posts, were considered to be part of the Roman dominion. If Roman lands were threatened, then the enemy had to be met before it pierced the frontier; it was then harshly punished inside its own territory. Supremacy extended to any place where Rome could in theory extend its military force.

The policy worked well until the end of the second century A.D. Dangers were met as they arose, with commanders moving troops from one frontier to the next as attacks progressed. It did not work in the third century, however, as enemy strikes became more common and were carried out simultaneously at times. The solution was to create a mobile field army (later several mobile armies were created). In varying forms, this strategy appeared first under Gallienus, then Diocletian, and finally Constantine (although one can argue that the troops Septimius Severus stationed in Italy were the nucleus of the Roman field army). The strength of the new army was its mobility. Thus the foot soldier, once the pride of the Roman military, gave way to cavalry. This also meant that the border troops were relegated to second-class status. Service in the mobile field army meant prestige, rewards, and promotion.

This emphasis on mobility led to important changes in frontier policy. Diocletian had strengthened the frontier borders with fortifications, adopting an elastic defense to hold the enemy in check at the frontier. Constantine abandoned the idea of stout border defense and instead sought to slow invaders by constructing a series of obstacles within the imperial territories. This strategy of defense in depth placed frontier troops and populations in great danger and eroded the principle that peace reigned throughout the Roman Empire.

By then, however, Roman power was clearly on the wane. And although the Roman armies were still powerful, their outright superiority slowly disappeared after Constantine. Under Augustus and his successors, the armed forces combined superior strategic skill with effective tactics. But this was not necessarily the case thereafter. The suppression of Boudicca's Rebellion, the capture of Masada, and the see-saw struggle against the German tribes are good examples. By the second half of the fourth century A.D. things would be different. The Romans could still hold their own and often defeated their opponents, as at Strasburg in 357. But as the quality of the troops declined, the onslaught from outside and the struggles within became in the long run impossible to restrain. Roman armies, especially the infantry, became the victims of disaster (e.g., Adrianople) and attrition (e.g., Ad Salices). And the traditional core elements of the Roman army practically disappeared. Friends and enemies greeted Rome from the same corners of the world.

The end of the Roman Empire coincided with population decline, polarization of society (many individuals took from but did not give back to the community), corruption at the highest levels, disappearance of the civic sense, and perhaps even the appearance of Christianity, which emphasized peace over military glory. As in the past, the key was the army: It was too small to patrol the border; was too expensive to maintain (even with heavy taxes); and was badly led by incompetent emperors. The final blow was the bifurcation into the Western Empire and Eastern empire, begun under Diocletian and completed after Theodosius. Practically abandoned by their eastern brethren, the westerners were overrun by the German tribes. The Romans in the east would last for another millennium.

Glossary

aerarium militare	treasury founded by Augustus to pay the military forces
as	(pl. *asses*) bronze coin
auxilia	non-Roman auxiliary men normally fighting as light soldiers
Capitol	one of Rome's seven hills. The others were the Palatine, Caelian, Aventine, Viminal, Quirinal, and Esquiline. The hills outside the walls were the Vatican, Janiculum, and Pincian. The Capitol was the religious center of the city. It housed the temple of Jupiter, Juno, and Minerva.
censor	Roman magistrate whose main duty was to draw up lists of Roman citizens
census	tax assessment, national levy
centurion	junior officer. There were sixty centurions per legion. The most senior was the *primipilus*, the centurion of the first century of the first cohort.
cohort	standard tactical section of the legion from the second century B.C. There were ten cohorts per legion. The cohort numbered 480 men, but probably around the second half of the first century A.D. the first cohort became double the size of the other cohorts.
colony	(*colonia*, pl. *coloniae*) communities founded on conquered enemy territory with lots of land allotted to Roman citizens and allies
comes	high-ranking military and/or administrative officer of the Late Empire
comitatus	(*comitatenses*) mobile force during the Late Empire, initially the emperor's retinue
consul	the highest administrative and military office during the republic. Each year two consuls were elected. The office continued during the empire but with much more limited powers.

curia	Senate house in Rome; also the city's ward
dilectus	annual military levy
dux	military commander in charge of the frontier troops, lower than the *comes*
equites	originally horsemen; later one of the dominant social and political groups making up Rome's ruling class
exercitus	army
flamen	priest
Forum	the political center of Rome and of every Roman city
gladius	legionnaire sword
hastati	heavy infantry soldiers of the first line in a midrepublican legion
laeti	soldiers recruited from barbarians settled in imperial lands
Latini	inhabitants of Latium and a consciously aware ethnic and cultural population. Rome eventually conquered Latium and united the Latins by granting them special rights like the ability to marry a Roman citizen, to trade with Roman citizens, and the right to gain Roman citizenship if settling in a territory under Rome's direct jurisdiction *(ager Romanus)*. The settlers of Roman colonies enjoyed Latin rights whether they came from Rome or from a Latin town.
legatus	imperial officer from the senatorial order in charge normally of a legion
legion	basic battle group of the Roman army. From the second century B.C. onward it numbered ten cohorts
lictors	attendants to magistrates with powers
limes	boundary, frontier
limitanei	frontier troops during the Late Empire
maniple	basic fighting unit of the Roman legion until the end of the Second Punic War. There were thirty maniples per legion. The maniples of the *hastati* (first heavy infantry line) and *principes* (second heavy infantry line) included 120 men; the maniples of the *triarii* (third heavy infantry line) counted sixty men. Each maniple was composed of two centuries.
Maximus	highest priest in Rome

mos maiorum	ancestors' customs
numerus	unit of foot or horse troops
oppidum	(pl. *oppida*) stronghold, fortified town
pilum	legionnaires' heavy javelin
plebs	commoners
praetor	chief magistrate
prefect	prefect of the praetorian guard, the commander of the praetorians
primipilus	senior centurion, head of the first century of the first cohort
Principate	Augustus's regime; also the historical period until the late third century
principes	heavy infantry soldiers of the second line in a midrepublican legion
proconsul	governor of a province during the republic in command of the legions in the province; governor of a senatorial province during the empire but without the command of any provincial forces
provincia	(pl. *provinciae*), conquered dependent territory outside peninsular Italy
rostrum	speaker's platform
scutum	legionnaires' shield
Senate	theoretically an advisory body for the state's magistrates; in practice the highest political body. Senators were appointed for life. The conditions for appointment changed throughout the period, but originally senators came from the aristocracy.
socii	Roman allies—Italian people allied to Rome by treaty. They fought bitterly against Rome (91–87 B.C.) to gain Roman citizenship. At the end of the war peninsular Italy south of the Po River was united in the sense that the inhabitants shared Roman citizenship.
spatha	sword
toga	garment symbol of the Roman citizen
triarii	heavy infantry soldiers of the third line in a midrepublican legion
tribune	the tribunes of the plebs *(tribuni plebis)* were ten annual magistrates whose task was to defend the people against any oppression. The military tribunes *(tribuni militum)* were elected by the people in cooperation with the consuls. Each legion had six

tribunes. Most of them performed administrative more than military duties. Normally tribunes came from the equestrian order.

triumvirate   First Triumvirate was the political union formed by Caesar, Pompeius, and Crassus in 60 B.C. The Second Triumvirate was the political alliance formed in 43 B.C. by Octavian (Augustus), Marcus Antonius, and Lepidus.

velites   light infantry in a midrepublican legion

vexillatio   cavalry detachment

APPENDIX I

Time Line, 218 B.C.—A.D. 476

B.C.

218–201	Second Punic War
172–167	Third Macedonian War
153–151	Second Celtiberian War
149–146	Third Punic War
143–133	Third Celtiberian War
133–132	Slave war in Sicily
133	Tiberius Gracchus's land law; murder of Tiberius Gracchus
121	Murder of Gaius Gracchus
113	Cimbri defeat the Romans at Norcia
112	War against the king of Numidia, Jugurtha
107	Marius opens the army to all Roman citizens
106	Marius and Sulla defeat Jugurtha
105	Cimbri and Teutones destroy Roman armies at Arausio
104–100	Second slave war in Sicily
102	Marius defeats Teutones at Aquae Sextiae
101	Marius defeats Cimbri at Vercellae
91	Social War begins
88	Civil war between Sulla and Marius
86	Marius dies but civil war continues
78	Sulla dies but civil war continues
73–71	Spartacus leads revolt
71	Crassus defeats Spartacus
70	Pompeius and Crassus elected consuls for the first time
63	Julius Caesar chosen Pontifex Maximus
63	Birth of Octavian (Augustus)
61	Caesar appointed governor of Spain

60	Caesar returns from Spain and forms First Triumvirate with Pompeius and Crassus
59	Caesar elected consul and given control over Cisalpine and Transalpine Gaul and Illyricum
58	Caesar defeats Helvetii and Ariovistus
57	Caesar defeats Belgae and Nervii
56	Caesar continues campaigns in Gaul
55	Caesar defeats German Usipetes and Tencteri; builds bridge on the Rhine River; lands in Britain
54	Caesar lands again in Britain
53	Parthians defeat and kill Crassus at Carrhae
52	Caesar defeats Vercingetorix at Alesia
51	Caesar brings rest of Gaul under Roman control
50	Caesar crosses the Rubicon (northern limit of Roman Italy); the civil war against Pompeius begins
49	Pompeians defeated in Spain and Africa
48	Caesar defeats Pompeius at Pharsalus; murder of Pompeius in Egypt; Caesar makes Cleopatra the effective ruler in Egypt
47–46	Caesar continues his victories against remaining Pompeian forces in Africa
45	Caesar defeats Pompeians at Munda in Spain
44	Caesar is murdered; civil war between Caesar's supporters and his murderers begins
42	Defeat of Caesar's murderers, Brutus and Cassius, at Philippi
31	Octavian (Augustus) defeats Marcus Antonius and Cleopatra at Actium
30	Suicide of Antonius and then Cleopatra

A.D.

4	Tiberius moves into Germany
5	Tiberius reaches the Elbe and explores Jutland
6	Revolt in Pannonia and Illyricum
9	Defeat of Varus in Germany
14	Death of Augustus; Germanicus's first campaign in Germany; accession of Tiberius (14–37)
15	Germanicus conducts two campaigns in Germany
16	Germanicus again invades Germany but is recalled to Rome
19	Death of Germanicus in Antioch
37	Death of Tiberius
37	Accession of Gaius (Caligula, 37–41)

41	Caligula is murdered
41–54	Claudius's tenure as emperor
43	Invasion of Britain
50	Claudius adopts Nero
54	Accession of Nero
61	Boudicca's Rebellion in Britain
66–73	Great Jewish Revolt
67	Vespasian in command in Palestine
68	Death of Nero; Galba proclaimed emperor; Vespasian besieges Jerusalem
69	Galba is killed and Otho is proclaimed emperor in Rome; armies in Germany proclaim Vitellius emperor; suicide of Otho after his defeat by Vitellius; Vespasian proclaimed emperor in the east; death of Vitellius
70	Fall of Jerusalem
74	Fall of Masada
79–81	Titus emperor
81–96	Domitian emperor
96	Assassination of Domitian
96–98	Nerva emperor
98–117	Trajan emperor
101–106	War against and conquest of Dacia
106	Annexation of Arabia Petrae
113	Trajan wages war against Parthia
114	Annexation of Armenia
115	Annexation of Mesopotamia
117–138	Hadrian emperor
122	Hadrian builds defensive wall in Britain
138–161	Antoninus Pius emperor
142	Antonine Wall in Britain completed
161–180	Marcus Aurelius emperor; continuous conflict at empire's borders
180–192	Commodus emperor
192	Commodus murdered
193	Pertinax, Julianus, and Pescennius emperors; Pertinax and Julianus soon murdered
193–211	Septimius Severus emperor
194	Septimius Severus defeats and kills Pescennius, proclaimed emperor by Syrian legions
198	Severus's son Caracalla proclaimed Augustus
211	Severus dies at York; joint control between Caracalla and his brother Geta

212	Caracalla kills Geta
217	Murder of Caracalla near Carrhae in the Near East; Macrinus proclaimed emperor
218	Macrinus is killed; Elagabalus proclaimed emperor
222	Murder of Elagabalus; Severus Alexander becomes emperor
223	Murder of Ulpian, prefect of the praetorians
231–232	Failure of campaign against Persians
234–235	Campaign against Alamans
235	Murder of Severus Alexander; Maximinus becomes emperor
236–237	Campaign against Dacians and Sarmatians
238–244	Murder of Maximinus and of other newly appointed emperors: Gordian II, Pupienus, Balbinus, and Gordian III; suicide of Gordian I
249	Decius, appointed emperor by his soldiers, kills the reigning emperor, Philip (the Arab)
251	Decius killed on the Danube; Trebonianus Gallus proclaimed emperor; his son Volusianus also proclaimed Augustus
253	Trebonianus Gallus murdered by his own soldiers; Aemilianus proclaimed emperor but murdered by his own troops; the new emperor Valerian rules with his son Gallienus as second Augustus
259	Valerian captured by Persians
268	Murder of Gallienus; Claudius proclaimed emperor
270	Plague kills Claudius; Aurelian becomes emperor after the Senate's choice, Quintillus, dies probably at the hands of his troops
275	Aurelian murdered by his own soldiers in Thrace; Tacitus proclaimed emperor
276	Tacitus dies either of natural causes or by the hands of his soldiers; Florian, probably Tacitus's half-brother, succeeds him, but Florian too disappears, killed by his own soldiers; Probus is the new emperor
282	Probus is murdered by his own soldiers; the new emperor, Carus, dies while on campaign in the Near East
282-onward	the Roman Empire is run by two Augusti (senior emperors), one in the west, one in the east, with the assistance of two Caesares (junior emperors)
284	Diocletian becomes emperor after Numerianus's death; a year later he defeats the other emperor, Carinus, Numerianus's brother; Carinus is killed
286	Maximian becomes co-emperor
305	Diocletian and Maximian abdicate; the new Augusti are Constantius and Galerius, the Caesares Severus and Maximinus Daia
306	Constantius dies at York; the soldiers proclaim Constantine emperor in the west while Maxentius, the son of former emperor Maximian, is proclaimed emperor in Rome

306–312   Complex events finally bring Constantine to defeat Maxentius at the Milvian Bridge; during his long reign (306–337) Constantine rejects the pagan religion and accepts Christianity

324   Constantinople is founded

337   Constantine dies

357   Julian defeats the Alamans at Argentoratum (Strasburg)

378   Goths defeat and kill the eastern emperor, Valens, at Adrianople

395   The empire is divided between west and east

406   Barbarians invade Gaul

408   Alaric invades Italy

409   Vandals invade Spain

410   Visigoths capture Rome

429   Vandals invade Africa

455   Vandals sack Rome

476   Odoacer becomes king of Italy after the deposition of the last western emperor, Romulus Augustulus

APPENDIX II

Roman Emperors, 27 B.C.–A.D. 476

Julio-Claudian Dynasty

Augustus	27 B.C.–A.D. 14
Tiberius	14–37
Gaius (Caligula)	37–41
Claudius	41–54
Nero	54–68
Galba	68–69
Otho	69
Vitellius	69

Flavian Dynasty

Vespasian	69–79
Titus	79–81
Domitian	81–96
Nerva	96–98
Trajan	98–117
Hadrian	117–138

Antonine Dynasty

Antoninus Pius	138–161
Marcus Aurelius	161–180
(with Lucius Verus 161–169)	
Commodus	180–192
Pertinax	193
Didius Julianus	193

Pescennius Niger	193–194
Clodius Albinus	193–197

Severan Dynasty

Septimius Severus	193–211
Caracalla	198–217
(with Geta 211)	
Macrinus (not a Severan)	217–218
Diadumenianus	218
Elagabalus	218–222
Severus Alexander	222–235
Maximinus	235–238
Gordian I (with Gordian II)	238
Pupienus (with Balbinus)	238
Maximus	238
Gordian III	239–244
Philip (the Arab)	244–249
Decius	249–251
Trebonianus Gallus	251–253
Volusianus	251–253
Aemilianus	253
Gallienus (with Valerian 253–260)	253–268
Claudius II (Gothicus)	268–270
Quintillus	270
Aurelian	270–275
Tacitus	275–276
Florianus	276
Probus	276–282

(From Carus onward there were two senior emperors, called "Augusti," and two junior emperors, called "Caesares")

Carus	282–283
Numerianus	283–284
Carinus	282–285
Diocletian	284–305
Maximian (joint ruler with Domitian)	286–305
Constantius	293–306
Galerius	293–311

Severus	305–307
Maximinus Daia	305–313
Maxentius	306–312
Constantine I	306–337
Licinius	308–324
Constantine II	337–340
Constans	337–350
Constantius II	337–361
Gallus	351–354
Julian (the Apostate)	355–363
Jovian	363–364
Valentinian I	364–375
Valens	364–378
Gratian	367–383
Valentinian II	375–392
Theodosius I	379–395

(In 392, the empire was partitioned between the Western and Eastern Empires. The following is a list of emperors up to the end of the Western Empire.)

Western Emperors

Honorius	392–423
Constantius III	421
Valentinian III	425–455
Petronius Maximus	455
Avitus	455–456
Majorian	457–461
Libius Severus	461–465
Anthemius	467–472
Olybrius	472
Glycerius	473–474
Julius Nepos	474–475
Romulus Augustulus	475–476

Eastern Emperors

Arcadius	392–408
Theodosius II	408–450
Marcian	450–457
Leo I	457–474
Leo II	474
Zeno	474–491

Selected Bibliography

Primary Sources

Unless otherwise specified, all translations are from the Loeb Classical Library.

Ammianus Marcellinus
Appian
Caesar
Cicero
Claudianus
Dio Cassius
Florus
Frontinus
Josephus
Livy
Orosius
Plutarch
Polybius
Procopius
Quintilian
Res Gestae Divi Augusti
Sallust
Strabo
Svetonius
Tacitus
Vegetius
Velleius Paterculus
Virgil
Zosimus

Secondary Sources

Adcock, F. E. 1981. *The Roman Art of War under the Republic.* New York (reprint of 1940 ed.).

Austin, N.J.E. 1972. "Ammianus' Account of the Adrianople Campaign: Some Strategic Observations." *Acta Classica* 15: 77–83.

_____. 1973. "In Support of Ammianus' Veracity." *Historia* 22: 331–335.

Badian, E. 1968. *Roman Imperialism in the Late Republic*. Ithaca.

Barnes, Timothy D. 1998. *Ammianus Marcellinus and the Representation of Historical Reality*. London.

Bartel, B. 1980–1981. "Culturalism and Cultural Responses: Problems Related to Roman Provincial Analysis." *World Archaeology* 12: 11–26.

Bekker-Nielsen, Tennes. 1988. "*Terra Incognita*: The Subjective Geography of the Roman Empire." Pp. 148–161 in *Studies in Ancient History and Numismatics Presented to Rudi Thomsen*. Aarhus.

Ben Adallah, Zeineb, and Yann Le Bohec. 1997. "Nouvelles Inscriptions concernant l'armée romaine." *Melanges de l'École Française de Rome* 109: 41–82.

Ben-Yehuda, Nachman. 1995. *The Masada Myth: Collective Memory and Mythmaking in Israel*. Madison, WI.

Birley, Anthony. 1987 (1st ed. 1966). *Marcus Aurelius: A Biography*. London.

_____. 1971. *Septimius Severus the African Emperor*. London.

Birley, Eric. 1953. *Roman Britain and the Roman Army*. London.

_____. 1988. *The Roman Army: Papers, 1929–1986*. Amsterdam.

Bishop, M. C., and J.C.N. Coulson. 1993. *Roman Military Equipment from the Punic Wars to the Fall of Rome*. London.

Blagg, Thomas, and Martin Millett, eds. 1990. *The Early Roman Empire in the West*. Oxford.

Blockley, R. C. 1977. "Ammianus Marcellinus on the Battle of Strasburg: Art and Analysis in the *History*." *Phoenix* 31: 218–231.

Breeze, D. J., and B. Dobson. 1987 (1st ed. 1976). *Hadrian's Wall*. London.

Brisson, Jean-Paul, ed. 1969. *Problèmes de la guerre à Rome*. Paris-La Haye.

Brown, Robert D. 1999. "Two Caesarian Battle Descriptions: A Study in Contrast." *Classical Journal* 94: 329–357.

Brunt, P. A. 1971. *Italian Manpower, 225 B.C.–A.D. 14*. Oxford.

_____. 1988. *The Fall of the Roman Republic and Related Essays*. Oxford.

_____. 1990. *Roman Imperial Themes*. Oxford.

Burns, Thomas S. 1973. "The Battle of Adrianople: A Reconsideration." *Historia* 22: 336–345.

_____. 1994. *Barbarians Within the Gates of Rome: A Study of Roman Military Policy and the Barbarians, ca. 375–425 A.D.* Bloomington, IN.

Campanile, Enrico. 1993. "La Gallia di Cesare." Pp. 17–28 in *La cultura in Cesare*. Ed. Diego Poli. Roma.

Campbell, J. Brian 1984. *The Emperor and the Roman Army*. Oxford.

_____. 1994. *The Roman Army, 31 B.C.–A.D. 337: A Sourcebook*. London.

Carrié, Jean-Michel. 1986. "L'esercito: trasformazioni funzionali ed economie locali." Pp. 449–488 in *Istituzioni, ceti, economie*. Ed. Andrea Giardina. Bari.

Cary, M., and H. H. Scullard. 1984 (rpt. of 3rd ed. 1975). *A History of Rome*. London.

Chassignet, Martine. 1987. "Caton et l'impérialisme romain au IIe siècle av. J.-C. d'après les origines." *Latomus* 46: 285–300.

Cheesman, G. L. 1914. *The Auxilia of the Roman Imperial Army.* Oxford.

Coello, Terence. 1996. *Unit Sizes in the Late Roman Empire.* Oxford.

Cogrossi, Cornelia. 1981. "Pietà popolare e divinizzazione nel culto di Cesare nel 44 a.C." Pp. 141–160 in *Religione e politica nel mondo antico.* Ed. Maria Sordi. Milano.

Cohen, Shaye D. 1982. "Masada: Literary Tradition, Archaeological Remains, and the Credibility of Josephus." *Journal of Jewish Studies* 33: 385–405.

_____. 1988. "What Really Happened at Masada?" *Moment* (July/August): 28–35.

Connolly, Peter. 1981. *Greece and Rome at War.* Englewood Cliffs, NJ (see also the contributions of B. Dixon and R. Tomlin in the same book).

_____. 1991. "The Roman Fighting Technique Deduced from Armour and Weaponry." *Roman Frontier Studies 1989.* Ed. V. A. Maxfield and M. J. Dobson. Exeter, pp. 358–363.

Corcoran, Simon. 1996. *The Empire of the Tetrarchs: Imperial Pronouncements and Government, A.D. 284–324.* Oxford.

Crump, G. A. 1999. "Ammianus and the Late Roman Army." *Classical Quarterly* 49: 91–103.

Cunliffe, Barry. 1997. *The Ancient Celts.* Oxford.

Curchin, L. A. 1997. "Roman Frontier Concepts in the Spanish Interior." Pp. 67–71 in *Roman Frontier Studies 1995: Proceedings of the 16th International Congress of Roman Frontier Studies.* Ed. W. Groenman-van Waateringe et al. Oxford.

Dabrowa, Edward. 1993. *Legio X Fretensis: A Prosopographical Study of Its Officers (I–III c. A.D.).* Stuttgart.

David, Jean-Michel. 1997 (1st French ed. 1994). *The Roman Conquest of Italy,* trans. Antonias Neville. Bodmin.

Davies, Roy W. 1989. *Service in the Roman Army.* Ed. D. Breeze and V. A. Mansfield. Edinburgh.

Davison, D. P. 1989. *The Barracks of the Roman Army from the First to the Third Centuries A.D.* BAR 472. Oxford.

De Blois, Lukas. 1976. *The Policy of the Emperor Gallienus.* Leiden.

Dejardins, Ernest. 1876–1893. *Géographie historique et administrative de la Gaule Romaine.* 4 vols. Paris.

Delbrück, Hans. 1975–1980. *History of the Art of War Within the Framework of Political History,* trans. W. J. Renfroe Jr. 2 vols. London.

Dench, Emma. 1995. *From Barbarians to New Men: Greek, Roman, and Modern Perceptions of Peoples of the Central Apennines.* Oxford.

De Sanctis, Gaetano. 1976. *La guerra sociale.* Firenze.

Develin, R. "The Army Pay Rises under Severus and Caracalla and the Question of the *Annona militaris.*" *Latomus* 30: 686–695.

Devijver, Hubert. 1974. "The Roman Army in Egypt (with Special Reference to the Militiae Equestres)." *Aufstieg und Niedergang der Römischen Welt* (ANRW) 2(1):452–492.

_____. 1989–1992. *The Equestrian Officers of the Roman Army*. Amsterdam.

Dobson, B. 1970. "The Centurion and Social Mobility during the Principate." Pp. 99–116 in *Recherches sur les structures sociales dans l'antiquité classique*. Ed. C. Nicolet. Paris.

_____. 1978. *Die primipilares*. Bonn.

Domaszewski, A. von. 1967 (2nd ed.). *Die Rangordnung des römischen Heeres*. Bohlau.

_____. 1972. *Aufsätze zur römische Heeresgeschichte*. Köln.

Drinkwater, J. F. 1990. "For Better or Worse? Towards an Assessment of the Economic and Social Consequences of the Roman Conquest of Gaul." Pp. 210–219 in *The Early Roman Empire in the West*. Ed. Thomas Blagg and Martin Millett. Oxford.

Duncan-Jones, R. 1978. "Pay and Numbers in Diocletian Army." *Chiron* 8: 54–60.

Du Picq, A. 1914. *L'étude sur le combat*. Paris.

Durry, M. 1938. *Les cohortes prétoriennes*. Paris.

Eck, W. 1960. "Die Eroberung von Masada und eine neue Inschrift des L. Flavius Silva Nonius Bassus." *Zeitschrift für die Neutestamentliche Wissenschaft* 60: 282–289.

Ellis, Linda. 1996. "Dacians, Sarmatians, and Goths on the Roman-Carpathian Frontier: Second–Fourth Centuries." Pp. 105–119 in *Shifting Frontiers in Late Antiquity*. Ed. R. Mathisen and H. Sivan. Aldershot.

Elton, Hugh. 1996. *Warfare in Roman Europe, A.D. 350–425*. Oxford.

Ezov, Amiram. 1996. "The 'Missing Dimension' of C. Julius Caesar." *Historia* 45: 64–94.

Feldman, Louis H. 1984. *Josephus and Modern Scholarship, 1937–1980*. New York.

Ferrill, Arther. 1986. *The Fall of the Roman Empire: The Military Explanation*. London.

_____. 1991. *Roman Imperial Grand Strategy*. Lanham, MD.

Fiema, Zbigniew. 1999. "Barriers, Barracks, and Beyond: Remarks on Some Current Military Studies." *American Journal of Archaeology* 104: 348–352.

Fink, R. O. 1971. *Roman Military Records on Papyrus*. Cleveland, OH.

Forni, Giovanni. 1953. *Il reclutamento delle legioni da Augusto a Diocleziano*. Roma.

_____. 1974. "Estrazione etnica e sociale dei soldati delle legioni." *Aufstieg und Niedergang der Römischen Welt* (ANRW) 2(1): 339–391.

Friesinger, Herwig, and Fritz Krinzinger, eds. 1997. *Der römische Limes in Österreich: Führer zu den archäologischen Denkmälern*. Vienna.

Fuller, J.F.C. 1965. *Julius Caesar: Man, Soldier, and Tyrant*. London.

Gabba, Emilio. 1956. *Appiano e la storia delle guerre civili*. Firenze.

_____. 1973. *Esercito e società nella tarda repubblica romana*. Firenze.

Galinsky, Karl. 1996. *Augustan Culture: An Interpretive Introduction*. Princeton.

Garuti, Giovanni, ed. 1979. *Cl. Claudiani De Bello Gothico*. Bologna.

Gelzer, M. 1968 (1st German ed. 1921). *Caesar: Politician and Statesman*. Trans. P. Needham. Oxford.

Giardina, Andrea, ed. 1986. *Istituzioni, ceti, economie*. Bari.

Gill, Dan. 1993. "A Natural Spur at Masada." *Nature* 364: 569–570.

Goffart, Walter. 1974. *Caput and Colonate: Towards a History of Late Roman Taxation*. Toronto.

_____. 1980. *Barbarians and Romans: The Techniques of Accommodation*. Princeton.

_____. 1989. *Rome's Fall and After*. London.

Goldsworthy, Adrian. 1996. *The Roman Army at War, 100 B.C.–A.D. 200*. Oxford.

_____. 1998. "'Instinctive Genius': The Depiction of Caesar the General." Pp. 193–217 in *Julius Caesar as Artful Dodger: The War Commentaries as Political Instruments*. Ed. Kathryn Welch and Anton Powell. London.

Grahame, Mark. 1998. "Redefining Romanization: Material Culture and the Question of Social Continuity in Roman Britain." Pp. 1–10 in *Trac 97: Proceedings of the Seventh Annual Theoretical Roman Archaeology Conference, Nottingham, 1997*. Ed. C. Forcey et al. Oxford.

Groenman-van Waateringe, W., et al., eds. *Roman Frontier Studies 1995: Proceedings of the 16th International Congress of Roman Frontier Studies*. Oxbow Monograph 91. Oxford.

Grönke, Eveline. 1997. *Das römische Alenkasteli Biricianae in Weissenburg. I. Bay. Die Grabungen von 1890 bis 1990*. Mainz.

Hackett, J., ed. 1989. *Warfare in the Ancient World*. New York (containing articles on Rome by P. Connolly, L. Keppie, B. Dobson, and R. Tomlin).

Hadas-Lebel, Mireille. 1997 (1st French ed. 1995). *Masada: Una storia e un simbolo*. Trans. Claudia Maria Tresso. Genova.

Hanson, W. S. 1989. *Agricola and the Conquest of the North*. London.

_____. 1997. "Forces of Change and Methods of Control." Pp. 67–80 in *Dialogues in Roman Imperialism: Power, Discourse, and Discrepant Experience in the Roman Empire*. Ed. D. J. Mattingly. Portsmouth, RI.

Hanson, W. S., and G. S. Maxwell. 1983. *Rome's North West Frontier: The Antonine Wall*. Edinburgh.

Harmand, Jacques. 1967. *L'armée et le soldat à Rome de 107 à 50 avant notre ère*. Paris.

_____. 1974. "Les origines de l'armée impériale: Un témoignage sur la réalité du pseudo-principat et sur l'evolution militaire de l'Occident." *Aufstieg und Niedergang der Römischen Welt* (ANRW) 2(1): 263–298.

Harris, William V. 1985 (1st ed. 1979). *War and Imperialism in Republican Rome, 327–70 B.C.* Oxford.

_____. 1990. "On Defining the Political Culture of the Roman Republic: Some Comments on Rosenstein, Williamson, and North." *Classical Philology* 85: 288–294 (the responses of the scholars mentioned are at pp. 294–298).

Hinard, F. 1997–1998. "Rome: Des origines à la fin de la République." *Revue historique* 121: 115–135; 128: 415–440.

Hodgson, N. 1997. "Relationship Between Roman Frontiers and Artificial Frontiers." Pp. 61–66 in *Roman Frontier Studies 1995: Proceedings of the 16th International Congress of Roman Frontier Studies*. Ed. W. Groenman-van Waateringe et al. Oxford.

Holder, P. A. 1980. *Studies in the Auxilia of the Roman Army from Augustus to Trajan*. Oxford.

Holmes, T. Rice. 1911. *Caesar's Conquest of Gaul*. Oxford.

Hopkins, K. 1980. "Taxes and Trade in the Roman Empire 200 B.C.–A.D. 400." *Journal of Roman Studies* 70: 101–125.

Hornblower, Simon, and Antony Spawforth, eds. 1996. *The Oxford Classical Dictionary*. Oxford.

Höscher, T. 1967. *Pax Romana*. Mainz.

Howarth, Randell S. 1999. "Rome, the Italians, and the Land." *Historia* 48: 282–300.

Ilari, Virgilio. 1974. *Gli italici nelle strutture militari romane*. Milano.

Isaac, Benjamin. 1990. *The Limits of Empire: The Roman Army in the East*. Oxford.

Jewish Theological Seminary of America. 1967. *Masada and the Finds from the Bar-Kokhba Caves: Struggle for Freedom*. New York.

Jones, A.H.M. 1964. *The Later Roman Empire, 284–602*. Oxford.

———. 1966. *The Decline of the Ancient World*. Harlow.

Jones, Richard Duncan. 1982 (2nd ed.). *The Economy of the Roman Empire*. Cambridge.

Kajanto, Iiro. 1970. "Tacitus' Attitude to War and the Soldier." *Latomus* 29: 699–718.

Kasher, Arich, ed. 1983. *The Great Revolt*. Jerusalem.

Keegan, John. 1993. *A History of Warfare*. Toronto.

Kennedy, David L., ed. 1996. *The Roman Army in the East*. Ann Arbor.

Keppie, Lawrence. 1998 (1st ed. 1984). *The Making of the Roman Army from Republic to Empire*. Norman, OK.

Kerneis-Poly, Soazick. 1996. "Les numeri ethniques de l'armée romaine au IIe et IIIe siècles." *Rivista storica dell'antichità* 26: 69–94.

Kerr, William G. 1991. "Economic Warfare on the Northern Limes: *Portoria* and the Germans." Pp. 442–445 in *Frontier Studies 1989*. Ed. V. A. Maxfield and M. J. Dobson. Exeter.

King, C. E., ed. 1980. *Imperial Revenue, Expenditure, and Monetary Policy*. BAR S76. Oxford.

Kromayer, J., and G. Veith. 1928. *Heerwesen und Kriegsführung: Handbuch der klaasischen Altertumwissenschaft*, by I. Von Müller. München.

Kunow, Jurgen. 1990. "Relations Between Roman Occupation and the *Limesvorland* in the Province of Germania Inferior." Pp. 86–96 in *The Early Roman Empire in the West*. Ed. T. Blagg and M. Millett. Oxford.

Le Bohec, Yann. 1989. *Les unités auxiliaires de l'armée romaine en Afrique Procunsolaire et Numidie sous le Haut Empire*. Paris.

_____. 1992 (1st French ed. 1989). *L'esercito romano: Le armi imperiali da Augusto a Caracalla*. Roma.

_____. 1998. "Vercingétorix." *Rivista storica dell'antichità* 28: 85–120.

Lecrompe, R. 1968. *César, De Bello Gallico. Index Verborum. Documents pour servir à l'enseignement de la langue latine*. Hildsheim.

Le Roux, Patrick. 1982. *L'armée romaine et l'organisation des provinces ibériques d'Auguste à l'invasione de 409*. Paris.

Levick, Barbara. 1985. *The Government of the Roman Empire: A Sourcebook*. London.

Lind, L. R. 1979. "The Tradition of Roman Moral Conservatism." Pp. 7–58 in *Studies in Latin Literature and Roman History*. Ed. Carl Deroux. Bruxelles.

Lintott, Andrew. 1993. *Imperium Romanum: Politics and Administration*. London.

Loreto, Luigi. 1993. "Pensare la guerra in Cesare: Teoria e Prassi." Pp. 239–343 in *La cultura in Cesare*. Ed. Diego Poli. Roma.

Luttwak, Edward N. 1976. *The Grand Strategy of the Roman Empire from the First Century A.D. to the Third*. Baltimore.

Macmullen, Ramsay. 1963. *Soldier and Civilian in the Later Roman Empire*. Cambridge.

_____. 1974. *Roman Social Relations, 50 B.C.–A.D. 284*. New Haven.

_____. 1976. *Roman Government's Response to Crisis, A.D. 235–337*. New Haven.

_____. 1980. "How Big Was the Roman Imperial Army?" *Klio* 62: 451–460.

_____. 1984. "The Roman Emperors' Army Costs." *Latomus* 43: 571–580.

Maier, Christian. 1995 (1st German ed. 1982). *Caesar*. Trans. D. McLintock. London.

Mann, J. C. 1982. *Legionary Recruitment and Veteran Settlement*. London.

Mantovani, Tommaso. 1992–1993. "Tra Romani e 'barbari': La *percezione della frontiera e il controllo del Danubio lungo il limes Valeriae*." *Rivista storica dell'antichità* 22–23: 107–135.

Marin y Peña, M. 1956. *Instituciones militares romanas*. Madrid.

Matei, A. V. 1997. "Limes Prolissensis—A New Defensive Line (Ditches, Wall, and Towers) Discovered in Front of the Military Site of Porolissum, in Dacia." Pp. 92–95 in *Roman Frontier Studies 1995: Proceedings of the 16th International Congress of Roman Frontier Studies*. Ed. W. Groenman-van Waateringe et al. Oxford.

Mathisen, Ralph W., and Hagith S. Sivan, eds. 1996. *Shifting Frontiers in Late Antiquity*. Aldershot.

Mattern, Susan P. 1999. *Rome and the Enemy: Imperial Strategy in the Principate*. Berkeley.

Matthews, John. 1989. *The Roman Empire of Ammianus*. London.

Mattingly, D. J., ed. 1997. *Dialogues in Roman Imperialism: Power, Discourse, and Discrepant Experience in the Roman Empire*. Portsmouth, RI.

Mierse, William E. 1999. *Temples and Towns in Roman Iberia: The Social and Architectural Dynamics of Sanctuary Designs from the Third Century B.C. to the Third Century A.D.* Berkeley.

Milan, Alessandro. 1993. *Le forze armate nella storia di Roma antica*. Roma.

Millar, Fergus. 1967 (1966 1st ed). *The Roman Empire and Its Neighbours*. New York.

_____. 1998. *The Crowd in Rome in the Late Republic*. Ann Arbor.

Millar, Fergus, and Erich Segal, eds. 1984. *Caesar Augustus: Seven Aspects*. Oxford (esp. pp. 89–128).

Millett, Martin. 1990. "Romanization: Historical Issues and Archaeological Interpretation." Pp. 35–41 in *The Early Roman Empire in the West*. Ed. Thomas Blagg and Martin Millett. Oxford.

Mommsen, T. 1889. *Das römische Militarwesen seit Diokletien*. *Hermes* 24: 206–283.

_____. 1976 (rpt. ed.). *Römische Geschichte*. 8 vols. Munich.

Murison, Charles L. 1993. *Galba, Otho, and Vitellius: Careers and Controversies*. New York.

Napoli, Joëlle. 1997. *Recherches sur les fortifications linéaires romaines*. Roma.

Nicolet, C. 1980 (1st French ed. 1976). *The World of the Citizen in Republican Rome*. Trans. P. S. Falla. London.

Oakley, Stephen. 1993. "The Roman Conquest of Italy." In *War and Society in the Roman World*. Ed. John Rich and Graham Shipley. London.

O'Flynn, John Michael. 1983. *Generalissimos of the Western Roman Empire*. Edmonton.

Otte, James K. 1998. "How Will I Feed My Legions? Provisioning the Roman Army along the Lower Rhine Frontier." Pp. 67–74 in *Design and Production in Medieval and Early Modern Europe: Essays in Honor of Bradford Blaine*. Ed. Nancy van Deusen. Ottawa.

Pani, Mario. 1993. *Potere e valori a Roma fra Augusto e Traiano*. Bari.

Passerini, Alfredo. 1939. *Le coorti pretorie*. Roma.

_____. 1971. *Caio Mario*. Milano.

_____. 1972. *Linee di storia romana in età imperiale*. Milano.

Perelli, Luciano. 1982. *Il movimento popolare nell'ultimo secolo della repubblica*. Torino.

Poli, Diego, ed. 1993. *La cultura in Cesare*. Roma.

Purcell, Nicholas. 1990. "The Creation of the Provincial Landscape: The Roman Impact on Cisalpine Gaul." Pp. 7–29 in *The Early Roman Empire in the West*. Ed. Thomas Blagg and Martin Millett. Oxford.

Raaflaub, Kurt A. 1980. "The Political Significance of Augustus' Military Reforms." Pp. 1005–1022 in *Roman Frontier Studies 1979*. Ed. W. S. Hanson and L.J.F. Keppie. Oxford.

Raaflaub, Kurt A., and Toher Mark, eds. 1990. *Between Republic and Empire: Interpretations of Augustus and His Principate*. Berkeley.

Ramage, E. S. 1997. "Augustus' Propaganda in Gaul." *Klio* 79: 117–160.

Randers-Pehrson, Justine Davis. 1983. *Barbarians and Romans: The Birth Struggle of Europe, A.D. 400–700*. Norman, OK.

Rich, John, and Graham Shipley, eds. *War and Society in the Roman World*. London.

Rich, J. W. 1999. "Drusus and the Spolia Opima." *Classical Quarterly* 49: 544–555.

Richardot, Philippe. 1995. "Un désastre romain peu connu sur le Rhin." *Rivista storica dell'antichità* 25: 111–130.

———. 1998. *La fin de l'armée romaine (284–476)*. Paris.

Richardson, J. S. 1991. "*Imperium Romanum*: Empire and the Language of Power." *Journal of Roman Studies* 81: 1–9.

Richmond, I. A. 1962. "The Siege-Works of Masada, Israel." *Journal of Roman Studies* 52: 142–155.

Rosenstein, Nathan. 1990. "War, Failure, and Aristocratic Competition." *Classical Philology* 85: 255–265.

Rossi, Ruggero F. 1980. *Dai Gracchi a Silla*. Bologna.

Roth, Jonathan P. 1999. *The Logistics of the Roman Army at War (264 B.C.–A.D. 235)*. Leiden.

Ruggini, Lellia Cracco. 1987. "Intolerance: Equal and Less Equal in the Roman World." *Classical Philology* 82: 187–205.

Runkel, F. 1903. *Die Schlacht bei Adrianopel*. Berlin.

Saddington, D. B. 1975. "The Development of the Roman Auxiliary Forces from Augustus to Trajan." *Aufstieg und Niedergang der Römischen Welt* (ANRW) 2(3): 176–201.

———. 1982. *The Development of the Roman Auxiliary Forces from Caesar to Vespasian, 49 B.C.–A.D. 79*. Harare.

———. 1991. "The Parameters of Romanization." Pp. 413–418 in *Roman Frontier Studies 1989*. Ed. V. A. Maxfield and M. J. Dobson. Exeter.

———. 1991. "Tacitus and the Roman Army." *Aufstieg und Niedergang der Römischen Welt* (ANRW) 33(5): 3484–3583.

Saller, Richard P. 1982. *Personal Patronage under the Early Empire*. Cambridge.

Salmon, E. T. 1967. *Samnium and the Samnites*. London.

Santosuosso, Antonio. 1997. *Soldiers, Citizens, and the Symbols of War from Classical Greece to Republican Rome, 500–167 B.C.* Boulder.

Saxtorph, Niels M. 1988. "The Emperor's Men." Pp. 162–165 in *Studies in Ancient History and Numismatics Presented to Rudi Thomsen*. Aarhus.

Seager, Robin. 1999. "Roman Policy on the Rhine and the Danube in Ammianus." *Classical Quarterly* 49: 579–605.

Simon, E. 1967. *Ara Pacis Augustae*. Tübingen.

Smith, R. E. 1972. "The Army Reforms of Septimius Severus." *Historia* 12: 481–500.

Soprintendenza Archeologica di Roma. 1978. *I Galli e l'Italia*. Roma.

Southern, Pat, and Karen Ramsey Dixon. 1996. *The Late Roman Army*. London.

Speidel, Michael P. 1975. "The Rise of Ethnic Units in the Roman Imperial Army. *Aufstieg und Niedergang der Römischen Welt* (ANRW) 2(3) 202–251.

———. 1980. "Legionaries from Asia Minor." *Aufstieg und Niedergang der Römischen Welt* (ANRW)2(7): 730–746.

_____. 1984–1992. *Roman Army Studies.* 2 vols. Stuttgart.

_____. 1994. *Riding for Caesar: The Roman Emperors' Horse Guards.* Cambridge.

1988. *Studies in Ancient History and Numismatics Presented to Rudi Thomsen.* Aarhus.

Swift, L. J. 1979. "War and the Christian Conscience." *Aufstieg und Niedergang der Römischen Welt* (ANRW) 23(1): 835–868.

Syme, Ronald. 1982 (rpt. of 1949 ed.). *The Roman Revolution.* Oxford.

_____. 1986. *The Augustan Aristocracy.* Oxford.

Tarassuk, Leonid, and Claude Blair, eds. 1982. *The Complete Encyclopedia of Arms and Weapons.* New York.

Terrenato, Nicola. 1998. "The Romanization of Italy: Global Acculturation or Cultural *Bricolage*." *Trac* 97: 20–27.

Thompson, E. A. 1965. *The Early Germans.* Oxford.

Tierney, J. J. 1960. "The Celtic Ethnography of Posidonius." *Proceedings Royal Irish Academy* 60: 189–275.

Tomlin, Roger. 1998. "Christianity and the Late Roman Army." Pp. 31–51 in *Constantine: History, Historiography, and Legend.* Ed. Samuel N.C. Lieu and Dominic Montserrat. London.

van Creveld, M. 1977. *Supplying War.* Cambridge.

_____. 1985. *Command in War.* Harvard.

Wallace, Jennifer. 1998. "A (Hi)story of Illyria." *Greece and Rome* 45: 213–225.

Watson, Alan. 1967. *The Law of Persons in the Later Roman Republic.* Oxford.

Watson, G. R. 1969. *The Roman Soldier.* Ithaca.

Webster, G. 1985. *The Roman Imperial Army.* London.

Weinstock, Stefan. 1971. *Divus Julius.* Oxford.

Wells, Colin. 1984. *The Roman Empire.* Stanford.

_____. 1986. "Celibate Soldiers: Augustus and the Army." *American Journal of Ancient History* 14: 180–190.

Wells, Peter S. 1999. *The Barbarians Speak: How the Conquered Peoples Shaped Roman Europe.* Princeton.

Wheeler, E. L. 1979. "The Legion as Phalanx." *Chiron* 9: 303–318.

_____. 1991. "Rethinking the Upper Euphrates Frontier: Where Was the Western Border of Armenia?" *Limes* 15: 505–511.

_____. 1993. "Methodological Limits and the Mirage of Roman Strategy." *Journal of Military History* 57: 215–240.

Whittaker, C. R. 1996. "Where Are the Frontiers Now?" Pp. 25–41 in *The Roman Army in the East.* Ed. David L. Kennedy. Ann Arbor.

_____. 1997 (1st ed. 1994). *Frontiers of the Roman Empire: A Social and Economic Study.* Baltimore.

_____. 1997. "Imperialism and Culture: The Roman Initiative." *Trac* 97: 143–163.

Wistrand, E. 1978. *Caesar and Contemporary Society.* Göterborg.

Woods, David. 1996. "The Saracen Defenders of Constantinople in 378." *Greek, Roman, and Byzantine Studies* 37: 259–279.

Wulff Alonso, Fernando. 1991. *Romanos e Itálicos en la Baja República: Estudios sobre sus relaciones entre la Segunda Guerra Púnica y la Guerra Social (201–91 B.C.)*. Bruxelles.

Yadin, Yigael. 1966. *Masada: Herod's Fortress and the Zealots' Last Stand*. Jerusalem.

Zanker, Paul. 1988. *The Power of Images in the Age of Augustus*. Ann Arbor.

Index